NEVER
DIE
EASY

The Autobiography of
WALTER PAYTON

NEVER
DIE
EASY

Walter Payton WITH Don Yaeger

Random House Trade Paperbacks
New York

ISBN 0-375-75821-6

Random House website address: www.atrandom.com

Printed in the United States of America on acid-free paper

4 6 8 9 7 5 3

Book design by Jessica Shatan

To Jarrett and Brittney

Football will not be my legacy. The two of you will. I love you both more than you'll ever know, probably more than I ever showed. I could not be more proud of where you two are headed. Keep straight and keep moving. And remember to tell your mother you love her.

—WP

To Denise

My perfect lifemate. Thanks for believing in me, for encouraging me and for sharing my dreams. More than anything else, thanks for loving me. I can only hope I'm as good for you as you are for me. ILY.

—DY

Foreword

As I stood there at Walter's private memorial service and listened to the speakers step forward to eulogize my friend, I was struck by an amazing thing: Almost none of the conversation was about Walter Payton, the greatest football player I ever saw. Instead, almost everything said was about Walter Payton the man. And that was perfect, because that was the Walter he would want us to remember. He was never really comfortable with his celebrity, especially around the media, but he was always polite. He didn't open up to people very much, but he always made time for as many people as pulled at him. I don't think most fans have any idea how tough that is, but no one handled himself with more grace than Walter.

What Walter did better than anyone I've met was treat people right—everybody. There aren't many athletes out there today—especially superstars—who know how to do that. He didn't focus just on the CEOs at a dinner, he paid attention to the waiters and waitresses who were working the event. He loved people and he loved to smile. He knew those teeth were magic when he flashed a grin. He loved talking to kids and asking parents for pictures of kids. He understood being a role model—in fact, he cherished the responsibility and the opportunity that it gave him.

I'm glad so much has been made about Walter's off-field and post-career achievements, because that was as important to him as football. He had a few business partners who really treated him special—friends like Mike Lanigan from Mi-Jack Products—and those relationships are what helped a guy who played football in the days before out-of-sight contracts leave behind a good life for his family.

Walter always said that records are meant to be broken—if anyone should know that, it was him—and years ago, he sent me a plaque reminding me that "Tomorrow Is Promised to No One." He wanted me to think about the future and live life to its fullest. That was his style.

When people ask me about playing with Walter, I tell them about his great work ethic. But that is what everyone knows. What Walter also knew was how important he was to us on the Bears and that 50 percent of Walter was better than most anyone else we had. One time, during a game in Dallas, he had a rib injury and his lip was quivering, and I could barely hear what he said. He put his hand out, and he said, "Help me get up." He didn't want to lay on the carpet—and he didn't go out of the game; he walked back to the huddle. He had torn cartilage to his ribs, but he just powered through it, just gutted himself through it. That kind of heart and guts matched his ability, and that is why I believe he was the best ever. Maybe Jimmy Brown had that, maybe Gale Sayers had that, I don't know. But I know that Walter had it.

We lost more than a football legend on November 1, 1999. We lost a great man. I lost a great friend.

Walter, I love you. Connie, Jarrett, and Brittney: always know that I'm here for you.

—MATT SUHEY
May 2000

Author's Note

Never Die Easy would have been a much easier book to write if things hadn't changed so dramatically in the week leading up to Walter Payton's death. Suddenly, the book that Walter was writing had to change or never be finished. As a result, a decision was made to surround the hours of Walter's interviews with the stories and thoughts of those who knew him best.

It was my good fortune that friends like Matt Suhey and business associates like John Gamauf and Mike Lanigan, who didn't open up to anyone after Walter's death, wanted to add their voices to Walter's book.

I hope this explains the format the book has taken. It is not your traditional autobiography. But Walter Payton wasn't your traditional man.

—DON YAEGER

Contents

Cast of Characters

Mark Alberts: business partner of Walter Payton

Charles Boston: former head football coach at Jefferson High School, and later assistant coach at Columbia High School, currently retired and living in Columbia, Mississippi

Jim Brown: Hall of Fame running back for the Cleveland Browns, currently an actor in Southern California

Pam Curry: sister of Walter Payton

Forest Dantin: Columbia High teammate, currently an attorney in Columbia, Mississippi

Mike Ditka: former head coach of the Chicago Bears

John Gamauf: Bridgestone/Firestone vice president, close friend of the Payton family

Ricky Joe Graves: Columbia High teammate, currently teaching at West Marion High School in Mississippi

Roland Harper: former fullback of the Chicago Bears, currently owns several businesses in Chicago

Franco Harris: Hall of Fame running back for the Pittsburgh Steelers, currently in private business in western Pennsylvania

Mike Lanigan: Longtime business partner of Walter Payton and close friend, president of Mi-Jack Products

John Madden: TV commentator, former NFL coach

Bill McGrane: former Bears publicist

Jim McMahon: former quarterback of the Chicago Bears

Jeanie Ortega-Piron: guardianship administrator of the Illinois Department of Children and Family Services

Brittney Payton: daughter of Walter Payton, currently a sophomore at Barrington High School

Connie Payton: wife of Walter Payton

Eddie Payton: brother of Walter Payton, currently golf coach at Jackson State University

Jarrett Payton: son of Walter Payton, currently running back at University of Miami

Les Peters: boyhood friend, went on to play football at Jackson State, currently a teacher and football coach at East Marion High School in Mississippi

Rodney Phillips: teammate and roommate of Walter Payton at Jackson State, went on to enjoy a six-year career in the NFL, currently a firefighter in Jackson, Mississippi

Ginny Quirk: executive assistant to Walter Payton and partner in Celebrity Appearances, Inc.

Mike Singletary: former middle linebacker of the Chicago Bears

Matt Suhey: former fullback of the Chicago Bears, currently a Chicago businessman and executor of Walter Payton's estate

Kim Tucker: executive director, Walter Payton Foundation; director of marketing, Walter Payton, Inc.; partner in Celebrity Appearances, Inc.

NEVER
DIE
EASY

1

The Greatest Bear of Them All

The young man from Columbia, Mississippi, would have been shocked, maybe even a little embarrassed, by all the attention. He certainly would have been humbled. In the hours after Walter Payton passed away on November 1, 1999, something special happened to the world of sports. For one shining moment, people forgot the problems that plague sports today—disrespectful athletes, teams holding cities hostage, out-of-control fans—and focused instead on what is good about sports, all of which was embodied by that young man from Columbia.

Few things can bring a city as vibrant as Chicago to a standstill. Fewer still are the things that can bring together a group of loosely organized people, a group like those involved in professional football. So forgive Connie Payton if she was, as she said, absolutely awestruck by the reaction that followed her husband's death. Sports fans will not soon forget where they were when they heard that the Greatest Bear of Them All was gone.

A zealously private man, Walter Payton had left pro football nearly thirteen years earlier and had only rarely attended games and participated in NFL-related events. Walter had grown to believe there wasn't much more he could do for the game he once played. There weren't many players he admired and even fewer whom he enjoyed watching. The game, he worried, was in trouble because so many players didn't understand the value of team, didn't understand what it was like to have played in "his time" even though it was really not so long ago. Walter had worried there was nothing left he could give to the game.

Nothing, Connie Payton found out, could be further from the truth.

During the first few days of November 1999, coaches, players, fans, and broadcasters from across the country took time out to talk about Walter Payton and what he had meant to them. What he meant was not 3,838 carries, 16,728 yards, 110 touchdowns. What he meant was more than that. Those eulogizing him chose instead to recall a story about a time they saw him sign an autograph for a fan in a hospital, spend pregame time talking to those in the stands or cuddling a child handed down to him from the crowd.

The grief and affection that flowed from all corners of America served as a billboard-size lesson of what the game once was and should still be. Yes, he held great records. Yes, his runs were often spectacular—even the runs that gained only a handful of yards. Yes, he was the most talented player of what many considered the most talented professional football team in the modern era. He showed that you could be a superstar and still be someone whom people could touch. He was down-to-earth, funny, always looking for a rear end to pinch. He loved to laugh, showing off that perfect smile, yet he wasn't afraid to cry. He was a man's man and every mother's dream. Payton had not just been a great football player, he had been a role model in an age when role models are in short supply.

Most would agree that the death of almost any other player would not have hit lovers of football quite the way Walter Payton's untimely passing did. The league asked teams to fly flags at half-mast. Moments of silence were offered at stadiums from Buffalo to San

Diego. Players remembered him by scribbling his name or number on their shoes. And while honoring him, those in pro football came together in a way that touched even the most hardened. Honoring his passing brought together the men who had played with and against him, the coaches who had tried to stop him, younger players who knew him only through video highlights, and fans, many of whom had never even seen him play. In that time of mourning, pro football rallied and became a community again.

And maybe that was Walter's greatest gift—not his athletic talent but his unmatched ability to touch all those who came in contact with him.

Connie Payton: Walter would have been shocked at the response from people all around the world upon his passing. I was quite shocked. When we were making the funeral arrangements, Ginny and Matt kept talking about security to help with crowd control. They mentioned checkpoints at the door of the church and finding a church large enough to hold the number of people that would be in attendance. I looked at them with this puzzled expression on my face and said, "What are you two talking about?" Their response to me was "Don't you realize how many people are going to want to attend Walter's funeral and the memorial service?" It was more than I ever imagined and knowing Walter the way that I do, I'm sure that he would have been just as surprised. I wondered what it was about him that made people respond the way they did. As quiet as he could be there must have been something magical about the way he reacted around others. Then I realized that it was nothing magical but his genuine spirit and his openness that set him apart from all the other athletes. It didn't matter who the person was that wanted his time. He would stop and talk, even when he didn't want to at times. About a week or so after he passed, my mother and I were at the car wash and we were approached by several people telling their personal Walter stories. There were also stories of encounters with Walter that had been told to them by friends or family members. The stories were as simple as: He held my baby, he touched my son's head, asked him how he was doing in school, made him give Mom or Dad a kiss, then said to them, That's what you are supposed to do. He did have a special way with kids and he loved babies. The stories could go on and on, but it's evident as to why people felt that they knew him personally.

Eddie Payton (Walter's brother): Walter's last days were pretty much the greatest days of my life, being able to be there with him at the end. It wasn't a sad time, but it was an emotional time. You had a mother, a brother, and a wife, a son and a daughter, taking care of him. He knew what was happening, was well aware of it, accepted it. He knew what his fate was, never asked me why, never bitter, enjoyed every day that he was with us. He talked and laughed and joked with people who came in to visit as long as he could. As long as his stamina would allow, and then he'd rest. Then he'd wake up and be ready to talk again. It was one of the most beautiful things that I'd ever witnessed and one of the greatest shows of courage that, in my short lifetime, I've ever witnessed. Because for a man to go with that much pride and that much dignity just says volumes about who he was. He crammed about as much as he could in forty-five years of life. I mean, he helped, touched, inspired, worked for the betterment of so many people. And then he was able to accomplish some of his lifetime goals. Got two great kids who are going to be great Americans. One's gonna be a hell of a football player. And he's instilled in them some of the things that our parents instilled in us. And when you look at your kids and see them doing well, or better than you did, you say, I've done something right. Walter said that before he finally died.

Connie Payton: Matt was spending a great deal of time at the house with Walter. On Saturday, nine days before Walter died, Matt came over to take him out for a ride, which he did often. It was a good morning for Walter. He shaved, got dressed, and the two of them went out for a little while. Several weeks before, we had started him on a liquid nutrition supplement, which was working out extremely well. He was feeling a lot stronger, doing more things around the house. We would take longer walks in the neighborhood. We all felt that he was getting better with each day. We also had nurses stopping in to do the treatments that we couldn't do at home ourselves. One of the things that we had to do often was to take his temperature. Walter had a PICC line in his right shoulder, which was used to draw blood and feed him his nutrition. It was also inserted there to make it easier for everyone involved because Walter had a fear of needles and wouldn't let anyone near him to draw blood from his veins, which had started to collapse. On that Saturday evening, the nurse found that he was running a slight temperature. She said that we should watch it and that she would take it again when she came in on Sunday morning. She came that morning and found that he was still running a fever. We were told to call the doctor, which we did. The doctor asked us to come to the hospital just to make sure that an infection hadn't set in.

We took Walter to the Midwest Treatment Center. My family and I thought that maybe it was time to change the PICC line because it was only a temporary line anyway. We didn't worry because he seemed to be in good spirits. As a matter of fact, on our way to the hospital we had a great conversation with one of his former teammates, Thomas Sanders, and his family, who were waiting outside our home. We talked for a while, then he and Thomas hugged and kissed before we went on our way. The doctors were waiting for us when we arrived at the hospital around two-thirty P.M. Walter got out of the car on his own. A wheelchair was waiting to take him upstairs.

When we went to the hospital, we had no reason to think anything but that possibly Walter had a minor infection, but little did we know that it was a bigger problem. His body was beginning to shut down. The fluid that he started to retain was because his kidneys were failing. I couldn't believe what I was seeing or hearing. In less than three and a half hours, my husband could no longer get himself up, he could hardly speak. He was aware that something more serious was happening to him. The doctors explained that they wanted to put him on dialysis. I then had to tell him what they wanted to do; his eyes were open very wide. I told him that we should consider it, do whatever we had to do to live. He said to do whatever I thought was right.

By Sunday night, his mother and I knew that his condition was getting worse. The doctor had started the dialysis to relieve pressure. The doctors knew medically there was not much more that they could do for Walter. We all wanted him to be comfortable. He was sleeping a great deal and we made the decision not to say anything to him about the grim outlook. Such dramatic changes in such a short period of time. Again I thanked the good Lord for our reaching the hospital before any of this happened.

On Monday morning, the doctors said to have Jarrett come home from Miami. I made the dreaded call to the University of Miami, spoke to the athletic director and coaches. I wanted them to know all the details so that they could help prepare our son emotionally. Jarrett was not told all the details, but he knew that it was important for him to get home. We made the travel arrangements, which got him home late Monday night. Once he arrived home, he, Brittney, and I had a talk about the turn of events. On Tuesday morning, we all went to the hospital to see Walter. It was very emotional for all of us. Brittney took it the hardest. The kids talked to him, held his hand, and kissed him. He recognized them, he even said a few words to Jarrett. I really think he knew that Brittney was upset, so he held on to her hand tightly. He was very tired, but was trying hard to stay with us. We told him to rest, that we would all be there for him.

On Wednesday, after talking to his doctors and being told that there was nothing more to do to better his condition, I decided to bring him home, where I knew he would want to be. Walter loved our home; after all it was our dream house. The hospital made all the arrangements to have hospice available and to get all the necessary hospital equipment set up at the house so that we could make him as comfortable as possible. I wanted everything to be perfect, nothing broken, nothing missing! Once things were in order, the ambulance arrived for the trip home. It seemed like a long trip home, so different than the trip to the hospital. The one thing that was the same for me is that I had the same faith to keep believing and trusting in God. After all, faith is believing in the things unseen, and we walk by faith, not by sight.

Walter was amazing. He fought to live. Our friends and I prayed long and hard. We were not giving up hope; as a matter of fact his condition seemed as if it was getting better. He began to respond to us more and his kidneys were functioning better also. He didn't seem as swollen and his eyes were not as jaundiced. We were very thankful for what was happening. We were so sure that he was getting better that I had planned to send Jarrett back to Miami on Tuesday, November 2.

We brought Walter home because the doctors said that there was nothing more that they could do for him. I knew this, yet I was not prepared for him to die. I wanted so badly for him to get better. He too wanted to beat this dreaded disease. There were so many things to do, for instance watching Jarrett begin his football career at UM, watching Brittney grow into a beautiful young lady with so much to offer the world that lies before her.

Eddie Payton: I got there Monday while he was in the hospital. I didn't go over and hang at the house, there were so many people hanging out at the house. At times, I felt that Walter felt awkward about all those people. I don't think he wanted people to see him, because the reason he didn't go out much after he got sick is he didn't want his fans to see him looking like that. He wanted them to remember him as full of life. He looked a lot worse than people can imagine. But the great thing about it, because of his condition just before he died, he filled up with fluid and he looked really, really well. We went to the mortuary to do some things, and he looked like he could get up and walk out any minute. Looked like he had never been sick. If you have a brother, you're going to remember the good, the bad, the ugly. Right to the very end, Walter gave me memories. The last thing I asked him when I last saw him is was there anything he wanted me to do. Anyone he wanted me to say anything to, anything needed to be done. He just looked at me and said, "Get the hell out the room." I'll always remember that. He had a big smile on his face. That's what keeps me on an even keel. I'll remember that last smile. What you want? Oh, get the hell out the room. What a smile! And that was Walter. That was Walter. He had done it all. Don't worry about him 'cause he knew that if he passed in the next two minutes, he was going to a better place that he was prepared to go to.

Pam Curry (Walter's sister): When I got the call to come to Chicago, it was devastating. My mother had called. She said that Walter's kidneys failed. When we got to Chicago, we got there late. And that next morning we went to the hospital, they knew how I had been before—very emotional. My momma said, "He needs your strength, more so than ever, he needs your strength." She said, "Don't go in there if you can't give it, don't go by what you look at, what you see." When I walked in the room, Momma said, "You know who this is?" He said, "Yeah." She said, "That's Pam." It was just hard to look at him.

It is a cruel disease, it was just cruel. When I look at how everything transpired, it is hard to think through. We found out that it was the liver, then we're told all we have to do is a transplant, then the door was closed because of the tumor. Then after it was the tumor, then we found out it had gotten into the lymph nodes, where it spreads like wildfire. It was just devastating, but he never gave up.

Walter, I knew that this was something that was tearing him up inside, but there's one thing that I've always known, the eyes can't lie. If you look at a person in their eyes, you see their soul, and he was hurting. He was hurting. I think that's what hurt me. It was just a burden that was hard for him to carry. He carried it as best as he could.

When we were coming out of the hospital and heading home with him, I was telling him, I said, "You don't have to fight anymore." He said, "Why?" I said, "I don't want you to give up, but I'm here now," and I said, "I'm gonna fight for you." I said, "I'm gonna play for you." He looked at me like, I'm not ready to die. He was such a fighter even to the end, when they took him home from Mt. Zion Hospital, they said twenty-four hours he would probably be dead because he had no . . . His kidneys had failed, it's over. And he lived six days after that. Think about that, medicine says you can't do that, but Walter did it. To the very end, Walter lived like he played football . . . tough.

I remembered that morning that he died, and you always think that if I had done this or if I had done that. But I had shaven him, I think that Thursday, I had given him a shave. That Sunday, he was getting the bristles back. And I said, I guess I should shave you tomorrow. But then I said, No, I better do it now, so I shaved him that Sunday. So a day later, when he passed, he was clean-shaven. Sounds silly, but it means something to me.

And so that Monday when he got up, he woke up and I was sleeping in the room with him, and Connie was sleeping with Brittney. He would wake up about three in the morning and say either "I want to talk," or "I want something to eat." And I would get him some ice or some of that stuff he was drinking—Boost—and I would give him some of that and he would go back to sleep. But that Monday morning, Walter started having hiccups. My husband had said . . . We were talking before about death hiccups and death rattle. I didn't hear the rattle, but the hiccups bothered me. I got ready to leave the room and Walter looked at me and asked where I was going. He was in control right to the end. They told us to expect hallucinating, but he had none of that. He was tough right to the end. He slept a lot—but when he was awake, he was functioning.

I was there in the room when he passed. We grabbed him and he seemed so light. It was almost like he just seemed like a feather, he seemed so light. He had such a peace on his face. I remember saying, "Look at him, look how he looks." He had a smile—about like you're smiling now—he had a smile on his face. Spiritually, my soul rejoiced. I was so happy that he was no longer in pain and the peace that he had on his face.

Connie Payton: Walter was very confident that he would beat his illness. Death was not a part of his vocabulary. He wouldn't talk about arrangements upon his death. It was not a comfortable topic. I would say to him that we really needed to discuss the subject because we will all die someday and loved ones needed to know precisely the details of one's wishes. There were also all the details on business ventures to discuss. It didn't mean that any of us were giving up the fight; these were matters that needed to be addressed. The subject would come up at the hospital, they wanted to know if Walter had a living will. I just wanted him to say what he wanted to happen to him if things took a turn for the worse in the hospital. The social worker tried to get him to see how important the living will was. He absolutely shut us out. I knew what he was trying to do, but at the same time I needed him to address the situation.

Jarrett Payton: When someone is hurting like my dad was for a long time and you're around, you know you want the pain to end. But what I'll always remember is his spirit, how he didn't want to complain and make any of the rest of us feel that pain. That's what probably has bothered me the most, keeping all that inside him. I couldn't take that. It was hard for me when I came home from school, it was hard to come home. Then when I went to the hospital to see him, I was like, Whoa. I didn't know what to do. I had all these weird emotions and didn't know what to do. I couldn't stay home when he came home, it was like I couldn't be home. I had to leave. I was leaving, coming home, leaving, coming home, because I couldn't stay at home. It hurt to see him in that condition. This was my hero. The toughest man I'd ever known. Remember, if you look at the videos, even when there was wide-open field calling him, my dad chose to initiate contact. He loved being tough.

One day that week, I left and went out to get my mind off of it. When I walked back in, he popped up and said, "Where have you been?" He always said that to me, always. He always would, no matter where I'd go, I'd come home from school or I'd go out with my friends or something, he'd always be like, "Where have you been?" From that point, after he did that, I had a different feeling, as if he and I had a connection before he passed away. I still smile when I think about it. That was actually the last thing that he said to me.

Brittney Payton: I went through it the hardest. I was Daddy's little girl, which I really enjoyed. The whole time he was sick I always thought it would be okay. The whole time I just kept praying. Even in the final days when I saw him fighting it so hard, I said he had it in him to win this thing. That Monday I said—like I did every morning—that I was going off to school, I'll see you later, I love you. I always gave him a kiss on the head when I walked out and I would hold his hand. He opened his eyes that morning and knew what I was saying. I went to school, and right around lunchtime I got a call to the dean's office at Barrington High School. I went up there and Miss Luna [Picart, the Payton family assistant] was standing there. From the moment I saw Miss Luna, I started worrying. I asked her if everything was okay and she said that Dad had gotten worse. I asked how much worse and she just said, "Worse." She said, "You should come home." It is about fifteen minutes from the school to our house and it was the longest fifteen minutes of my life. I tried to block out any negative thoughts and just rode along in silence. When I came in the house, I dropped my bag and started heading to my room. My parents' room is down the hall from mine and I couldn't see anything because people were in there, so I went to my room. When I walked in, my mom and my brother were there sitting on my bed. My mom had been so strong through all of this, so when I saw her crying, I knew. I knew what had happened. The three of us just sat there on my bed and cried. I'm not even sure anyone said anything.

For days after, it was still hard for me. I was numb. It really didn't hit me for a while. I didn't want to believe my dad was gone. All my friends were such a big help to me, and especially all the people who stayed around our house. My friend Nicole Ellis stayed with me for several days afterward. I would talk on the phone all the time with another friend, Katie Schmidt. Kelly Strout, who has been a friend of mine since preschool, and her mom would come by every day to see how we were doing.

Mike Singletary: The last few days I saw him, there was a struggle. There was a struggle and a fight for survival. There was pain. That morning when I went, I just . . . I hate going through this part because I don't think people understand it. I just went in and I began to pray like I had the few days before and just reading Scripture and just holding his hand and talking to him and praying. I got up, and please understand that I'm not saying that it was because of my prayers, but he was just so peaceful-looking. I just went in there and I hadn't really looked at him. I just kind of went in and got on my knees and began to pray as I held his hand. When I finished praying, I got up, and his face could have been like that before I got in the room, but when I got up and I looked at him, I said, I can't believe this. I can't believe this. I'm looking at his face and there was such a peace on his face, it was unbelievable. I didn't know that was the last time I'd see him alive. As a matter of fact, I didn't really think of him dying. I couldn't even think of him dying. I just thought, I'm not gonna even think that way and Lord, if there is some way that you see fit for him to live, if you could heal him. So I never thought about him dying, never really did.

Two weeks before he passed away, Walter said he wanted to make sure that his book and his life might offer some lessons for others. He wanted others to remember the importance of appreciating what they have, of remembering that no matter what you've accomplished, you are not better than anyone else, that every opportunity you have to meet someone is an opportunity to leave a piece of yourself behind.

Connie Payton: We had discussions in the past about situations like this. We both said that we didn't want to be kept alive on life support. If there was nothing medically available to save our lives, we would want to die with dignity. So when that time came, I knew exactly what to do.

The lessons learned from Walter's life are many. I believe that we should never take life for granted, to live life to its fullest because as the old saying goes, "Tomorrow isn't promised to anyone." I believed that Walter realized that it didn't matter how much money one had or how famous one was. If you didn't have good health, none of it mattered. He would have given it all back to feel healthy. I also realize how much time we waste doing things that are trivial in life. The things we need to do like spending quality time with family and good friends are often overlooked. This brings balance and goodness to one's world. I'm thankful every day for good physical, mental, and emotional health.

Walter was always a healthy person. His body from an outward appearance seemed strong and vibrant. If someone had told me that he would have contracted a rare liver disease with an even rarer form of cancer, I would not have believed it. In my eyes he was supposed to live forever. The realization of his death hasn't sunk in yet. It feels like a dream. I think of him daily. When the phone rings, I still expect to hear his voice at the other end.

When we first learned of his illness, it was said that he would have two years to receive a liver transplant before anything drastic would occur. Walter had a great attitude throughout the entire illness. He didn't want our family to worry about anything. He said that he would receive the transplant and go on to live a full life. We believed this to be true. I would tell the kids that things were going to be fine and they should take advantage of each day because none of us know what each day will bring. I knew that Walter was no different than the next person, but he wasn't supposed to die so young. We had so much life ahead of us. It amazed Jarrett that his dad had only missed one football game in thirteen years, had been so strong, how could this be happening to him? The reality hit that it didn't matter how healthy you were or what you had achieved, none of us know our destiny.

Walter wanted this book to inspire others. That should be the inspiration. Live every day, every moment, to its fullest and be as gracious as you can be. That was Walter. To the very end.

"Begin with the end in mind," Walter Payton used to say to children, admonishing them to think through the consequences of their actions. There's no way, when Walter Payton began his whirlwind life in a tiny Mississippi town, that he could have had this end in mind. Or know that he would touch so many lives in so short a time.

2

Growing Up

Back in the day before Walter Payton danced on its playing fields, Columbia, Mississippi, was a sight to see. The Pearl River, which still churns its muddy self right through town, was in the early 1900s a formidable waterway, wide and deep and perfectly suited for bringing barges and trading ships the ninety miles up from the Gulf of Mexico and into Columbia.

The ships came for the lumber that Mississippi's thick piney woods could offer in abundance. The loggers hauled the wood into town, where the barges lined up to chug it out. In their wake they left cash, prosperity, and more jobs than the locals could fill. They also left a sense that Columbia, so otherwise isolated in the hilly red clay terrain of southern Mississippi, was someplace. Someplace better, or more important, maybe, than Prentiss to the north, McComb to the west, or Poplarville to the south.

So Columbia surged—with jobs, people, and material wealth. A number of meat-processing plants sprung up, changing street names to Bone Alley and Beef Alley. Oh, it was no New Orleans, not even

Hattiesburg, but in this eternally poor area of the country, Columbia was wealthy. There were no vacancies in the storefronts in the bustling downtown. The county erected a magnificent courthouse in the city's center square, serving as both a house of justice and a symbol of Columbia's uniqueness. The town was hailed as the "City of Charm on the Pearl River."

But the river that brought so much to Columbia would soon turn a cruel cold shoulder on the city. Silt slowly built up in the Pearl, filling its shipping lanes with mud and eventually making the river impassable for the big, commercial vessels needed to haul out the area's chief resource. Marion County still had plenty of lumber available for harvest. It just no longer had an easy, central way to ship it out.

The town naturally dried up as the river filled up. The jobs and people and wealth departed, leaving behind the survivors but little in terms of opportunity. By the 1950s, industry was limited. There was farming, service work, and the Pioneer Recovery System, a parachute factory that touts itself as the world's largest and was the town's main employer. But for most residents, particularly Columbia's blacks, becoming a teacher or a preacher was about as large as a kid could dream of ever becoming. Which isn't to say that life in Columbia was such a bad thing for most of the 7,500 residents. You may not have gotten rich there, but Columbia was wealthy in those Norman Rockwell charms of the era. It was a simpler time. Not necessarily better than today, not necessarily even good. Just simpler. A time when everyone knew everyone, you could walk the streets at night, and you didn't mind if your child scrambled down to Mr. Earl's, who sold groceries off his front porch, or Miss Jeanette's, who had all the penny candy a belly could hold.

And wasn't the food good! Salted pork and biscuits and syrup and tender smoked barbecue chicken, so sweet you could smell it cooking clear over in Foxworth. Then there were Mom's beans and slaw and corn bread and cracklin' bread, not to mention all the great things that came from the garden—onions, cabbage, sweet potatoes, turnips, watermelons. And if you threw a hook into any body of water you were sure to pull out a catfish so tasty it could make you weep.

Jobs and money weren't plentiful, but how would you know the difference if you grew up in the 1950s and '60s, like Walter Payton did, in Columbia? Everyone was sort of the same. The whites had more money than the blacks, but not by a lot. And it's not like there was a lot of social interaction. The north and west sides of town were where the blacks such as the Paytons lived. The homes were simple structures, small, single-story, wood-framed houses placed on small, tight lots on dirt streets. They were decorated in modest but prideful ways.

The Paytons lived on Hendrick Street, second home on the left, just a few steps from John J. Jefferson High School, then the black school in town. Nationally, in the days of Payton's adolescence, the cauldron of social and racial inequities was slowly boiling over. In 1954, the United States Supreme Court deemed the "separate but equal" academic systems like the one in Columbia unconstitutional because nothing separate could inherently be equal. A few years later a woman by the name of Rosa Parks refused to give up her seat on a bus in Alabama, prompting a prolonged boycott of public transportation. In 1964, just up the road in Philadelphia, Mississippi, three civil rights workers were slain, prompting national outrage. A year later, marchers were beaten as they worked to get blacks registered to vote in Selma, Alabama.

It was a tumultuous time throughout the South, but like so many isolated, insular, rural southern towns, Columbia was on the outside of the action. Although many people, particularly blacks, opposed the segregated high schools and Jim Crow laws that kept them down, there was never that spark to cause a fire of organized protests.

The kids of Columbia, particularly black kids, entertained themselves in traditional ways. This was well before PlayStations, the Internet, and television made the young sedentary. The Payton children—brother Eddie, sister Pam, and Walter—spent their time outside of the home playing in the woods, fishing, or trying to put together sandlot football or baseball games.

They walked everywhere, since their father, Edward Payton, was usually using his truck, either to get to the parachute company for work, or driving to the five-acre garden he farmed outside of town. Left on their own, the kids played to stay out of trouble, often gathering on the sports fields of Jefferson High to compete. They all also took up instruments, Walter becoming so proficient at the drums that he would concentrate on the school band, never even playing organized football until his junior year at Jefferson.

To make extra money, the Payton children worked, performing any odd job they could find around the town. If Alyne Payton found an idle hand, then they would help her in the yard, which she took pride in, or around the house, which she kept immaculate despite working the second shift at the parachute company herself.

The Payton home was a solid one, led by demanding, determined parents and full of happy-go-lucky kids. The family wasn't wealthy, working long hours just to scrape by. But they were like everyone else in Columbia, just trying to raise a family in a tough situation in the Deep South in the 1950s and '60s. One thing was certain— Edward and Alyne Payton were determined to raise children with morals, common sense, and the kind of work ethic that would prove legendary later in life.

Walter Payton: Growing up we played sports nonstop. I mean every single day. As soon I got done with breakfast I was ready to go. My mom was amazing. She would work from four P.M. to eleven P.M. every night at the local parachute company, where just about everyone worked, and she'd come home tired, but she'd be up early every morning to cook the best breakfasts for us. She'd always say we needed to be prepared for the day. She probably would have liked to sleep in, but that wasn't my mother. She was up for us.

As soon as breakfast was done, we'd be out the door. I was always tailing my brother, Eddie, and sister, Pam, who were older than I. They would be out the door looking for something to do and I would be right behind them. If we didn't our mother would find something for us and that usually meant work. Since none of us wanted to do housework or help in the garden, we were gone—though sometimes I hid in the outhouse we had because there wasn't indoor plumbing. Mostly we went looking for the chance to play.

Competing in sports back then was everything. No matter what the game was or how much older and stronger the other kids were, we were taught to give it everything we had until it was over. Never give less than one hundred percent. If you start something, you shouldn't quit, that is what we were taught. If you're going to play, you might as well play to be your best. That was Daddy's rule.

In a small town you just enjoyed playing. You were kind of isolated from a lot of the things that were going on, especially in the sixties. There wasn't so much a lack of interest as a lack of exposure. We didn't even know what was going on elsewhere, or what the rest of the world was like. And we didn't have all the stuff kids have today. We didn't have any money, although we barely knew it at the time.

My daddy worked two jobs just to get by. He would work at the parachute factory, as a custodian, during the day shift. Then Mom would go in. They said that way the kids always had a parent around. But Dad had a truck, so he spent a lot of his afternoons and weekends doing odd jobs. Plus he'd haul dirt and grass and do whatever someone would pay him for.

That's the way it was then. If you had a truck, you did odd jobs and it was like owning your own business, which was the best anyone could say about you. You did whatever it took to put food on the table for your family. Dad had a garden outside of town, maybe four or five acres, and he'd go up there and work a lot also. Often in the afternoon he'd grab one or two of us and we'd have to go up there and work in the garden until dinnertime. It was hard work. We didn't have a mule, and it was a real garden. We had a hand plow that had a disk on this wheel that you used when you didn't have a mule. It was designed for smaller gardens. You push the wheel, and the disk goes down, and that was it. Like I said, it was hard work, appreciated now. But that was my dad's passion and he brought us along. He brought in a lot of food for us off of that garden. Fed us a lot of meals out of that garden. It was hard work, but even when we were real little, Daddy expected one hundred percent out of us. There was nothing he hated more than someone not giving one hundred percent. It made no sense to him. Just do it right, he would say.

Daddy would work, work, work, and made the money and gave it to Momma. Momma would work, work, work, and manage the money that both of them made. I guess because Daddy was kind of common labor and Momma worked in houses with people who made a lot of money, was privileged to a lot of information, a lot of ways to invest, the value of putting your money in the bank and being able to borrow and pay back and then borrow on what you had. She was a businessperson. Often I would have to work in the garden because Eddie had lined up all of the neighborhood lawns to mow. He'd get out there with those old push mowers, the old spinners, and cut every lawn for miles, making any bit of change he could. He had a monopoly on the business, I couldn't get in.

We got our love of playing and our love for the outdoors from our parents. My mother loved working in the yard, and Daddy, when he wasn't working, he was hunting and fishing. My parents just never sat around, they were always doing something and that came down to us.

In the summer, when we didn't have school, Mom would always be concerned that we would find some trouble out there. I am not sure what she thought we would find, but she was always concerned, so she tried to keep us occupied. And that meant yard work. My mother was a yard person and every summer to keep us out of trouble she'd have this guy to come in and dump this hundred pounds of topsoil in the driveway. She'd want us to spread the topsoil all over the yard.

We had one shovel and a wheelbarrow. And it was a little wheelbarrow—it wasn't a big wheelbarrow, it wasn't an industrial wheelbarrow—it was a little-bitty sucker. So I would fill and Eddie would push.

It was hard work and we were so small then, I was six, seven, eight, Eddie was a couple of years older. But there we were, trying to shovel and push all of this topsoil everywhere. Making things worse was the summer rains. It rains like you wouldn't believe during the summer in Mississippi, and the whole yard would get wet. That caused the wheelbarrow to sink in the wet soil. We'd have to put boards throughout the yard and push the wheelbarrow to the end of them. I'd fill it, Eddie would pick it up and take it out and dump it, and Momma or Pam would spread it. At the time we thought it was good for the yard. We, or least I, didn't know until much later that Mom had the topsoil delivered to keep us out of trouble in the summer.

If you want my opinion, there was no reason to spread all that top-soil except to keep us occupied and around the house. I was never so happy as when a guy named Ezekiel Graves started Little League baseball when I was ten. That got me from hauling all that dirt. Little League got Eddie and me out of a lot of yard work. I look back on it now, though, and I think that yard work taught me a lot. I learned about working hard and staying with something even though the project seemed overwhelming.

You have to imagine how big that huge pile of dirt appeared to a seven-year-old. I used to think we would never finish. We'd just try to make dents in it every day. Which is how you have to approach any kind of work. You have to take things one day at a time. The same is true for training for football. I used to work so hard that I would often vomit after working out. This was whether I was at Jackson State or with the Bears. People would ask me why I would work like that even after I was a starter in the NFL, an all-pro. I always had a difficult time working out with other people who didn't share that belief. And I always thought, That's just the way you do it. You work as hard as you can for as long as you can and the small gains you make will eventually pay off. Eventually that mountain of dirt will be gone and you can go play baseball or go hunting.

The other thing all that dirt hauling did for Eddie and me was make us strong. I never lifted a weight until I got to college. At Jackson State the other players would ask how I got so strong if I never lifted a weight and I'd tell them about the pile of dirt Mom would have hauled in each summer.

Our neighborhood didn't have much, but it was a close-knit group. All of us went to school together, all of us lived in the neighborhood. We walked to school, went to basically the same churches. Nobody on the surface had any more than anybody else, so nobody kind of looked down at anybody. We were all in the same boat, so there's really not a lot of competition or egos. It was just a small community raising their kids. We didn't even think we were poor.

What is poor? We had food. We dressed well. We didn't have a lot, but what we had fit, and it was always neat. When you look back at it you can say, Yeah, sure, we were poor and there were even poorer in Columbia. You go down to the other side of town and you cross a track, and you see people living in shotgun houses and eight of them in three rooms. You open the door and you can see all the way through, but at that time what you had wasn't as important as who you were.

Everybody was doing the best they could to provide for their kids, so there really wasn't a class system. We all went to the same schools and did the same thing. Most of our parents worked at the same places, so they were all making the same thing. When everybody has nothing it's not as big of a deal.

In our community the teachers and the preachers were the only people that you considered had more than everybody else. Those were the people you looked up to. There weren't any black doctors or black lawyers. Nobody black owned anything other than convenience stores or the Dew Drop Inn. You have to imagine that neighborhood. There were really not even any stores. If you wanted candy or something you had to go to Mr. Earl's house on our street. Mr. Earl was blind and he had the front of his house face the school, so he would sell stuff off the porch. He said, Hmmm, this is not bad, so he built about a ten-by-ten building, and he sold everything out of it from nickel cigarettes to gum and candy. We'd go to Mr. Earl's just about every day. But that was the extent of business in our neighborhood. I guess I knew the white people owned everything, but I didn't think about it. I was just a kid and that's the way things were. I accepted it.

Eddie Payton: We didn't know what racism was back then. There was not a racial issue when I was a child. It's just the way it was. I really didn't understand the differences until I got to college. When I was in high school, there was no discussion of it. It was like, This is just the way it feels, the way it's been. You don't think about it. You go to this school, they go to that school. You go to this church, they go to that church. They go to the country club to play golf, you go to the country club to work. That's just the way it was. Even in the late 1960s and early '70s.

In Columbia, we worked all the time. We worked all summer, even during the football season. I used to work as a caddie at Columbia Country Club, even though it dawned on me that I couldn't play there. But I needed the job. We'd practice sports and then go caddie. We'd play high school games on Saturday night and we'd be down there on a Saturday morning caddying and doing maintenance.

We'd work all day and play all night. Conditioning was never a problem for us. The thing about the Columbia Country Club was that it was this dinky nine-hole golf course and they still wouldn't let blacks play there. It wasn't like this was some great golf course. Later, when Walter and I were in the NFL, we both had no problem being able to play a couple hundred of the top courses in the world. But we were never invited back to either play or be a member of the little Columbia Country Club. We used to laugh about that.

They did invite me once, but they told me that I could come but I couldn't bring a friend. They invited me because of something that came out in an article. I had mentioned that even after I was in the NFL and Walter in the Super Bowl we couldn't play on the golf course in Columbia. They called and said, "Well, it ain't like that. We want you to come down and play. We're proud of you, we want you to come down."

I said, "Fine, I'd love to come down to play." They said, "The only thing is you have to come by yourself, you can't bring any of your friends." And I'm going, Hmm. So I thought about it for about eight seconds and I said, "Well, I'm no different from my friends. If I can't bring my friends to be a part of my enjoyment, I don't want to play with you guys." So if they ever change, I'd love to go back and play, but they haven't changed, so it doesn't bother me.

But back then, we didn't know much about it. We were too busy playing and working and trying to have fun. We occasionally got in trouble, but it was always harmless stuff. I remember we had a neighbor, Reverend Hendricks up the street, who had big plum trees. He was a preacher, and he had big plum trees that were in the middle of his garden. It had to be about fifteen yards from the fence around the yard to the tree. We used to jump the fence and help ourselves and then jump back over the fence. But one day he caught us. He said, "Hey, you boys get out of there." We took off running and he yelled, "Don't run, I know who you are."

We got home and kind of worried about it. I guess about four o'clock our parents got home and Reverend Hendricks started coming down the street. As he came down we said, Oh, crap. I went to the door and he was sitting there talking to my daddy, he was saying, "Mr. Payton, I didn't catch them but I know it was your boys, at least one of them I'm sure was one of your boys."

So I'm armed with this information, and remember, I'm two years older, so I run back and I say to Walter, "Look, Reverend Hendricks says he saw you take the plums off his tree. He's not sure who the other guy was and this is what we're going to do. When Daddy comes in here and asks, you tell him yeah, you did it. He's gonna get angry and when he starts whipping you, I'll stop it. I'll stop him and say, Don't do it, Daddy, it was my fault and if you gotta whip anybody, whip me, and then he'll let both of us off. He'll like that we stuck up for each other."

So Walter, he said, "Okay, that'll work, good plan." So sure enough Daddy came back there, he had his belt in his hand, he wasn't just upset, he was really p.o.'d. He said, "Which one of you boys was on that damn plum tree?" Walter said, "Daddy, I did it, but

I'm sorry." Daddy didn't say a word, he just grabbed him by the hand and whap, whap. He didn't ask him to explain who was with him or anything. Walter jumped around crying and he just caved, he yelled, "Edward Charles was with me too."

I'm back in the corner, going, Oh, no. There ain't no way out. So Daddy let him go and went to whacking on me. Needless to say we didn't speak to each other for a while. Nor did we sit down for a while.

Pam Curry: The one thing about when we were growing up was that we always knew what our parents expected. They were not like parents, at least not like parents today. They said what they meant, and they meant what they said. There was no escaping. So you knew right off the bat that there are certain consequences to your actions. Even though we did them, there were consequences.

We were mischievous, but we were not bad children. We were more mischievous because we didn't have the luxury that kids have today, the Nintendos, the electronic games. The things that we played with and we did, we had to come up with things ourselves. We would go fishing. There was a pond behind the house.

We got our work ethic from our mother and our father. They were sticklers for doing a job right. Once a week we all had to wash the dishes, and if you missed one plate, if it wasn't clean enough, then you had to wash all the dishes in the house including the pots and pans. So you do it right, or you do it over until you get it right. Nobody does that anymore. And I think the children lose a lot, they really do, because their expectation at home, compared to what you get in the workplace, is totally different.

To me, growing up in Columbia was really, really wonderful. We were very poor, but we didn't know it. We were happy. We got our needs met, but we didn't get everything that we wanted. Being the only girl with Eddie and Walter was tough. They'd tease me because I was a girl, I would get in the way. I couldn't be where they were, so I always had to prove to them that I could do whatever they could. Every time we got in trouble, I got caught and they always used the excuse that the only reason why we went wherever we got in trouble was to keep me out of trouble. So I was the scapegoat, but we got whippings in threes.

My daddy was the head of the house, but he allowed my mother to run it like she wanted to. We didn't get too many whippings from Daddy. When we did, however, it was serious. He was the disciplinarian, but she carried it out. In some ways you could get around him. One thing we used to do with Daddy was ride in his truck, we took rides and we rode and we talked. For some reason when I was about, I would say, seventeen, I had wanted to start smoking. My daddy smoked, but I hadn't dared try in front of him.

Eddie had brought up the subject one time. Walter and I always watched Eddie because he had a boldness about him. He would always get in trouble with his mouth with Daddy. So one day we were all at home and he put his feet up on the counter, on the coffee table, and he asked Daddy for a cigarette. Walter and I looked at each other like Eddie was fixing to die now. And Daddy said, "What did you say?" And Eddie, he was a senior in high school, said, "I'm grown." So Walter and I started easing out of the room because we knew my daddy was about to blow his stack and you didn't want to be around that because he might decide to give all three of us whippings. And sure enough, he went off. He almost killed Eddie.

I don't know what made me want to try smoking, but we were riding in the truck and he was telling me something and I said, "Yeah, Daddy, I know exactly what you mean." I said, "Pass me a cigarette." He passed the cigarette. So that's how I started smoking, riding in the truck with my daddy. My mom never knew it. I think she had to know because she probably could smell it. But he let me get away with it.

Walter Payton: Daddy had a different level of discipline for all of us. Eddie did get away with a lot because he was the oldest and because he was Daddy's namesake. Pam got away with things because she was the girl. Maybe every kid feels this way, but I definitely believe my daddy was harder on me than the other two. He told me he expected more of me because Eddie was blazing a trail. He made it kind of hard because at times he made it feel like a competition.

Despite all of the work our parents made us go through, we found the time to get out and play. We'd play everything—basketball, baseball, and of course football. We'd hunt and fish—Eddie and I used to tie a string to a branch because we didn't have a fishing pole—and play in the woods. We were just very active. I really grew up with nothing. I worked very hard to be where I am now. Hard work and determination have always been the keys to my success. But back then I had nothing to play with. I grew up next to the city dump. Eddie, Pam, and I would go to the dump and pick out stuff and go and turn it in if it was bottle caps or bottles.

Hopefully we'd have some money so each of us could buy our own favorite things that we'd want to buy, our own favorite treats. As a child, even, I was very much a loner, I always have been. Until I got older, I literally would play all by myself. One of my favorite games was the game of war. I would play the good guy, and then I'd be the bad guy. It confused people that I could play both roles. I would see these cars driving by and I am sure they'd look over and look at me and say, "There's that crazy Payton kid."

I look back at my style of playing football, and that evolved from my childhood because I loved the game of war. When I held the football and somebody was gonna take my football, I was going to hit them back first. I worked for that position and I wasn't giving it up or backing down. When the kids in the neighborhood would play "it" I hated to get caught. I started then learning how to juke and spin to make me impossible to catch. That all came from my childhood. That is something that a coach did not instill in me, that particular style.

And that's my style and that's why my style is different from other athletes, because it didn't come from athletics. It came from playing a childhood game. Later, when I got older, more organized playing became a big deal. Little League was huge for us and Eddie and I were pretty good at baseball. We eventually played some semi-pro baseball when we were in high school with our coach at Jefferson

High School, Coach Charles Boston. We had a semi-pro team called the Columbia Jets, and even though I was only sixteen, Coach Boston put me in the outfield and told everyone that I was just young-looking. Eddie played shortstop. Everyone else there were men.

We'd play tag or tackle football on the Jefferson field in Columbia in the summer, but we wouldn't have enough players to field a whole team, so we would only use from the hash mark to the sideline of a regular field. You didn't have a lot of room to move around, so you had to learn how to shed tackles, dodge guys or go right over them. I think a lot of my style that I used in organized games, even in the NFL, I learned during those endless summer games on a dusty field in Columbia.

If we had more players we'd move to this old sandlot nearby. When it got windy it would get so dusty you had to turn your back. But we played as much as we could. And there were great athletes there. We had a number of kids go on to college, the black schools throughout the South, schools like Jackson State or Alcorn State, and even the NFL. It wasn't just Eddie and I who made the NFL. We just were all always out there competing. Almost every day.

Les Peters (boyhood friend): I played all the time with both Walter and Eddie. I was probably five years older than Walter, but we would all play sports together. We played semi-pro baseball together. We played over in Laurel, Hattiesburg, all over Louisiana. After we got out of church on Sunday, we'd head off to play.

Walter was good, but actually Eddie was a better baseball player. I actually think that Eddie probably was the best all-around athlete, but Walter was right there, too. Eddie could have played professional baseball. We thought he had a great arm, great quickness, great skills. Walter was so young, but he played with the big boys. This was the late 1960s. I got through Jackson State on a football scholarship in '68 and I would come back home to work, they would play with me in the summer.

We would train together and play together in the summer. They would train with all of us older guys. They were right with us when we were training to go back to college for the fall—they were training for high school, practicing for high school. The thing that drove both Eddie and Walter to the NFL was the competitiveness. Neither was that big, but they played that way because the competitiveness between them was unreal. We used to tease them all the time. We'd tease Eddie. "Eddie, you can't handle him, you can't handle him." Then we'd say the same thing to Walter. It was just a competitiveness that they had.

You should have seen them. I've seen Walter make catches in the outfield that were better than anything you'll see on TV. He covered so much ground out there. And I've seen Eddie field some balls in short left field from shortstop and throw you out at first. His arm was so strong that I've seen him knock a board off the wall on the fence behind first. He overthrew first base and knocked the board off the wall.

Back then neither were great hitters, because they were teenagers playing against men, but they could bunt. Eddie could just naturally bunt. He could go like he was going to swing, and then drop that bat and bunt it out there. Walter would almost have to square around to bunt. But for ninety feet getting down that base path, you want to see elegance in action, you should have seen those two humans. Eddie's thighs, you'd have to look at Eddie's thighs in the young days. Eddie's thighs were just so compactly built. Walter looked like he was chiseled.

But guess what? In high school, he didn't have any weights. Walter looked like Mr. America but he never lifted a weight. God gave him talent. We didn't have any weights in Columbia. I didn't know what weights were until I got to college. And then you lifted if you wanted to, it wasn't mandatory like now. We got it mandatory in high school now, mandatory in college. Weight lifting is like a religion now. If you don't go to weight practice, they're not going to fool with you.

Walter was strong anyway. And fast. If Walter would have hit a slow ball to the infield, they weren't going to throw him out. You ought to see him getting down that line. He was just one of the great athletes in Columbia we played with. There was another guy called Prentiss Thomas, he played quarterback along with Eddie when Eddie was a tailback. Joe Owens, who used to play with the Saints, he played along with us then. Then there was Claudius James, who played with the Green Bay Packers. He was one of the first guys that got a Super Bowl ring from around this area. Jim Dunaway, who later played with the Buffalo Bills, he got one also, but Claudius James got a Super Bowl ring first. Then, of course, there was Walter with the Bears.

We played sandlot football and we played baseball in cow pastures. Now they have the infield. When you have an infield like there is now, how can you miss a ground ball? We'd go and play in pastures, and we had a great time. We had great crowds. Eddie and I used to call our park Duckworth Park. That's where most of the black kids play. We played football up on their end of town. It's amazing. I tell people there was an old plant they had over there, they used to call it a stock plant. A big old dust bowl like that we used to play in. We used to dream of playing in the NFL, just like every other kid. Dreamed of playing in the majors, just like other kids from a small town. But then we were just in cow pastures and dust bowls. Who would have thought we'd all make it so far?

3

High School

The year Walter Payton was born, 1954, the United States Supreme Court ruled in the landmark case *Brown* v. *Board of Education* that segregated schools were unconstitutional. By 1963, most school districts throughout the southern states of Tennessee, South Carolina, Georgia, and Texas began admitting black students after a strong federal order by President Kennedy.

It was a tumultuous time in the old Deep South. In 1963 in Jackson, Mississippi, the state capital ninety miles north of Columbia and the town where Walter would attend college, a man named Medgar Evers, the secretary of the Mississippi chapter of the National Association for the Advancement of Colored People, was shot to death in the dark outside of his home. A year later, three civil rights workers were murdered in Philadelphia, Mississippi, a small town much like Columbia, just a little over one hundred miles to the northeast.

There were pockets of resistance to integration and to equal rights all over the South, particularly in Alabama and Mississippi, which held to their traditional beliefs. In Alabama, Governor George Wallace ran for election in the 1960s on the campaign promise "Segregation today, segregation tomorrow, segregation forever." That promise would be broken when President Johnson dispatched federal troops to force integration in the sometimes intense, violent, and very public battles of integration in the Alabama cities of Huntsville, Tuskegee, and Birmingham in the mid-1960s. But despite all of that, it was not until 1970 that officials in Columbia, Mississippi, decided to integrate their city's high schools.

Until then, white students attended Columbia High. A mile down the street, black children attended John J. Jefferson High School. Although late to make the change, Columbia experienced only mild opposition when the school board decided to integrate the schools midyear, shuffling the Jefferson students to the newer, more modern Columbia High in January.

At the time, Walter Payton was a junior, coming off a brilliant season of playing football at Jefferson. Ironically, although he was a gifted athlete and the small black school needed all the players it could get, Payton had not gone out for football until his junior year. He instead was a member of the vibrant Jefferson marching band, where he played the drums. Eddie was the star tailback for Jefferson before accepting a scholarship to Jackson State University.

The belief around Columbia was that Walter never wanted to compete with his older brother on the Jefferson playing fields. For his part, Walter said he was more into the band until he realized that girls paid running backs more attention than drummers.

Whatever the reason, when Walter burst on to the Jefferson team he was an instant star, displaying the same kind of powerful, elusive running style that would propel him to the NFL Hall of Fame. Although not the biggest player on the field, Payton wasn't always interested in avoiding tacklers. He often lowered his shoulder and simply plowed through a linebacker.

When the schools integrated there was natural tension but very little animosity. Most people in Columbia had come to view integrated high schools as the future, and besides a few protesters—who nonetheless got their picture in *Newsweek*—contention was minimal. The schools integrated, at least outwardly, peacefully.

But there would be some battles. For years a quiet rivalry had developed between the city's two high schools. Because of the low enrollments the small town offered, Columbia High could not be considered a juggernaut football program, but it fared well in the intensely competitive Little Dixie Conference, which included schools from Gulfport, Jackson, and Hattiesburg.

In Columbia, the white high school was the one that got all the mainstream media attention—written up in the local paper and discussed on the radio—even though the team hadn't been a consistent winner in nearly two decades. It played on Friday nights to good-size crowds, while Jefferson played on Saturday nights on the Columbia High field.

Although interaction between students from the two schools was limited, there was a belief around Jefferson that it annually had the better team. The students also suspected, correctly, that Columbia High had far better equipment and resources. Indeed, Columbia had blocking dummies and sleds and better uniforms and protective equipment, although characterizing either school as plush, with modern, top-of-the-line equipment, would be wrong. In fact, neither school had much. Both schools were underfunded.

But with integration, Columbia High suddenly had a chance to become a very good football team. Word about the great junior back at Jefferson, the small kid named Payton, had swirled through the white side of town. People were curious to see how things would mesh, and players on both teams were prepared to prove that their school played better football.

Ricky Joe Graves (Columbia High teammate): When we first integrated, we didn't know them and they didn't know us. We were kind of two separate entities out there. All we knew was that we were Columbia High and they were Jefferson High. Although there wasn't any trouble with integration, there was some tension. I re-

member that everything was real tense the first two or three weeks
and some of the players would try to talk to each other and that kind
of stuff. But not much. You could tell that the atmosphere was tense.

I'll never forget the first day of spring practice, all the blacks were
on one end of the field, and all the whites were on the other end of
the field. Of course, we had heard that Walter was supposed to be
pretty good. We were all sitting around talking, bragging about
what are we gonna do, all this kind of stuff.

We were bragging, "Yeah, I'm gonna put him on the ground,
blah, blah, blah." Of course we were just little old white boys, we
didn't have any idea of the speed they had. And we didn't have the
ability they had. But at the time we didn't know. We were just playing on pride.

Back then our coach had a habit of running the same play over and
over and over again in practice. He'd run it until we got a play right,
so we would have to run it again and again. Repetition, he used to
say. I was a linebacker and a good tackler. Since I played linebacker,
I realized that since I knew what play the offense was going to run,
because they kept running it over and over, this was my chance to
strut my stuff, to show that I could handle Walter. I even shot my
mouth off about it.

So they ran this one particular play and I knew that Walter was
gonna get the football and I knew where he was gonna be. There
wasn't any reading to it. All I had to do was get to a point. When the
ball was snapped, I just took off and was gonna meet him there.
Well, I did meet him there and, boy, I laid into him. I thought, Man,
I got this sucker. And I just laid everything into him. I had him almost on the ground, almost horizontal. I wrapped up on him and
everything. The next thing I felt were his knees hitting me right
under the chin and he was up running again, and I'm sprawled out
on the ground after being dodoed. And he was gone for a touchdown. Walter just ran over me. It was just unreal the balance that he
had.

I thought, Man, look at this. I knew I couldn't hit him any better.

From that moment on, it was like, Hey, what can you do? How do you stop this guy, you know? There's just no stopping him.

We just knew that he was unusual. All of a sudden we realized our team could be pretty good. All the bragging was over. I felt like we were a team right then. During that summer, we used to go and play. We played touch football from the hash mark to the sidelines. That's not very wide and you had twelve kids out there messing around, trying to tag each other out. Long runs were rare, it was too hard to get free. But not for Walter. Nobody could touch him. He would just get around, it was almost no fun because you couldn't grab him. You'd be right there and he would be gone.

As far as high school, he was so much above, head and shoulders above, anything anybody had ever seen.

Forest Dantin (high school teammate): I don't know if I even knew Walter's name when we first heard the schools were going to be integrated. We just knew there was a real good back coming over from Jefferson. Most of the students weren't overwhelmingly excited about integration, but mainly because it was the merger of the two schools. The way we looked at it, frankly, was a lot of these guys don't want to come over here, they want to stay at their school. We weren't mad at them or upset at them, because that was adults doing stuff. Back then in Columbia, whites and blacks didn't have much interaction, but that doesn't mean there was a great deal of tension between the races.

We had heard a little about Walter's ability, but we had no idea how good he was. I had never seen him play. I had met Eddie the year before. Some of the players on the Columbia team were getting ready for the football season, and Eddie was out running getting ready for Jackson State and we played with him.

But with Walter, we looked at it as, How good could this player be? We looked at it like, This is our school and we're good, too. We have good players. So we kind of wanted to show that we could play also.

I remember it was the first day of practice and we got out there and we had a scrimmage. Ricky Joe Graves was definitely the best tackler we had on the team. We had some really good players, but he was the surest tackler and he played middle linebacker. They ran a play and Ricky thought he was going to tackle Walter. There was this huge collision between Walter and Ricky. Ricky really hit him hard and it looked like Walter was down and then, all of sudden, he wasn't. He was off, running to the end zone.

We said, "Ricky Joe, what happened?" He said, "I don't know. I had the guy, I had him wrapped up." He said he was lying on the ground with Walter's knees on his chest and then Walter stepped on him and he was gone. It was a fantastic run, we couldn't believe it.

All of a sudden we figured out that the former Columbia High team had a good line, but we were lacking in skill people. The former Jefferson team had some linemen, but they were really strong with the skill people. Where each team lacked, the other filled in with a backup. Plus we had Walter and he was better than anyone had ever seen. It was something that just worked out wonderful. We had a 7−0 run before we lost a game.

Walter Payton: When we first heard our schools were going to integrate, we were more concerned with the simple things, that we had to change schools, that things weren't going to be the same, not really the big, racial aspects of it. Growing up we just accepted that blacks and whites attended separate schools. It was just the way it was, we had our school, they had theirs. It wasn't something that you really thought about as a kid.

So when we heard that they were going to integrate the high schools it wasn't a big social victory, just a new thing. I am not sure we were even that excited about it, although we understood it was a step forward. But when you are a teenager, new things are not always welcome.

But we had no grudges against the kids from Columbia High. We looked at them as just kids, there wasn't any animosity or distrust. We never thought it was their fault that this was happening. We did, though, have some school pride. When you merge with your rival you definitely want to prove that you are better, I think that is just natural. You want to prove yourself to your new classmates or teammates. We wanted to show we played sports better, we played instruments better, everything.

I definitely sensed the tension the first few weeks of school and especially when football practice began. I have always been a practical joker, so I tried to loosen up the locker room by playing practical jokes on players of all races. Didn't matter what color you were if I could light you up with a firecracker on the way to the practice field! I was just trying to lighten things up so that everyone could get past the initial stuff and become a team. I knew we had the makings of a good team if we could play together. The one thing I have always found about different races is everyone likes to laugh. It is universal. Comedy can really bring people together, so that is what I tried to do.

At Jefferson, playing football was a big deal. There wasn't as much interest or exposure as they got at Columbia High, but in our neighborhood it was important. So we just played; we played for the respect of the community and the pride of the town. We had our little sixty-, eighty-mile circle of people that we played and to us, we upheld the city of Columbia as being the best in athletics. We just went out and played.

The big thing at Jefferson was that the best running back got to wear the number 22. I got to wear it after Eddie graduated and I remember Don Bell was the player who wore 22 before Eddie, and he was the best running back. Don went on to play at Alcorn State. When you got the number 22 at Jefferson, it made you grow up. It was kind of like a badge of honor in our town. Whoever wore 22 was *the* back. It was expected of you.

Playing football at Jefferson was something that everyone did. If you didn't play, there was almost something wrong with you. I bet almost 80 percent of my senior class played football. We had small teams, forty guys, so we needed every player. My first two years I didn't play, I concentrated on playing in the school band instead. I was a drummer, and some people gave me a hard time because Eddie was so good at football they figured I had to have some talent.

Our school was so small that often the football players would join the band at halftime and perform in uniform. We'd have linebackers playing the trumpet in shoulder pads and guys marching around in full uniform. At a small neighborhood high school like Jefferson you had to do whatever it took.

We were always confident that Jefferson had the best football team in town, even though Columbia had more students and better equipment and facilities. They'd play on Friday nights and sometimes we'd sneak over and watch them and we thought they weren't very good. They had some players, but we never thought they were good enough to beat us. We felt we could beat them at any time. We just wanted the chance.

The newspaper in town only came out once a week, so they would write up the game the week before and it would appear on Wednesday or Thursday. And there was a little radio. Like I said, obviously not like playing for the Bears, but back then it seemed like something.

We didn't get a lot of media coverage, but in terms of fan support our entire neighborhood would come out to the games on Saturday. Our stands were always full, everyone would walk over to the Columbia High stadium. So the people that we were playing for, the people we knew, they may or may not have taken the paper. But they were there and they knew what happened. Those are the people who respected us and appreciated what we did.

We weren't the biggest or most publicized school, but I think everyone who played at Jefferson, or attended Jefferson, takes a lot of pride in it. It was our neighborhood school and we represented the neighborhood.

Ricky Joe Graves: In those days Jefferson High School didn't get the new equipment. The white schools got most of the equipment. It was supposed to be separate but equal, but actually it was just separate, not equal. I didn't realize that, until they came over and we had equipment that they had never seen before. Things like blocking sleds, and stuff like that.

It was a new time and the type of person Walter was really helped smooth things over. He was a fun-loving guy, he liked to joke around. He just was real easygoing, everybody liked him. When we integrated, it could have been bad. The first part of the year, we had some two or three kids that came out there and demonstrated, and the media came and they picked up just on those kids. The rest of us didn't care. We didn't want to have anything to do with protesting.

Walter's ability to get along with everybody made that time in that town a lot different from how it was in a lot of other places in the South. He was just a real intelligent person. He was as far as I can remember an A and B student, and was a lot of fun to be around. He loved to lighten things up in what could have been a tense locker room.

I've never seen an athlete like him, and later, when I was a high school coach— I've coached against some really good ones. He was the only person I've ever seen that could walk on his hands about as well as he could on his feet. He was so coordinated and so balanced that it was just phenomenal. He didn't just walk around on his hands, he could turn corners, go up stairs, things like that. Part of what made him a great runner was that balance. Not only could nobody else on the team do it, I have never heard of anybody being able to do it.

Some of us would marvel at the condition he was in. Walter used to jog to and from practice, it was probably a mile, mile and a half from his house. He'd jog a mile and then practice. We knew he didn't lift weights or anything and he was always quiet about any training he did. What we as teammates did know was that he used to wear a pair of old army boots to go running in. He ran in the woods—dodging trees as if they were defenders—down some little old trails and stuff. He'd go down there and run in his army boots, which made wearing cleats seem like running barefoot.

Forest Dantin: The biggest play Walter ever made was in the first game against Prentiss, and that's the one probably everybody still talks about. You have to remember that integration was a tough subject and not everyone was for it, even though things were peaceful. We were trailing in the first half 6–0 when Walter got the ball in just a little simple dive play, and he went for ninety-five. Took a simple play and scored a touchdown because he was Walter. Just as he cleared around the 30-yard line he just kind of coasted. Then somebody on the other team kind of showed up in the background, and he looked behind him and saw him. It was just like he hit another gear. He was gone. He was in the end zone.

Columbia won 14–6 that day and Walter scored another touchdown from sixty-five yards out. Another simple play that he just made. That really put the subject of integration behind us. People were so excited at how good of a football team we had and what a good person Walter was that it eased things over in the town. It's funny that as charged up as people were about integration, a simple thing like a football team could put all that behind them. That's exactly what happened in our town.

Charles Boston (former head coach Jefferson High, assistant coach Columbia High): To me, that first game did a lot for integration. When people saw Walter carry the football, I don't think they considered him a black boy, but rather a Columbia Wildcat. The way he ran was so exciting that there was no way people couldn't root for him.

It gave people a chance to see that black children had special gifts too, and maybe they had been missing those gifts. Walter was special, he was gifted, anyone could see that. And it took Walter to show Columbia that all children have gifts, whether it be carrying a football or doing schoolwork or whatever. I think it helped Columbia realize that it should celebrate all of its children's gifts.

When we first integrated, the kids at Jefferson were concerned. They were not afraid, just a little skeptical, since we didn't know the other people. We knew integration was coming. I remember when Eddie was at Jefferson, there were white people in the stands that came to see us play. I had heard that the people from Columbia were watching him. They knew he was a good football player and they were going to try to recruit my best athletes from Jefferson. So naturally I wanted to play Columbia then. I figured if I played them, then I could show my boys that we can compete with them and I can keep my players. But that never happened and Eddie never left Jefferson.

Well, after integration in January, the first thing we did was we had spring practice. As fate would have it, I was about to run out of linemen at Jefferson. I had one tackle and one guard and I didn't know what I was going to do to field the team. But I had some backs. I had Edward Moses, a little guy who took a lot of pressure off of Walter that year. He was a 165-pound scatback. He could really run. He ran wide most of the time. I also had a quarterback, Archie Johnson. And, of course, Walter.

But anyway, we had spring practice with no problems. I wasn't surprised because I knew my guys and I knew that they would not be a problem. They wanted to play football. I think there might have been a little animosity or something. Some guys were not going to be in the backfield, probably because we've got some guys here who're better than they are.

We get to that first ball game, against Prentiss, a city twenty-five miles up the road. Kept up with Columbia High pretty good. I'd listen to them on the radio. So I knew this was a kind of rival game, Prentiss and Columbia. This is the first game after integration, so everybody's all excited. The people were there, maybe 2,500 people at the stadium. I mean, we've got a crowd.

Well, we kicked it off and battled back and forth before Walter rips off one, something like ninety-five yards. Later he breaks another one, goes sixty-five yards for another touchdown. Now, during these two runs, Walter would break out into the open and he knew, I'm gone now. One time he's got quite a distance between him and the next guy, he did something like run with his fist raised in the air. Well, that offended somebody, they thought it was the black power signal. I don't know what it was. To me he was saying, I'm gone, bye-bye. Some guy asked me about that after the game. We had just defeated the archrival 14–6 and Walter scored both touchdowns on long runs. The guy said he didn't like him giving the black power signal. I just politely told him if he runs the ball like that, he can give any signal he wants. Everyone agreed. The guy left me alone. I never heard another word from anyone.

I'm not saying it was just Walter, but that football team had a lot to do with integration here in Columbia. We didn't have any problems, I believe, because of that team. We won football games, we won seven straight that year. Columbia High hadn't been doing that. They hadn't been winning that many ball games, so the fans were just excited they were winning. Then there were no fights. In football practices, sometimes you'll have a fight. I had them at Jefferson. Sometimes it just gets a little heated. But we didn't have one on the integrated team.

I was even happy when they stopped playing "Dixie" at the Columbia High football games. I thought that was a sign of progress within the city. I think people began to see the kids as the Wildcats, instead of a black boy or a white boy or whatever. I think that really helped integration here in Columbia. I think it was a big reason there was no trouble here.

Ricky Joe Graves: As good as he was, I don't think any of us knew until after high school how special he was. We just didn't have a frame of reference. It wasn't until he was at Jackson State that anybody realized what kind of athlete he really was. He probably scored more touchdowns and made more yardage in high school than any other athlete who had been there up to that time. And we had big Jim Dunaway, who played for Ole Miss and then the NFL, and we've had several pro athletes who have come through Columbia.

Whenever Walter had the urge to score, or the urge to run with the football, he did. There used to be a joke, so to speak, that when he really felt like doing something, he would just look over at the other halfback and wink at him, and it was over with. And he'd just say, "I'm gone," and he would do it. He just did those kinds of things. I don't know if it was that he knew he could do it, or he was just feeling the urge at the time, or what. But he could go when he wanted to. With the team, that team would have won the conference championship, but a play was sent in by mistake in the championship game.

We were down 7–3 to Monticello, and we needed a touchdown. Walter carried us all the way down to like the 15-yard line. We were running out of time and Coach sent in a play, it was supposed to have been the option, a run/pass option type play, and the ball was supposed to have been handed off to Walter. But the signal kind of got mixed up and they threw a pass instead.

Of course the ball was not caught and time ran out and that's how the game ended, with that play. But I really believe in my heart that if Payton would have had one more chance there, we would have won that championship.

Walter Payton: The players on the team used to ask me how I stayed in shape in high school, because I never lifted weights or trained with the other players. I always laughed. I used to tell them that I played four sports in high school—football, basketball, baseball, and track—plus I was always working in the yard or in my daddy's garden. I didn't have time to work out, but I didn't need to. I was always doing something.

Not to mention that we used to have to walk all over town. We didn't have cars and there wasn't any buses, so if you wanted to get somewhere you walked or jogged. I would jog about a mile and a half each way to school. In the summer I would jog over to practice, play football, and then jog back. That's almost three miles a day of jogging. We would jog to play sandlot ball or over to this pasture where we played baseball. We walked or jogged everywhere.

It is not like it is now, where kids don't walk anywhere. Back then in Columbia, if you waited for a ride, you'd be waiting all day. And all our activities were physical ones. We used to play some cards—I was a great Tonk player—but other than that it was outdoor stuff. Playing sports, working, hunting, and fishing.

I would sometimes go for long runs in the woods, wearing a pair of old army boots I got from the city dump. I'd put those on and take off into the woods that surround Columbia. I had a number of trails and sometimes would run along the Pearl River in the soft soil. It's an incredible workout when you run in the wet sand. You really have to work pretty hard to get going.

But that wasn't really why I did those runs. I appreciated the hard work, but it was to get out into the woods and be by myself. I loved the quiet of the Mississippi woods and the animals out there and how peaceful it was. I was always a loner as a kid and I think that is one reason I liked just running off where no one else was.

One of the best things that happened to me was learning that work ethic and coming along slowly. I wasn't a star athlete right away. Too many kids today are a superstar at twelve. Everyone is telling them how great they are. People are giving them things. They have no appreciation for what it really takes to stay there. They have so many people telling them they're great that they quit working. I'm lucky I didn't ever have that. And remember, Michael Jordan was the same way. He didn't make his high school basketball team until he was a junior. And I didn't play high school football until I was a junior. I think that makes a difference in work ethic.

Besides, all that running served me well when I joined the track team. I had good speed and was always a good baseball player because I could cover a lot of ground in center field and could leg out some infield hits and steal bases. Track was a little like that. Coach Boston used to coach all the sports at Jefferson and he encouraged me to go out for the track team.

It was fun. I was a sprinter, but sometimes I had to step up and do other events. One day we were at Hazelhurst for a track meet and our long jumper got hurt. Coach Boston said he needed somebody to take part in the long jump because they needed to get some more points so we could win. He said, "Walter, I need for you to do it."

I said, "Coach I've never done that before, I don't know the form or anything." I hadn't even long jumped once in practice. Coach said, "Just run as fast as you can and jump right before the line." He showed me the form real quick. So I took a couple of practice runs and then it was my turn up. So I went running down there and jumped as far as I could and I not only won that event, but I set the track meet record. All on my first try. And we won the meet. That was just one of many days where life in Columbia gave me the confidence to do bigger things later on.

4

Jackson State

Paul "Bear" Bryant, the legendary football coach at the University of Alabama, offered a simple but noteworthy opinion in the mid-1960s when he was asked if he would ever integrate his high-powered but then all-white teams in Tuscaloosa. "Well," said Bryant, who would win four national titles as coach of the Crimson Tide, "I won't be the first. But I won't be third."

The implication was obvious. Bryant knew that the South was home to an incredible slew of black athletes who, once one Southeastern Conference school began recruiting and playing, could overwhelm any team silly enough to rely solely on white players. While Bryant wasn't ready to be a pioneer in race relations, he wasn't dumb enough to hold out and lose. Eventually, when the floodgates opened, Alabama, while not pulling the linchpin, would be ready.

This was the era in which Walter Payton and all of the South's black athletes grew up. Despite being outrageously gifted, they were largely ignored by their big state schools, which the media fawned over. Through most of the 1960s, Alabama, Auburn, Mississippi State, Ole Miss, Louisiana State, and so on fielded all-white football and basketball teams. In 1966, Texas Western College basketball coach Don Haskins started five black players and defeated all-white SEC powerhouse Kentucky for the national championship. A few weeks later a black basketball player named Perry Wallace accepted a basketball scholarship to Vanderbilt, breaking the conference's color barrier in that sport. On September 30, 1967, Nat Northington became the first black to play SEC football when he suited up for Kentucky in a game against Ole Miss.

But progress was slow. At first, SEC schools would only take a few blacks, carefully selecting the players, often not going for the very best. Instead, black athletes were forced to choose between heading to big schools in the Midwest or West or enrolling at the smaller, predominantly black schools of the South—institutions such as Grambling State and Southern in Louisiana, Prairie View A&M in Texas, and Alcorn State and Jackson State in Mississippi—which in 1974 would form the Southwestern Athletic Conference.

Since many of the black players were from small towns or rural backgrounds, they often chose to stay closer to home rather than head off to California or the Big Ten. The result was a level of football played in the SWAC that was on a par with anything played by the traditional schools the media focused on.

Consider Jackson State, where both Eddie and Walter Payton played. In 1968 the Tigers had eleven seniors drafted into the National Football League. During Payton's stretch at Jackson State he played with twenty players who would eventually be drafted by the NFL. That included first-round picks Jerome Barkum (1972, New York Jets), Donald Reese (1974, Miami Dolphins), and Robert Brazile (1975, Houston Oilers). This was common throughout the SWAC, where strong programs such as Southern, Grambling, and Alcorn all boasted similar levels of talent.

In 1971, SEC schools were accepting only a few blacks. As mind-boggling as it is now, it was no surprise when Walter Payton graduated from Columbia High School that he had only three scholarship offers: the University of Kansas, Alcorn State, and Jackson State. Despite an overpowering senior season where he was named all-state in the SEC, not even the local schools Mississippi and Mississippi State, let alone Bryant's storied 'Bama program, ever came a-calling.

Walter considered attending Kansas. He even went to the Jayhawks' Lawrence campus for a brief spell before changing his mind and returning closer to home. Although Coach Boston was an Alcorn alum, Walter decided to accept a scholarship offer from Jackson State, where Eddie was already established and a lot of Columbia players and students went.

There was a great deal of excitement surrounding the Jackson State football team when Walter arrived, because word had it he was even better than his older brother, Eddie, who was not only a star but would go on to his own career in the NFL. As Tiger teammate Jackie Slater once said, "Many of us could not understand how it could even be fathomed that Walter could be better than Eddie, because Eddie was just a fantastic little tough guy. But then we saw it." Walter's freshman year he often lined up alongside Eddie, causing fans to dub the Jackson State backfield "Paytons' Place."

The Tigers were coached by the gruff, tough Bob Hill, a Mississippi coaching legend, who was a longtime presence within Jackson State football. In Payton's four years, JSU would go 33–11–1. Payton would become Jackson's all-time greatest player, rushing for 3,563 career yards, averaging 6.1 yards per carry, and scoring a national-record sixty-six career touchdowns. Upon graduation in 1975, he was drafted at age twenty in the first round by the Chicago Bears, one of five JSU Tigers selected in the draft that year.

Today, what with the heavy recruitment of black athletes to nearly every school in the nation, the SWAC teams have fallen behind in competitive terms. Although they still compete at the Division I level in basketball, the SWAC now plays at the Division I-AA level in football, where they often field strong teams. Jackson State has captured ten SWAC titles since Payton graduated, and regularly leads I-AA in attendance, including a I-AA-record 38,873 per game in 1997. At the end of each season, the Player of the Year in Division I-AA is awarded the Walter Payton Award, that level of football's Heisman Trophy.

Charles Boston: Walter wasn't recruited very heavily coming out of high school. Even though he was a very good player, only three schools recruited him, Kansas, Alcorn State, which is where I went to school, and Jackson State. None of the SEC schools came. I know my theory on why. It might not be right, but I think there were quotas back then and I really believe that if you had two, three, whatever, then that was it.

It's not like that now. But I really think that they believed you could just have so many blacks on a team and that was it. Most of them were probably backs or defensive backs or what have you. When you think about it, that was just a big mistake. Imagine what a player such as Walter could have meant to Mississippi State or Ole Miss! He would have changed the program.

We had a white player on the team, Steve Stewart, who was a good receiver, and he eventually graduated from the University of Houston. But first he went to the University of Southern Mississippi. USM is only about thirty miles east of here, in Hattiesburg, Mississippi. This has always stuck out in my mind because they came over to scout Steve before they signed him. They sent assistant coaches to watch our games. They saw Walter play, they saw the things he could do, the runs he could make, and they still didn't want him.

I talked to the recruiter myself. Steve was a good ballplayer, but I said, "What about Walter?" And the recruiter said, "We just want Steve." And I said, "But what about Walter, don't you need a player like that? He's one of the best players I've ever seen." And he said, "We just want Steve." I was like, Okay. It was the times. Imagine a program like Southern Mississippi not wanting a player like Walter

Payton, who makes all-state and becomes the NFL's all-time leading rusher and he grows up thirty miles away.

Forest Dantin: When it came to the spring and Walter was picking a school to go to, we thought it was stupid that none of the Southeastern Conference schools were recruiting him. My dad is an Ole Miss alum, both undergrad and law school. He ran for governor of Mississippi a couple of times, so he was a well-known alumnus. I was going to attend Ole Miss the next fall and we tried to generate some interest in Walter by the school.

They had an Ole Miss alumni meeting in Columbia the spring of our senior year. They held it at Tays Restaurant and my dad and I went. There was an assistant coach down here and we tried to convince him about Walter. We said, "Look, there is a guy that is on our team who you need to be looking at. He's the best high school football player we've ever seen."

He didn't want to hear too much about it. All he would ask is "How are his grades?" And we said they were all right. We didn't really have a clue, but I am sure they were good enough. But they never checked and they weren't interested. I just thought it was idiotic. Here was a great player right in the state of Mississippi, and Ole Miss wasn't even looking at him. The only offers he had were from Kansas, Alcorn, Jackson State, and some junior colleges. A player that good with only three schools offering him a scholarship. It's unbelievable when you think about it. Imagine the recruiting war they'd have now!

Walter Payton: I've always said that the best thing that happened to me was going to a school like Jackson State. I am really glad that it worked out that way, that schools such as Alabama or Mississippi State or Louisiana State didn't recruit me. Obviously I do not support the reason why those schools wouldn't recruit me; the idea that they didn't want black kids to attend or play at their schools was reprehensible. They turned their back on so many great kids and great players. They really denied people opportunities they deserved.

But I needed a school like Jackson State to keep my feet planted. I didn't need to go to one of these schools that had all this money and received all this attention. I remember looking at the players at those schools, and I thought the schools made prima donnas out of some of these guys. I played against guys in high school, or when I was on the Mississippi all-star team, who had a great deal of ability, but they went off to one of those big SEC schools and they ended up not being worth a dime.

It was because of the culture at the schools. All the players could think about was the fame and the fortune and the money, and when am I gonna get in the spotlight. They were surrounded by money, the boosters and comfortable facilities and the adulation. It spoiled them, it changed their work ethic. The media was always there telling them how great they were, making them famous. They would believe they were great, believe they were famous. But then here we would come. It's why the SWAC produced so many pros. While those players were becoming soft, we kept working. They thought they were the best players in the country. But they weren't playing against the entire country.

It wasn't like that at Jackson State. Our coach, Bob Hill, he kept it real. I don't care how good you were, you were treated like everybody else. You weren't put on a pedestal by Bob Hill.

It is why I am so happy that I went to a school like Jackson State and met a man such as Bob Hill. Coach Hill's whole focus helped make me. I don't know exactly how Coach Hill felt about me, but when I was there I always felt like a son. I had that special kind of a relationship with him. I always, always knew that he had my best interests in mind when he made decisions. I think that at some of these programs, with coaches being paid so much money, and the pressure from the media and boosters is so great, that they don't always have the players' best interests in their heart. They have to win, they have to make people happy, they fall for that.

Another thing that I took from Coach Hill was how a man should carry himself on the field. I never appreciated the guys who would do little jigs in the end zone and stuff like that. You see guys on television today, they make a five-yard gain and they have to do a dance. Or they make one tackle and they all celebrate. That's not football and that's not what you are out there for. I used to watch these guys, disgusted, I'd say, "Look at them, it's all about showing off and stuff like that." It's not about football.

I really have a lot of disrespect for players like that. I've never liked it and never understood it. I think I got a lot of that from Coach Hill. If he saw you do anything on the field, you were off the field. It was all about playing the game, not drawing attention to yourself. He'd say players like that were a joke, but they were such a joke they didn't even realize what fools they were. Coach Hill, in case you hadn't realized, is old-school. But that's the best school.

Another thing Coach was big on was not running out-of-bounds unless you were hit out. That had always been my style. I'd say, I'm not gonna run out-of-bounds before I hit somebody first. I wanted to make them feel me a little. I took great pride in that. A lot of guys are afraid of injury. Personally, I liked contact. I enjoyed it. My whole thing was, I'll give it to them before they give it to me. It's a system that works. Every play, I wanted to go full blast, 110, 120 percent. What I try to do is I try to neutralize his attack by attacking him. If you don't explode into him, by the law of physics you're gonna take most of the impact.

One of Coach Hill's mottos, one I took to heart, was "Never die easy," which is, obviously, also the title of this book. I took that as a motto for my game and my life. Never die easy. Why run out-of-bounds and die easy? Make that linebacker pay. Make him earn your death. It carries into all facets of life, and it is something both my dad and Coach Hill taught me. It's okay to lose, to die, but don't die without trying, without giving it your best.

I used to tell Jarrett the same thing when he started playing football. I used to say that not going out-of-bounds will actually help you later in the game because those linebackers are gonna think twice before they come after you again, because if you hit one one time or two times, they have second thoughts about having to tackle you the next time. Suddenly, it's, Ah, maybe not, because I remember what I got the last time I tried to tackle you.

So you put the punishment on them before they give it to you. It makes them think a little bit the next time they come after you. And if they are thinking, you are winning. You can't be afraid of a linebacker, just hit them before they hit you.

These are all things that Coach Hill taught us. It is why Coach Hill is one of the greatest coaches of all time. People don't understand how great of a coach he was, how great of a coach most of the guys in the SWAC were. Eddie Robinson at Grambling got some deserved recognition later in his career, but for the most part the fans and the media ignore those coaches like Coach Hill, just because they didn't coach at a white school.

Well, back then there were no black head coaches. Sadly, that is still true, which shows how far college football still needs to come. I'll tell you, if a school like Ole Miss or Mississippi State had been progressive enough or smart enough and hired Coach Hill, they would be the powerhouse program in the SEC, not Tennessee and Florida. He could coach as well as anyone in the game. I know they never would have done it, but if you put Coach Hill against Bear Bryant or any of those guys, he'd win. They could still do it. Those schools that are always complaining they aren't as good as Alabama or Florida, maybe they just haven't hired the right coach. All these years later and the SEC still has never had a black head coach. Can you imagine how big of a deal the first one will be?

At Jackson State, Coach Hill just wanted me to stay planted and not really get suckered into that other side because once you do, that's it. Once you get soft, once you take success and let it go to your head, you are done. Coach would keep the temptations away from us, by running us so hard and making us do all this stuff that he kept us so busy that we were too tired to do anything. At night, we couldn't wait to go to the room and go to sleep. We didn't have time to get in trouble. And believe me, we were afraid to get in trouble, because he would treat you like a parent would. He probably would have taken you out and spanked your butt just like a parent would do. Or he would call your parents and tell your parents, and the parents would make you come home and spank your butt. So he just kept everything in perspective for these guys. It is why so many of Coach Hill's former players from Jackson State did so great as professionals. We knew about hard work, keeping our noses clean, and to not let success go to our heads.

Those are the things that ruin a great number of athletic careers. Guys stop working, they get in trouble, or they begin to think they are better than they are. And suddenly, it is over. Those are three things players for Coach Hill did not have happen to them.

It's just as well, because Coach Hill would have cuffed us around if we had. Even though he was older and we had come back as professional athletes, I don't know any players who didn't fear the man. He was tough. Tough enough to scare the daylights out of any NFL player.

I remember Eddie telling me that the reason he went to Jackson State was that on his visit to campus he attended the Jackson State–Alcorn State game. Before the game Coach Hill and the Alcorn coach, Reno Castle, got into a fight in the middle of the field. Both benches emptied and there was this big fight. The coaches really went at it, and when they separated everyone, Coach Hill had his shirt torn off. He ran off the field, leading his team to the locker room, and he was waving his shirt around above his head.

You have to understand this was a big, big rivalry, as intense as any rivalry at any school in the country. Forget Alabama-Auburn, UCLA-USC, Michigan–Ohio State or any of those games. Alcorn-Jackson was huge, bigger than any of them. Almost all of the players were black kids from Mississippi. We all knew each other, we played with or against each other. It was a heated rivalry. You have never heard of a bench-clearing brawl at the Alabama-Auburn game with the coaches leading the fight, have you? Imagine if the media covered the SWAC! They'd have gone nuts.

Well, Eddie, he's in the stands trying to decide whether to go to Alcorn or Jackson. Alcorn was popular at Jefferson High because our coach, Coach Boston, went there, and because the town of Alcorn is a small one, a lot like Columbia. But Eddie was being recruited by both schools, so he watches the fight, watches Coach Hill run off the field waving his ripped shirt, and then watches Jackson win 7–6 and says, "I'm going to Jackson."

Coach Hill was a big reason why I wanted to go to Jackson, but so too was the fact that Eddie was there. We wound up rooming together when I was a freshman. Jackson State was a popular place for Columbia players to go and play. It was close to home and I knew a lot of people there. One of the people Eddie and I respected as an athlete was one of our friends from Columbia, Les Peters, and he played at Jackson State.

He was from home and a little older and he'd work out with us, he'd act as an assistant coach, and I just admired the passion he brought with him. He'd say stuff that coaches would say. "Die hard; be quick or be dead," stuff like that. That excited me.

Les Peters: We weren't recruited by the bigger schools, but it wasn't something that bothered us too much. We knew that if you could play in the SWAC you could play anywhere in the world. All you have to do is go back and look at the history of the SWAC, you'll see how many great players and teams there were. It didn't faze us, because it was like in high school, we knew the black teams were often better, no matter who got the publicity.

When I got out of Jefferson High in the late 1960s, Southern Illinois and Indiana were recruiting black players. I had a chance to go to either, but I chose Jackson State. The bigger schools in the area, like Ole Miss, Mississippi State, Southern Mississippi, Alabama, they weren't doing it. They weren't interested in us. When Walter came along, they'd take a couple guys, but that was it.

They really missed out on it, you know. And not just on good football players, but great people. You had to be around Walter and his family to really understand what type of human being he was. I hate that God couldn't let him stay longer, but he was a great athlete, a great human being, a great person.

Even though the big schools weren't recruiting us, you can't imagine how exciting playing college football was for us. I will never forget the day we played at Texas Southern and I walked on the field in the Astrodome. That was something, to have a little old country boy like me in the Astrodome. Everybody wanted to make the travel squad because none of us had ever been anywhere. This was our chance.

We had so much talent back then. In 1968, we had eleven guys drafted, it tied a record set by Southern California. Every team we played was stacked with guys who would go on to the NFL. Those teams were great, the players were so good. We just didn't get a lot of attention.

The Heisman was a joke back then. It was ridiculous. Archie Griffin won it two years back-to-back when Walter was at Jackson State. Now, Archie Griffin was a great back, but he wasn't half the football player Walter Payton was. And we knew that, everybody who had ever seen Walter knew it. But we knew, coming from a predominantly black school and a small school in a small state, that he was eliminated.

Walter was great, in part, because of what Bob Hill made him do. Bob Hill wanted complete players, you had to be able to block, fake, catch the ball. Bob would have Walter blocking Robert Brazile—who would go on to play with the Houston Oilers—and the other big linebackers. That's the reason Walter could block so well. Walter could block better than a fullback. One time I saw Walter block Teddy Hendricks, when Teddy was with Oakland and Walter was with the Bears. Walter just crushed him. John Madden still talks about it. But that was what we learned at Jackson State. It was pure fundamental football. Not a lot of glory, just great football. And if you couldn't play the game the right way, you didn't play. If you couldn't block, you learned, or you sat on the bench. I don't care how good you were at something else. That was Coach Hill, he never backed down from what he believed. The man was amazing.

Walter was the greatest football player ever lived. Now, there might have been some better running the ball, there might have been some faster, but Walter was the best football player all-around, could do it all. Block, catch, run; if you put him on defense, tackle, pass, kick, punt. Now, Walter would kick our point after touchdown, and field goals. He could do it all. You just wouldn't believe the type of person he was. They're not born every day.

It wasn't all hard work at Jackson State. For Walter it was a time to grow up and get his feet under him outside of the tight family and small town he'd left behind in Columbia. He began taking life and football more seriously. For many black children growing up in the South, the opportunity of a full athletic scholarship to a university was not taken lightly. Players were expected to make the most of their studies, ensuring a solid future, most often as a teacher and coach back home. College was viewed as a ticket to middle-class stability and a way out of a life of manual labor.

Payton did take his schoolwork seriously. He also found time for a healthy social life. Walter developed a reputation as not only a popular student but a great dancer. With his balance, light feet, and athleticism, it was no surprise. As a sophomore, he even entered a local dance contest, which was broadcast on a Jackson TV show called *24 Karat Black Gold.* Walter and his partner performed the "Cock Walk," a forefather to today's hip-hop moves, and won the contest. That earned the two of them a free trip to Los Angeles where they appeared on the legendary dance show *Soul Train.* Walter and his dance moves were broadcast nationally in the *Soul Train* line before he became a household name as a running back.

As Walter realized when he was in high school, girls tended to pay attention to football stars. That was until Coach Hill, looking to channel Payton's attention away from the many female admirers he had on campus and into football and schoolwork, introduced him to Connie Norwood. Hill's idea was to slow Walter down off the field, in an effort to speed him up on it. It worked. Connie and Walter began dating seriously from the start, before spending the rest of their lives together.

Connie Payton: I didn't know Walter when he appeared on *Soul Train*. The funny thing was, I watched that contest because *The Walt Boatner Hour* was a show I used to dance on, and a couple I knew from New Orleans won a similar contest and also appeared on *Soul Train*. So even though I had no idea who Walter was, I watched. He was in the contest with some girl. We have the video of it, it is funny. Walter is in jeans, and they had wide legs, real big bell-bottom jeans. He had a shirt cut up like a midriff shirt, so you could see his stomach with all the muscle tone. He also wore these big platform shoes. His shirt had long sleeves and he always wore these big caps. They were his trademark. They used to call them apple caps. It's like a cap, or even like a baseball cap, but the brothers wore them. They have a real wide front. Walter was known for those, even when he came to the Chicago Bears. He wore apple caps all the time. That's what he had on. It was some kind of outfit, but it was the mid-1970s, remember.

Bob Hill first introduced me to Walter my senior year in high school. Bob was dating my aunt Betty and would come down and visit from time to time. For whatever reason, he just thought that I would be a real nice, sensible girlfriend for Walter. Bob looked at Walter like a son and was very close to him. So one weekend, Bob wanted to know if I would come up with my aunt Betty to Jackson and he would arrange for the two of us to meet. Walter came over to his house that evening and as far as I was concerned, there was no attraction at first. I thought he was very polite, very nice, and I ended up feeling sorry for him because he really liked a girl whose parents didn't like him for some reason. And so we spent that evening just kind of talking about her and that whole situation. I ended the weekend thinking, He's a nice guy, he's here, I'm going back home. That's it, and I just hope he gets back together with his girlfriend.

Then later that spring, Walter wanted to come down and visit me in New Orleans for spring break. That was a surprise because I think we may have talked a little bit here and there on the phone, but even at that, I still didn't think it would be a relationship. So needless to say, we go to the airport to pick him up, and we had all kinds of car trouble coming home. My mom swears it was all his fault, so right off the bat she didn't like him, thought he was trouble.

Walter was real quiet in front of my parents and my three brothers. When it was dinnertime, he wouldn't eat with my family at the table. When everybody was through with dinner, he would want me to then go with him and get something to eat. It was like he was too shy to eat with everybody else. My mother just didn't understand that.

I didn't have any plans to go to Jackson State once I graduated. I was going to stay home and go to Dillard. I didn't want to be in a dormitory, I wanted to just commute to school every day, back and forth. However, Bob Hill had me come up to Jackson State over the summer to see if I would like it. While I was up there I got talked into trying out for the Jaycette dance team. And so I made it and decided to go to Jackson State. That was Walter's junior year.

I knew Walter was a good football player then, but I didn't really pay any attention to the football team during the games, because as a Jaycette I was more focused on how our dance routine was going to be. But Walter was incredible and a joy to watch. Bob knew that Walter was going to really make a name for himself and do something. I think that was the reason why Bob wanted him to pick out a levelheaded young lady who could probably pretty much keep him in line and wasn't going to take advantage of him. Bob was pretty much right, that was the kind of person I was.

Rodney Phillips (college friend and teammate): On the field Walter was impressive. A couple of those patented moves he used in the NFL, he always had them, even from the first time I saw him. I remember watching him for the first time in the Mississippi all-star game, and you don't see many high school kids physically developed the way he was. He was strong beyond his years.

He and his brother always claimed that one year his mom got a couple of dump-truck loads of dirt and dumped it in the yard, and made them spread it out. That's where he got his muscles from. I never bought it. I know Walter and he liked to work out in secret.

He roomed with his brother his first year. The next year he started out rooming with Ricky Young and part of the way into that, Bob Hill sort of changed us around. He put us together and we roomed the next three years together. We became great friends. Walter was more complex than he let on. He had a lot of serious moods. When something upset him he got a little quiet or a little sullen. He was very concerned about what people thought. He liked people and he liked to kid around. He was mischievous, he liked to be doing something all the time. If you were just sitting around, he would think of something to egg somebody or agitate somebody.

Walter was the star player and eventually people pulled at him from a lot of different directions. He was a cautious individual. He was always down-to-earth so he took that hero worship with a little bit of skepticism. He didn't go for people telling him how great he was. He was never into that.

His mother was a strong influence. It was obvious that he loved his mother and he was very close to her. His father had a great influence on him too, but he didn't talk about his father as much as he did his mother. His mom used to bake cookies for him, bring a gallon jar of cookies. Oatmeal and raisin. Those were some good cookies. She didn't know it, but she was probably bringing them more for me than him. He was also very close to Eddie, his brother, and Pam, his sister. Pam used to come by all the time and throw rocks at our window to get us to come out and see her.

We were all very determined back then. Being in the South, and this is not only Walter, but this is by and large athletes from that era in the South, we were more focused and determined than kids today.

It was because we came from so little. Football was everything. Sports were big in the community. That was one factor, if you grew up and the community saw you as possessing physical attributes or physical prowess, then you were expected to participate on that level. Discipline was big, but there were not as many distractions in those days. In the newer South, things were going on, but they weren't as prevalent as they are now.

Sports allowed you to be accepted. That helped create an atmosphere where a coach had a better opportunity to grasp the attention of a kid, and instill discipline, direction, and focus in them. A lot of those things were already within Walter. He had his own desire for success. I think those things were placed there and groomed by his mother. But they were expanded by athletics.

As a player he was just incredible. You couldn't believe the things he did. He made some great moves that were elusive, but unlike a Barry Sanders, he wasn't attempting to avoid all contact. He'd run over you. You didn't know what he'd do. One tackler he'd slip, the next he'd plow over. It kept everyone off balance. He just wanted to gain leverage. I've seen him make some karaoke moves, you know that drill in practice? I've seen him running straight down the field and all of a sudden, just karaoke around him, and the guy would fall down on his face. I've never seen anybody do that, and that was very impressive.

It used to bother Walter a little that he didn't get much national recognition. By the time he was a senior he was easily the best player in the country, but not a lot of people were talking about him. Not many people nationally had heard about him. I remember one Saturday we were sitting there in our room watching an Ohio State game on television. They played on Saturday afternoon and we played at night. Walter and I were reclining in our beds and the TV was kind of up, and we were looking and all of a sudden Walter sat up on the edge of the bed and you could tell he was upset.

I said, "Man, what's the matter with you?" He said some expletives, and then he said, "Archie Griffin can't carry my jock." Jackson State was pushing Walter as a candidate for the Heisman Trophy, but realistically, knowing that we were at a small college and Archie was at Ohio State, we knew Walter's chances were very slim. We knew Archie would get it. But by the same token, we knew that while he had the ability, he wasn't the best player. Walter Payton was.

Walter Payton: At the time it was disappointing to watch other players get the awards, get the notoriety, who I felt I was better than. But, in truth, as I've learned, it doesn't matter if you go to a small school, or are from a small town, or anything like that. It's what you do with the ability that God has given you.

It's one thing that you always realize, that nothing is complete. Nothing is complete, not even in society. At the time I didn't get the recognition, but obviously I would. The same is true with so many of my teammates, who didn't get named All-American but then would be drafted ahead of all the guys who did. I look at some of the other great players from small towns and schools in Mississippi, players such as Jerry Rice. You just have to remember it will come. The recognition will come in due time.

When I was a senior, I finished fourth in the Heisman Trophy voting and people said, "You know what, if you had gone to a larger university, you would have probably won the Heisman Trophy." But I tell you what I gained at Jackson State in terms of knowledge, in terms of being able to socialize and the education I got—I wouldn't trade it for all the Heisman Trophies in the world.

I was able to learn from my parents, my teammates, and Coach Hill, and there is no trophy as valuable as that. I thank God for them because without them I wouldn't have made it. So for all you young people who are out there who have dreams, hopes, desires, it doesn't matter where you are as long as you hold tightly to those, because it can come to fruition if you don't give up and if you persevere. It doesn't matter where you are in the race now, it is where you will end up. Don't give up because you are not where you want to be. Everything that you want, if you can visualize it, you can have it. And I hope that you never lose your vision. I was lucky I didn't and it worked out.

Rodney Phillips: Some of the greatest plays Walter ever made were short gains. He'd go up to the line of scrimmage and there was nothing, he would slam into the line and bounce off of them and spin and break three or four tackles just to get back to the line of scrimmage. He'd get maybe a two- or three-, four-yard gain. But getting a couple of yards out of a loss was a great run.

He was more than a great runner too. I did a lot of blocking for him, but a lot of times he blocked for me because he was a great blocker. And he could catch the ball so well. He used to be able to catch the ball with one hand. He was just so flexible, agile, and he had great balance. Everybody knows this by now, but back then, we were kind of amazed many times.

The first time he really impressed me was his freshman year. I grew up in a little town in southern Mississippi called Mendenhall, but I signed with the University of Cincinnati, only to transfer to Jackson State after one year. I was sitting out as a redshirt that year and I was watching practice. They put Walter out on the practice field with the older guys and they gave him the ball and he just started running over people. Those he didn't run over, he ran around, and then nobody could catch him. Everybody else had been working out and practicing and were older and he came out there the first day and blew them all away. And you have to remember how good the other players were. There were probably a couple dozen future pros on that field, a lot of future first-round NFL picks, NFL starters. So this was no simple thing.

When we played in games we used to give the ball to Walter over and over, especially when things were clicking. I remember this one time, I was on the sidelines, Ricky Young was at fullback, and Walter was running the ball. Bob Hill sent me in with a play. I came in and Walter was kind of leaning over and he was breathing hard. He had run the ball about five or six times in a row, and I came in with a play to give the ball to Walter. I looked at Walter and he had snot running down his face, sweat, he was breathing hard, and Ricky looked at me and then at Walter, and we looked at each other. He was dead tired. But we called the play, and he ran it down and scored a touchdown. He knew how to dig deep within himself no matter if he was tired or fatigued.

I played in the NFL for the Rams and the Cardinals and played with and against many great players, but Walter was easily the best player I've ever been around. When I came to the Rams, they had John Cappelletti, the Heisman Trophy winner. Then when I went to St. Louis, there was O. J. Anderson. O.J., as a pure runner, he had some tremendous moves. He was big and strong, but still he couldn't do all the things Walter could.

What made Walter different was that he was a great runner but there were so many other things he could do. He was a great blocker, a great pass receiver, he had the best arm on the team, could throw the ball to any of us. He could also punt the ball, kick it as far as anyone I've seen. He could do standing back flips, walk on his hands. He could stand up under the rim and dunk the basketball without getting a running leap. You name it. He was just a phenomenal athlete.

He was always in the best shape, just incredible shape. Bob Hill's practices were kind of grueling. One thing Bob believed in was conditioning. He believed in toughness and conditioning. Walter made it through practice like it was no problem.

There is an interchange around Jackson, Highway 220, and when we were in college it hadn't been completed yet. They were building it. We used to go out on one of the higher embankments and we used to run up and down that hill. It was like probably sixty yards almost straight up. To get up and down that, that was tough. And then there was a place down the hill, along the Pearl River, under the bridge. It would be all sand. Grueling stuff to run in, and we'd train there. This was early in our pro careers. Walter was always the leader; if you could keep up with him, you were doing good.

Walter was incredibly humble, considering how good he was. And the thing that keeps some good athletes from being great athletes is that they read their own press clippings. It's hard to be a great athlete and not have the ego. That's the downfall of many. Walter got past that.

Walter was even more intense, he believed in fundamentals, he believed in hard work, and then he had the talent to go along with it. There were people who were faster, there were people who were quicker, there were people who were stronger, but there was nobody who was all of those, because he could get in a footrace and he wouldn't be embarrassed. He could get in a strength contest with strong people and he wouldn't be embarrassed. He could get in a quickness contest with superquick people and he wouldn't be embarrassed. But no one else could do all the things as well. I think he could have been a decathlete and a world-record holder. He probably could have set a world record that would never be matched.

5

Going to Chicago

For a kid from little Columbia, Mississippi, who played college football in Jackson on a team where big road trips were to places such as Itta Bena, Mississippi; Normal, Alabama; and Grambling, Louisiana, the idea of moving to Chicago—3 million population, one-hundred-story-plus buildings, bitter windchill whipping in off of Lake Michigan—was one that took a moment to get used to.

Certainly, Walter knew that the NFL would take him to the nation's largest cities. He even knew that one of them would become his new hometown. But Chicago, the City of Big Shoulders, seemed so removed from what he had grown accustomed to in the small towns and back roads of the Deep South. The slow-smoked cooking of Miss Laetha's Bar-B-Que Inn in Foxworth was suddenly out. Deep-dish pizza from Gino's East and Uno's was in.

Walter was only twenty when the Bears drafted him. He had completed his degree in special education at Jackson State in just three and a half years and was physically ready for the NFL. But was he emotionally ready? Was he mature enough? Linebackers didn't scare

him. The big city, however, would be something of a challenge—
although nothing was capable of dousing his excitement.

While Walter didn't know the Bears were planning on using the
fourth pick overall on him in the 1975 draft, it really should have
been no surprise that Chicago would go for a running back. For as
long as the oldest Chicago Bears fan can remember, the franchise had
been blessed with great running backs. As much as its home city is
built on hard work, the Bears are a team of running backs and linebackers.

The list of ballcarriers read like a who's who of backs, all tough,
strong, and shifty runners who rallied the city behind the team. Red
Grange. Paddy Driscoll. Bronko Nagurski. George McAfee. Beattie
Feathers. Rick Casares. And, of course, Gale Sayers, who had retired
four years earlier.

It is no surprise that the City of Big Shoulders would prefer
strong-willed, blue-collar runners who churned out yardage as opposed to flashier, passing-first-skilled players. The Bears have always
been a running team, in part because the team mirrors its fan base
and in part because of the winter weather that makes throwing the
ball difficult as the season wears on. As the wind howls in off of Lake
Michigan and into Soldier Field, it is best to have a sure-handed,
swift-footed back who can control the clock and push toward the
end zone.

This is a team built on running backs and linebackers (this is also
the team of Dick Butkus and Mike Singletary). And thus when the
1975 draft arrived, the new coach, Jack Pardee, and the general manager, Jim Finks, combed the nation looking for the best running
back available. The big name was Ohio State's two-time Heisman
Trophy winner, Archie Griffin, who played in the nearby Big Ten.
But the Bears had been a franchise that didn't mind taking chances
on small college players—each of their previous three number-one
picks came from small schools—and no one could ignore the numbers or the highlights that Walter, a two-time Little All-American,
was producing down at Jackson State.

The first pick was property of the Atlanta Falcons, who chose Cal quarterback Steve Bartkowski. Dallas was next, and a heated debate ensued within the Cowboys coaching staff. Defensive coaches wanted Randy White, the great lineman from Maryland. Offensive coaches wanted Payton. Tom Landry went with the defense and White became an All-Pro in Dallas. Next up was the Baltimore Colts, who took North Carolina guard Ken Huff. Chicago wasted no time, selecting Payton immediately.

The Bears were banking on Walter becoming the next great running back the team could be built around. Although admittedly nervous about the prospect of not only playing professional football but heading to Chicago, Payton was the definition of confidence. He didn't shy away from the inevitable comparisons to past Bears greats.

"If the people of Chicago give me some time and are patient, I'll give them a new Gale Sayers," he said boldly on draft day. Soon after, Payton became a wealthy man, signing a three-year contract worth nearly $500,000. That included a $126,000 signing bonus, which was even bigger than the one that University of Mississippi quarterback Archie Manning received from the New Orleans Saints in 1971.

Walter appeared confident, but he later admitted that the idea of heading off to such a big city, in such a cold climate, was enough to make him nervous deep inside his southern heart. He let no one know about it, and at the tender age of twenty the Columbia kid was headed off to the bright lights of Rush Street, to the hard-core fans of Chicago's working neighborhoods, and into the fierce weather of Midway in winter. He was billed as a savior. But first he had to prove he could survive.

Walter Payton: When I was drafted by the Chicago Bears it wasn't the best situation at the time. They weren't a very good team, they were changing coaches, and I was leaving the Deep South to come to Chicago. It was the site of the 1967 riots and everything else. But mainly I knew it was cold there, and that is what I was thinking about most. How cold it was truly was a big factor. It was a culture shock for me, being from the South and coming to the Midwest. I know it sounds silly today, but it wasn't then. But I went back to my mom and talked to her about it and she said, "Listen, son, this is what has been dealt and you need to play your hand out." I often went and talked to my mother when I wasn't really sure about something.

Again, the idea of coming to Chicago, when all I had known was Mississippi, was more of a cultural shock to me. Growing up we thought Hattiesburg or Jackson was a big city, and now here was Chicago. But when I came up here, I felt it immediately. I felt the greatness of this city. I felt it when I started playing and I didn't have performances as good as they should have been. I felt the wrath of the city then.

That was very hard on me. But that was okay, they were just demanding. It really taught me to toughen up, and it just shaped me. I was motivated to just go out there and show everybody that I was going to make it. There was a lot of pressure being the number-one pick, and the fans, rightfully, demanded a lot from me.

At the time, they didn't know I was good yet. But they hung in there and hopefully they're proud of the results. But just the way that people are treated in Chicago is amazing. Even with the early pressure, I fell in love with Chicago and that's why I never moved back to the South. I loved it here, I loved the people here. This became my home and I will never leave Chicago. And I stay here not because I'm loved by the people now. I stay here because I love the people, the attitudes, and how friendly everyone is to each other. Plus I've gotten used to the cold. I have a big coat collection now.

That first summer, Vernon Perry and I headed north to attend training camp and we stopped in Memphis to stay with Eddie. Vernon was a teammate of mine at Jackson State and he had been invited to the Bears camp. That was nice for me because I knew at least one person. We decided to drive up together.

Eddie was teaching and coaching high school in Memphis. It would be another year before he was offered a chance to play in the

Canadian Football League, and then another one before he was finally given the chance to play in the NFL himself. But you have to remember, back then the reason we went to Jackson State wasn't to make the NFL but to get a degree and become a teacher and a coach. My mother always wanted Eddie to be a teacher. She wanted my sister, Pam, to be a nurse and she wanted me to be a preacher. I have no idea why she wanted me to be a preacher, but she did. But that's what it was then for boys, use football to go to college and become a teacher or a preacher. There is always steady work in those fields.

Vernon and I were excited about going to camp. I was just excited about the chance to play, the chance to prove myself against the best. I guess I was like any athlete, you're apprehensive when you go from one level to the next. You don't know how good you are, how good you were, and all of a sudden you're going to another level. I thought I could handle it, but until you strap it on and excel with people who are supposed to be good at that level, you're always apprehensive about how good you'll be.

But they were going to pay me over $100,000 a year to go play football. That was just incredible. I guess we knew that if you were a first-round pick in the NFL you were going to make a lot of money, but when you come from the background I did, growing up poor in a place like Columbia, Mississippi, you don't believe it until you have it. And even then you don't believe it.

We always feared they'd take it away or something. But any apprehension you have goes away when you can make that kind of money. I was going to camp to compete and play as hard as I could. I was going to give it everything I had, just like my dad had always demanded of us.

I remember being in Memphis with Vernon and Eddie just before camp and Eddie gave some advice about the NFL. He told me to hold on to the ball. He said, "Walter, just don't fumble. The only way they'll cut you is if you fumble. So don't." Now, I've received a lot of advice in my life, but that was about as plain, simple, and true as it gets.

Connie Payton: When Chicago picked him, I actually felt sorry for him. "Gee whiz, you got drafted by Chicago? Oh my goodness, isn't it real cold there? You've got to play outside in all that cold weather? Oh I feel sorry for you."

I honestly thought he had the worst deal of everybody, just because of what I had heard about Chicago. All I had heard was that it was this big bad city and there's a lot of crime. That was just the southern mentality of ours. "Oh, I can't believe you are going to live there, the houses look like birdcage houses, they all hook to each other."

And his teammate Ricky Young was going to San Diego, where it's nice and warm, in California. And another teammate, Robert Brazile, was going to Houston, where it's nice and warm. I didn't know much about New York, where two other teammates, John Tate and Charles James, were going. We didn't know who was going to pick him. Bob Hill had called and said that Chicago was interested, but you never know if that is true. Then Bob called back and said Chicago was going to take him. It was exciting. Even with the doubts we had about Chicago not being a very good team, it was very exciting for us.

Honestly, it's amazing that he ended up the most successful of all those guys from Jackson State, the only one that got a Super Bowl ring. On draft day, with him going to Chicago, I don't think anyone would have believed that. At the time, those other guys were on better teams than Walter. But he's the only one who had a career that lasted thirteen years, he had the stability with one team, he eventually got the Super Bowl ring, and nobody else did. We were truly blessed with a great city and team full of history.

When everybody was told where they were going, all of the Jackson State guys went back to the dorm. Somehow we had lined up all these motorcycles to ride. It was unusual because nobody owned a motorcycle, but somehow everybody wound up with these motorcycles. When everybody knew where they were going and what round and it was all over, we all got on these motorcycles and we just went riding on them all day. It was the coolest thing, and they were happy and excited. Walter was really excited about Chicago. He was happy about being picked in the first round, the fourth person picked overall. He was all grins.

Even if he had apprehensions about Chicago, Walter has never been one to say much. Even if that's what he felt, he never said it. I think he knew that Chicago had a lot of history, especially with Gale Sayers. He knew about all of that and much more. So he never once said he was afraid, didn't like it, thought it might be too cold, or anything like that.

Obviously he was a small-town boy, that's for sure. But if he was afraid of heading to a big city, he never said it. I never knew it.

I stayed behind his first year to finish school. I went up to visit with his mother. We would go up for games and we'd travel together. He came back to Mississippi after the season was over. That rookie year I think he was lonely in Chicago. He wasn't having the best games and it was all so new. Every time we would go up for a visit he would ask me to stay. I knew I had to come back for school, and I knew I couldn't stay there, because my mother would have killed me and his mother would have been upset too. It's not something I even believed in. Then I noticed him getting quiet right before he headed back for the second season. You could tell he was going to be lonely up there again. When it was almost time for him to go to training camp for his second season, he says, "You gotta come." I said, "No, I can't." He said, "Why can't you?" I said, "I can't. I'm in school, and my parents would kill me if I was to leave and say I'm going to live with you and we're not married or anything like that."

He said, "Why do we have to be married?" I said, "Let me tell you something. My family's old-fashioned and I am too. Now, granted we might have broken some of the ground rules, which kids do, but when it comes to marriage, I don't think so. I'll come and visit you, and that's all right." And so he realized that I really meant it. So he said, "Well, let's get married, then." He actually said it like he was mad. That was his proposal. Next thing I knew, we were going to get a license. We didn't tell anybody. We just went and filled out the application and got blood tests taken. We were married July 7, 1976, the day before he had to be at training camp.

I'm glad we did it that way, and I'm glad we didn't make a fuss. The truth of the matter was that we were supposed to come back after the season and have a wedding. But after being married and being up there for the season, I said, "You know what? We don't have to do all of that. It's fine, we're already married." Plus I have never been a real big party person anyway.

I went to summer school and did almost a full semester. Then I went up for the season, then we came back to Jackson. I actually never ended up graduating. I enrolled in Roosevelt University in Chicago and to this day I am only a few classes from being finished. My mother gets on me every day, still. I am gonna do it, but I have to do it when I'm ready to do it.

Before we had the kids we used to travel a lot, and that's the only reason I didn't finish then. We had all kinds of trips that we would be invited to go on, all kinds of cruises and golfing tournaments and tennis tournaments and speaking engagements, so we were traveling a lot. That was a lot more fun than classes. Then after about four years, I decided I wanted to go on and get pregnant. Then I got pregnant with Jarrett.

Les Peters: Back in Columbia we were so excited. A guy from our town being picked so high in the draft and then signing a contract like that. It blew us away. Football made Walter a millionaire and there aren't many people who come out of Columbia and become millionaires.

The whole draft process was fun. At first we were all surprised by Chicago. Everyone thought Dallas was going to draft him, but then Dallas took Randy White, who was a great football player, an All-Pro. But that was where Walter and Connie had been looking at. Connie would say, "Walter, you're going to need your suntan lotion." We'd all laugh about that.

But then he goes to Chicago and everyone is laughing about get-

ting your cold gear out because it's freezing up there. Walter had
never been there and he was a little nervous, but then he got up there
and he loved it. Chicago has been great to him. He would talk about
going to live in a big place like that. I remember talking with him
after he first saw Chicago and he said that it just really wrecked his
mind. He said, "This is amazing." You have to understand our background. Comparing Chicago to Jackson is not even as close as apples
and oranges. But after he got adjusted, he loved it. He'd always say,
"There's no place like Chicago."

Still, it's a long way from Hendrick Street, Columbia, Mississippi.
I remember Walter riding these old roller skates he probably got at
the dump up and down Hendrick Street. You know he had great balance, so you should have seen him up on those skates. We didn't have
all the good ones they have now. The ones we had were metal and
struck fire. Up and down Hendrick Street and now he was headed to
the NFL. A wealthy man headed to play in the NFL.

The most prolific runner in the history of the National Football
League started his storied career not with a bang but with a bust.
Eight carries for zero yards as the Bears lost 35–7 to the Baltimore
Colts. After the game he cried.

"Zero yards, but it was like I'd just watched someone gain 150,"
said teammate Mike Adamle that day. "He made a couple of moves
in the backfield after he was stopped for losses, just to get back to the
line of scrimmage, and I said, 'This guy's great.' And he got zero
yards."

Indeed, Payton's initial performance for the Bears didn't harken
back to the day he brought race-divided Columbia, Mississippi, together with his long, exciting runs, nor the many five-touchdown
days that thrilled the fans at Jackson State. It was how the entire season would go, as Payton posted career lows (during nonstrike years)
in yardage (679) and yards per carry (3.5), and scored only seven
touchdowns. He even duplicated his zero-yard performance against
the Colts, when the Lions shut him out on ten carries.

But while the numbers weren't there as he played for the hapless Bears, the skills and determination that would lead him to the Hall of Fame were clearly on display. Payton was his normal self, scrapping for every yard no matter how far in the backfield he was initially hit, no matter how many opposing linebackers were leaping on top of the pile, no matter how far behind in the game the Bears were. He fought for extra yards on late-game third-and-longs during blowout losses as if it were first-and-goal in the Super Bowl.

It was that "Never say die" attitude that began endearing him to the Bears' fans and made him a hero among his teammates. Bears backers were tough that first year, wondering why the number-one pick wasn't sweeping down the field like Gale Sayers. Heck, he only started seven games. But as the season went on, their respect for this running back grew. With every no-quit run, the legend of Payton grew. It was cemented in the season finale against the New Orleans Saints, when Payton rushed for 134 yards on twenty-five carries. It was the best performance by a Chicago runner since Gale Sayers was healthy in 1968. Unfortunately, the Bears finished the season 4–10.

Walter Payton: Like any rookie, I wanted to get to Chicago and prove I could play, prove to my teammates, my coaches, the other players in the league, and the fans that I was good player, that I was an NFL-caliber player. I believed I was, but that first day was tough. Zero yards. I thought I was prepared and had run well, but nothing opened up for me. It was just one of those things.

Still, zero yards for the number-one pick? I was so embarrassed. I was worried. Fortunately my teammates really picked me up. They told me that I played well and to not change a thing. The veterans were saying that my day would come and not to get discouraged. That really helped.

I wasn't going to quit or anything, I wasn't going to change the way I did things, in fact it made me take preparation all the more seriously. When I worked that hill, training and killing myself over the years, I often began by saying, "Zero yards." That was to remind me of that game. I remembered how I felt that first day, and really that entire season, and tried to use that in my leadership later in my career. People often asked how I never got discouraged during some of the lean years and how I continued to be a professional. Well, that's why. I learned that first year that you can play well and not put up the numbers or win games. But you need to continue to do it your way and good things will happen.

I think a lot can be learned from my rookie year. As a team we definitely had some tough years to follow, but none was worse than that first year. We were 4–10 and I gained only 679 yards. It was a bad year for the team and me individually. Plus Connie was in Jackson and I was alone in Chicago, still learning to fit in.

But I knew that even though nothing was happening immediately, that if I continued to exert maximum effort, if I continued to work hard, if I kept a positive attitude and I continued to work with my teammates, that good things could happen. Sometimes you learn more through adversity than through success, and my rookie year was proof of that.

Just like I'm not convinced I would have enjoyed a Hall of Fame career if I had experienced great success early in my high school career, or gone to a big, famous college and not Jackson State, I'm not sure I would have been as good a leader later in my career with the Bears if I hadn't experienced that first season. There is a famous line: "Tough times don't last, tough people do." Well, it's true. It is also true that sometimes you need to go through tough times to prove you are a tough person. There is just nothing more humbling than playing as hard as you can and gaining no yards and losing the game. But the faith I kept through that, the faith that my family and teammates had in me, made me better. I may not have always gained two hundred yards and certainly we didn't win every game, but they never shut me out after that first season. I wasn't letting that happen again.

6

The Early Years

The Chicago Bears of the late 1970s and early 1980s were not a particularly successful franchise. Actually, they weren't good at all. They lost more often than they won. They were occasionally humiliated by stronger opponents. They were never a serious factor in the chase for a Super Bowl championship. For Walter, the stretch was tough. He was an old-school competitor who would trade any individual glory for a win, and the mounting losses grinded him. But game in, game out, he showed up and played with the heart of an All-Pro, which most seasons he was.

Despite the many losses and occasional rough individual outing, the greatest indignity Payton suffered during his career occurred not on the field, but in a game in which he wasn't allowed to play. It came during his rookie season when then Bears coach Jack Pardee held him out of a game against the Pittsburgh Steelers so he could nurse a bad ankle. Payton wanted to play and never accepted that he had to sit out. It proved to be the only game in his career he ever missed.

Walter Payton: I had hurt the ankle the week before, but I was ready to go on Sunday. There was no question in my mind that I was going to play. But Coach held me out. He said that I needed to rest the ankle. I was like, "Excuse me, an ankle?" In college once I played after my ankle was hurt worse than that. I got it taped three times. I taped the skin without any prewrap because they said it would hold better. Then I put on my sock and taped it again. Finally I put on my shoe and they wrapped it up. I gained one-hundred-something yards and scored a couple of touchdowns that day. I figured if I could do it at Jackson, I could do it in Chicago. What I learned that day was that I didn't get to make that call.

You had to just play through any pain. You had to forget about it and go on like you normally would. That missed game always bothered me. I always figured that if you were ready and willing to play, and the coach won't let you, does that count as a game missed due to injury? Individual statistics were never the most important thing in my life. I didn't count up my yardage or touchdowns scored or anything like that. Once you let selfishness take over, you invariably hurt the team. You can't work towards two different goals—individual and team. You have to play for the team goal.

But playing in every game, never missing one due to injury, now that was something I was selfish about. I figured if there was one individual statistic that I should be selfish about, that I should take personally, that was it. I wanted to get out there and play, and not doing so is something I always regretted. I never counted it as a game missed due to injury, because I was ready to go. Just like every other week.

Payton never missed another game, although at times it seems amazing he could handle some of the beatings he received. On a team that consistently struggled, Walter was the guiding light. By year two, 1976, now married to Connie, he began hitting his stride, rushing for 1,390 yards and thirteen touchdowns, finishing just behind O. J.

Simpson for the league rushing title. In his third season, at age twenty-four, Payton was named the league's Most Valuable Player, the youngest person to ever receive the honor. He earned it, scampering for 1,852 yards and fourteen touchdowns over the course of the NFL's then fourteen-game season. He averaged 123.6 yards per game. That included a 40-carry, 275-yard game against the Minnesota Vikings, still an NFL record for yards gained in a single game. He did it all that day despite suffering from the flu. Payton was the centerpiece of a Bears team that rallied from a 3–5 start to finish 9–5 and earned a rare play-off bid, where they fell to the Cowboys.

The Bears wouldn't return to the play-offs very often, but the Payton train chugged on, year in, year out, dominating defenses with his humbling, punishing running style. Fans loved his style of running through, not away from, tacklers. He gained 1,395 yards in 1978; 1,610 in 1979; 1,460 in 1980; 1,222 in 1981; and 596 yards in the strike-shortened season of 1982, when Payton passed the 10,000-yard mark for his career. In 1983, the 11,000 mark went down as Walter churned on for 1,421 yards. All the while he established himself as not only the league's top runner but one of its best receivers (he even led the Bears in receiving for a few seasons). In a game against the Saints in 1983, Payton threw for a couple of touchdowns. In 1984 he played quarterback in one game.

He also developed into the league's finest open-field blocker. Blocking was a skill Walter paid great attention to because he believed a good block was a combination of heart and form. He had learned the form under Bob Hill at Jackson State, who demanded that all of his players lay a nice one-on-one, open-field block. The heart, however, Walter learned from his parents. Thus he considered throwing a block an action not just of practicality, but of pride.

His complete, all-out style of play made him a fan favorite not only in Chicago but throughout the league. In 1981, the struggling Bears played a powerful Dallas squad on Thanksgiving in Texas and lost 10–9. Payton was never better, running like a man possessed, determined to win one on national television despite playing for a team lacking talent. He finished with 179 yards on thirty-eight carries, and as he left the field, head down in defeat, he received a rousing standing ovation from Cowboys fans awed by his effort.

It became a weekly occurrence, Walter receiving huge ovations from opposing fans who appreciated his abilities and style. He became one of the league's most popular players despite toiling for a losing team. The ultimate sign of respect came in Green Bay—home to the Bears' ancient and despised rivals—where, as his career wore on, he began receiving standing ovations from the Lambeau faithful during the pregame introductions. It was the first time a Bear had ever been cheered in Green Bay. And the last.

But that kind of national admiration never got to Walter. He always considered himself just a member of the team, not a superstar. On his first away trip as a Bear, he sat in the first window seat on the left side of the plane in the coach section. At the time, the veteran players, particularly the stars, took the first-class seats and the rest of the team sat in coach. Walter sat in that same seat for every flight for his entire career. Long after he could have moved to first class and stretched out, he stuck with the rank and file of the team and flew coach class. It was those simple gestures, away from the media and the public, that made his teammates respect him so.

But despite all of his individual success, the respect he gained, and the iron-man streak he built up by playing full-throttle no matter how small the stakes, the Bears never materialized into much of a championship contender. From 1975 until 1983, the Bears were a combined 58–71, making only two play-off appearances where they failed to win a game. In hindsight, some of the results seem impossible, misprints in the history books, perhaps. Consider that in the 1977 game against Minnesota where Payton rushed for 275 yards—personally making it up and down the field nearly three times—the Bears' anemic offense managed to score only ten points.

During those seasons Walter fought through thoughts of early retirement. He used to say he wanted to quit the game at age twenty-eight, before the on-field beatings left him hobbled for the rest of his life. He considered leaving the game like Jim Brown, at the pinnacle of his career. But each fall brought a new challenge, new hope, and another chance to play the game he loved. The bruises he could deal with. Leaving the game without ever winning a single play-off, let alone the Super Bowl, he could not.

By 1983, Chicago was on the third coach of Payton's pro career, Mike Ditka. There was a movement among Chicago fans that maybe the Bears ought to give their loyal hero a chance and trade Walter to a contender team. For all he had given them, they argued, he was owed a shot at glory.

Eddie Payton: Chicago was really the perfect place for Walter to play. Chicago is a working man's city, it is a blue-collar town, and they respected players who played hard. They knew when a guy wasn't giving his all and they would get all over a player like that. But they also knew when a guy was playing hard, and they supported him.

That's why it was a perfect fit. Chicago fans, if they are not the greatest fans in the world, then they are the second-greatest fans in the world. They can appreciate effort. For so long the Bears were pretty mediocre—what they didn't have was effort. What Walter brought was a period of effort. Even if they didn't win, the effort was there every week. And the people of Chicago embraced that, I mean they loved the way he played—win or lose, you knew what you were going to get every play, every Sunday from Walter Payton, and that's why he became a favorite son.

And Walter appreciated that. He appreciated that his effort and his professionalism were being noticed. It's why he grew to love Chicago as much as Chicago grew to love him. It is why he never wanted to leave, even during the tough years. It is why he never demanded a trade or complained. He loved Chicago and he loved the Bears.

Walter Payton: You had to just keep going, playing for pride. Personal pride, team pride, organizational pride, and city pride. You had to go out and play for Chicago, because those people were behind us. I enjoyed a great deal of individual success during those years. I really came into my own in the league. The thing was, I was quick but not fast. That's why I developed a stutter step to help me break long runs. I was able to break away for thirty yards or forty yards, but if I had to go sixty, seventy yards, I'd probably get caught. I just wasn't fast enough.

So I'd stutter-step. Opponents didn't know what you were going to do. They didn't know if you were going to go straight, if you were going to come at them, or if you were going to stop. If you break free and are running down the sideline, the defensive guy who has an angle on you is already calculating in his mind where he's going to hit you at. He knows where you are going to be at a certain time because he's judging your speed. So that's when I start my stutter step, because it made him change his speed. When you do that he has to think and then it gives you that edge and you can go right by him. It is a way of breaking long runs when the other player is faster than you.

I had to do all sorts of tricks like that because there's no question that for a number of years I was a marked man. Everyone knew our offense was Walter right, Walter left, then Walter up the middle. Some of my friends around the league said teams actually started feeling sorry for me. I knew everyone was gunning for me, but you have to just keep playing. And when guys are eyeing you, you learn to either avoid taking the full hit by turning your body a little, or you try to hit them first. It is the only way to survive. You can't just let yourself take a beating. You have to dish a little out also because everyone knew it was going to me on the next run and we'd be right back where we were. You can't let a man hit you twenty times a game without knowing he's going to take some hits also.

Connie Payton: Walter never complained. I promise you, he never complained, even through all those years when things weren't going well. In fact, his reaction was that he worked out that much harder, and trained that much harder, so he could stay healthy and be even more productive. He understood it was a team thing. But he knew the only one he had control over was him. I think it meant a lot to him to just go out every game in spite of the team failures and still do his very best. I think he got a lot of gratification from that. Sure he wanted to try to win, but he was still able to go out, do his best, and put forth this good effort whether they won or not. Sometimes I wondered why he never said a thing. He never took the easy way out when he was asked how many yards he might have gained if he'd played for a better team. He always said the right things.

Roland Harper: Walter always knew how to lighten a situation. During even the toughest years, when we couldn't buy a win, he'd always make everyone laugh. He was famous for his fireworks. I think he loved M-80s because they were the loudest. One time he set one off in the lobby of our training camp in the middle of the night. It was during two-a-days, so everyone was exhausted. The police and fire departments came and the police knew Walter had done it, so they went to his room. By the time they got there, he had snuck out a window and had set the sirens on their cars off.

Another time I remember it was a cold day at practice, and when it ended he ran back to the locker room, locked the door behind him, and took a long shower while all of us were outside freezing. He was always doing stuff like that.

Hunting was the thing Walter loved to do on our off days. We'd put a sign up and take whoever wanted to go with us every Monday to this camp just over the Wisconsin border. Because we knew how to hunt, we'd let the others get off a first shot, then we'd finish the deal for them. One time we took one player and he couldn't hit nothing. Finally we came on a bird that wouldn't take off. It was just running around on the ground. He was chasing it with the barrel of the gun up, just waiting for it to take off so he could shoot. The pheasant started running right towards me and Walter, and we looked up just in time to see this guy coming at us pointing his gun. We hit the floor so fast it hurt. Sometimes it is a miracle we made it back. But those trips really helped those teams build camaraderie.

He used to pride himself on trying to lift everyone else to a higher level, even when we weren't winning a lot. He used to tell me that he wanted to make sure our opponent "at least knew we were there." That was his way of trying to feel good about the situation. He wanted opponents to know they had been in a dogfight after they played us, even if we didn't win. Walter made sure the team didn't give up just because we couldn't make the play-offs or whatever.

Jim McMahon: The fact that Walter survived thirteen years in the league, missing only one game, especially the beating that a running back takes, it's probably the most amazing thing. It is simply the most amazing stat. Jim Brown also never missed a game, which is an amazing stat. And Walter missing one, he actually could have played in that. Shit, I've missed eight games a year. He was the strongest guy I've ever met in my life. He was pound for pound, he was muscle everywhere. He took a lot of pounding, but he dished out a lot of pounding, just like Jim Brown used to do. He's a solid rock coming at you.

Walter Payton: Probably the best individual performance day I ever had was when I set the single-game rushing record against Minnesota. It was like being in the zone. You know, everybody always talked about how Michael Jordan used to get in a zone. Well, Michael was in the zone every time he got on the court. He was amazing. But for me, there are times when you got out on the football field and you never tire. Every move that you make is just like the last one, with the same speed, with the same enthusiasm. Every time the play is called, you know exactly what you are supposed to do and you do it. It happens.

One thing I always worked for was the perfect game. All the time that I played the game of football, I was shooting for that perfect game. It never happened. A perfect game is making every block, making every fake, catching every pass, doing everything you have to do. People said I had the perfect game against Minnesota because I rushed for 275 yards. But that was a long way from perfect.

In fact, the games when I was closest to perfect weren't the big-yardage games. I think it was a game where I didn't have very many yards, but my blocking was there, my passing was there, my faking was there. Those are the games you look at. It is difficult to pinpoint specific games, but I think one of them was against Green Bay and one of them was against the Lions. Those were the two best games I ever played, the closest I ever came to playing a perfect game. And no one talks about it, but I knew it. It's not all the yards you get and everything else, because you don't get that by yourself.

The game of football is about 85 percent mental. Sure you have to be able to physically play, but you have to deal with the losses and get yourself mentally ready to go back for another week. It is especially important to be mentally strong when you are on a team that struggles. It is difficult to stay consistently motivated when you are losing. That's when it is easy to slip, to give in for a moment. It is why I made myself train so hard in the off-season.

When you play professional football, everything is based upon winning. If you don't win you have failed. You work all week for a game plan, you work on it and then you go into the game and you lose, then you have to get yourself mentally ready, real fast, to start the next week. What you have to do is look at it as a big task. It is like running ten miles. Every time you complete one mile, you can't think about how you've just completed one mile. You've gotta think about the new mile you are just starting. Because if you start thinking, I've run two miles, I've run three miles, then you start to get tired, mentally and physically tired. So that's the same approach you use in football, 'cause every week it's a mile.

It is a little like that big pile of topsoil my mother used to dump in our yard for Eddie, Pam, and me to move. You had to take every wheelbarrow-full like it was a brand-new wheelbarrow. You had to focus on that. If you thought about how much of the pile you had already moved, you'd get tired and then it would take longer to get it done.

One thing people always asked me about during my career was how I dealt with the pain. When you have pain, what you do is you focus on nonpain. You focus your mind on soothing. You focus your mind on creating a healing form. I've had injuries that for some people it would have taken them three and four weeks to heal from, but with me it would only take three and four days. What reasons would you apply to that? You can't say it's medicine, because a lot of times I didn't take medicine. The reason I healed quickly is that I didn't dwell on the pain. Rather I would dwell on thinking positive, like, It's going to be okay, it's going to be well, it's getting well, it's feeling better. And then it happens. The only other way to explain it is to look at the brain and analyze the percentage of the brain that we use and the percentage that we don't use. I would attempt to some way tap into that, utilizing it to making the body produce its own enzymes for healing. We can do that, you just have to use the brain.

We know that certain things happen and we know there is a chemistry in our bodies that produces healing enzymes. You just have to harness that. If we take it a little bit further, than we learn to utilize that brain we're carrying around in the top of our heads. If you utilize all of it, to produce, to end pain, to numb pain, to speed healing, it will happen.

So that's how I played so many games without missing one with an injury. It wasn't that I was Superman, made of steel. It was because I utilized my entire brain to heal fast.

Mike Singletary: I came to the Bears in 1981 and immediately I saw several things about Walter that stood out. First I saw what being a professional means. The man taught me what a professional was, what a professional athlete should be, how a professional athlete should prepare, the entire mentality of a professional athlete.

As a person, I saw a guy who was very giving even though the Bears were a struggling team. There were a lot of demands on him. I remember people wanting his autograph after practice, crowds of people. Most of the time he'd stay out there and sign every autograph request. He didn't care how long it would take. The coaches would have just finished running us to death, and he would stay out there and sign autographs, joke around, play around with the fans.

He was that kind of guy. He loved being a professional athlete. He loved being a businessman. He loved and cherished his part as a role model. He did it with a lot of class. He really took the load and he did it with a lot of class.

Walter never gave us a lot of speeches about what it took to be a professional. He never took rookies aside and discussed it with them. He led by example. It is the best way to teach people. Little things are always caught by people. Even my own kids catch things. That's something I have to remember myself, to lead by example. It's a lot easier to talk, but man, I tell you what, walking that talk is very, very difficult. And Walter walked the walk every single day and the rest of us watched in awe.

I think he was frustrated by all the losses, but I think he also understood that's what being a professional athlete is all about. It really made me respect him more. He didn't whine about not winning more. You think about all the reasons he had to whine, and I don't ever remember him whining about us not winning. You'd lose the game, and he'd say, "Doggone it, we should have won the game." But as far as being a part of the Bears organization, he took a lot of pride in that even when we were losing.

He never pouted, he never asked for a trade, he never spoke bad about teammates in the newspapers. That's one of the things that really made me respect him more. In the midst of adversity, being on a team that wasn't as successful, he'd still shine.

Even though he was Sweetness and he could have done anything he wanted, he wasn't one of those guys where every time you turn around he's in the media, every time you turn around he's saying something, every time you turn around he's doing something a little off-color, paying attention to himself. He wasn't like that. He never put himself above the team, even though he could have. I never felt like Walter was above the team. I never felt any air of supremacy or anything like that.

He went out and he did his job. He put it on the line. He worked, he did the thing that he was supposed to do and more. And that's all you can ask from a player. I think there was a heck of a lot more in

Walter's mind than being the greatest back of all time. He was motivated by more than just being the best player.

He was also motivated by being on the best team. As Payton's career progressed, the desire to win a Super Bowl grew. The MVP awards, the huge statistical days, the All-Pro selections were nice, but every January he'd watch the Super Bowl on television and wish he were there. It was just the kind of attitude that Walter's final Bears coach, Mike Ditka, coveted in his players.

The former Chicago Bears great arrived in Midway in 1982 from the staff of the Dallas Cowboys intent on rallying the assembled talent and bringing a Super Bowl back to Chicago. He wanted a bruising, aggressive defense led by tough, skilled linebackers such as Mike Singletary, and he wanted a ball-control offense anchored by the tireless Payton. Ditka knew Chicago hadn't won in a long time. But he knew he had inherited a foundation for a team that could become champions one day.

The Bears didn't become immediate champs, but the team's attitude changed. By 1984, the season Walter would rush past Jim Brown's career rushing record, Chicago was the NFC Central Division Champion, finishing the regular season with a 10–6 record. In the play-offs, the Bears beat Washington in the first round—Walter threw a touchdown pass—before falling to San Francisco in the NFC title game. Walter finished the season with 1,648 yards rushing.

Mike Ditka: Walter was one of the first, if not *the* first player I spoke with when I became head coach. I remember telling him what my goals were, how I wanted the team to be looked at. I wanted them to be like Mr. Halas wanted the Bears to be: tough, no-nonsense, pound the ball, and keep on running. I wanted a physical defense, a defense that would intimidate opponents. And I said to him that day, "We'll win games."

I think that when I first came in there, a lot of those guys didn't know what to expect. They knew I was an ex–Bear player and I had been coaching Dallas. But that was it. I think they were kind of taken aback by my attitude. I remember one of the first things I told the football team was "We're going to win the Super Bowl here and we're going to win it pretty soon, and here's why we're gonna win it. First of all, you're as good as these other people in the league. Second, we're going to play a brand of football that's going to show everybody we're as good or better. It's gonna be good football, tough football, Chicago Bears football, and we are going to win with it."

I know that's what a lot of the guys remember about that first meeting, which is good because that was my goal. It had always been my lifetime dream to go back and coach the Bears. And to have a collection of guys like I had, I knew we had a great opportunity. We just needed to get everyone to believe like Walter did.

What I tried to get across to those guys is that Bears football was different from other kinds of football. I wanted them to know this was gonna be different. It was gonna be what Mr. Halas wanted. It was gonna be no-nonsense, hard-nosed, ask no quarter, give no quarter, that mentality. And I think they really bought into that. I remember telling them one time before we were gonna play somebody that "You worry about the playing and I'll take care of the coach. I know I can kick his ass." They laughed about it, but we went out there and we won that football game. That was a great game.

Walter Payton: When Mike came in he said that we were going to win the Super Bowl. Everybody just looked around and "Yeah right." But you could tell he meant it. He said, "You can come along for the ride, or you can get off. Either way we are still going."

I loved that. I really wanted to win a Super Bowl and I wanted to give the people of Chicago a winner to get behind. They had been great to me and I wanted to give something back. From that first day, you could tell things were different. Everyone believed, we began focusing on perfection, which I believe is how you have to play the game. You have to set your goals impossibly high. And winning the Super Bowl is the ultimate goal. Mike changed everything in Chicago.

Mike Ditka: It could have happened quicker in Chicago, but before you can win, you gotta really believe. And not everyone believed when I took over. Walter always did, and that was key because guys followed him and that's one reason things changed. We started believing in each other and then suddenly the chemistry hit and it was "boom." In the first year, 1982, we should have won more games, but we were making progress. Then an interesting thing happened in 1983. We were like 1 and 7 and we won seven out of the last eight games to go 8 and 8. That's what it was. And then the next year we went 10 and 4 and we went to Washington for the play-offs.

In the Washington game, they stacked the defense against Walter. And I tell you what, I've never seen a guy run harder. He just ran harder and harder and got after them and stayed after them. They were cracking him with hits too, you could hear it all over the stadium. Incredible collisions, and Walter would just get up and say, "Hey, I'm coming right back at you." He'd run back to the huddle and never show that they stopped him or hurt him. The way we got to them in that game was actually when Walter threw a touchdown pass off the reverse to Pat Dunsmore. It was a great play, a perfect throw. He could do it all the time, he loved to throw the ball. I actually played him at quarterback one game.

In 1984 we had a bunch of injuries at quarterback. I played like five different ones and then I finally said, "Forget it, I'm putting Walter in there." We had to go into the shotgun but that was okay. I just went with Walter and he handled it. He could do anything on the football field. He was the complete player. And he showed it in that game against Washington, when we won a play-off game. That's when I knew we were getting close. We were on our way.

7

The Record

Soldier Field, Chicago, October 7, 1984. It was vintage Payton. The record for which he will so long be remembered came on a run that typified his entire career. Unlike Ricky Williams, who broke the NCAA career rushing record at the University of Texas in 1998 with a long burst that resulted in a touchdown, Walter broke Jim Brown's NFL mark on a simple six-yard pitchout on the second carry of the second half.

It was a workmanlike conclusion to a workmanlike pursuit of football's glory record. Brown had set the record in nine years with the Cleveland Browns, rushing for 12,312 yards. Brown and Payton had similar running styles, a hard-driving, straightforward attack. It was a macho, old-school style that deplored taking the circuitous route to a first down and never backed down from a potential collision.

It was one of the reasons the proud Brown nodded approvingly when Payton approached the mark and why he called afterward to offer congratulations. That call was broadcast live over the radio in

Chicago. Brown had made national news the previous summer when he appeared on the cover of *Sports Illustrated,* wearing a Los Angeles Raiders uniform and declaring that he might come out of retirement at age forty-seven to keep his record from being broken.

Brown was not excited by the prospect of Franco Harris, the Pittsburgh Steelers great who had just signed with the Seattle Seahawks, breaking the record. Entering the 1984 season, Harris had amassed 11,950 career yards. Payton had 11,625. Both, obviously, had moved close enough to Brown's record. Brown was critical of Harris's running style, which he believed was tainted because Harris ran out-of-bounds too often, avoiding contact with would-be tacklers. He also commented that Harris was hanging on past his prime in an effort to eclipse the rushing mark.

Harris was entering his twelfth NFL season, highlighted by four NFL titles with the Steelers, a record eight 1,000-yard seasons, and nine Pro Bowl selections. But during the second half of the 1983 season he averaged only fifty yards a game and, after a holdout with the Steelers, found his way to Seattle to make a last push for twelve thousand yards and the Brown mark.

"France's had a great career, but it's not there, it's very obvious he doesn't have it together anymore," Brown told a CBS audience early in the 1984 season.

Payton made the whole controversy moot, however. Entering the 1984 season, he wanted to not just surpass Brown's record, but to do it before Harris. That meant erasing a 325-yard gap in a matter of a few weeks, something Payton felt was "unrealistic" but worth pursuing anyway. Harris, who missed training camp with Seattle due to the holdout, stumbled early, gaining only eighty-two yards in the season's first four weeks. Payton, meanwhile, streaked ahead of Harris in week four, when, ironically, the Bears and Seahawks met in Seattle. Payton gained 116 yards that day. Harris got only twenty-three. The Bears defense had assured Payton they would help his cause pregame.

That set up the historic game at Soldier Field on October 7, when Payton entered the game just sixty-six yards behind Brown. Payton wanted the record, but he wanted to do it right. The Bears had planned to stop the game when he passed Brown and conduct a three-minute ceremony to honor Payton. Walter vetoed it and made sure there would be nothing more than a simple announcement to the crowd. No stoppages, no presentations.

And so it would be. When the record fell, Payton took some pats from his team, ran over and shook the hand of the New Orleans Saints coach, Bum Phillips, and then ran to the Bears sideline, where he handed the game ball to the running backs coach, Johnny Roland. Payton would finish the game with 154 yards on thirty-two carries, part of a 1,684-yard season, the second-best of his career.

Later there was fanfare, with Brown and President Ronald Reagan calling in congratulations. Payton, then still only thirty, even discussed pushing forward, saying he eventually wanted to set the bar at sixteen thousand yards so the next guy to make a run at the record would have to practically die to make it. Surrounded by his family, teammates, and friends, Payton was on top of the world.

Walter Payton: At the time I could barely comprehend what it meant. I couldn't conceive of what it meant to break that record. I tried to keep things low-key and not get too off the ground with it, but breaking Jim's record was just something else. It was always the ultimate individual goal because it represented not just great individual performances, but the culmination of years of consistency and sustained excellence.

I've always thought that consistency is the most difficult thing to attain in life. Anyone can be good for a day, or a year. But can you consistently be great? That is so much more difficult. It requires a person to continue to work hard even after they have achieved success. It requires sacrifice, even after sacrifice is no longer required. It requires a hunger in a person that is about more than just making it. It is about staying there.

Whether it is an athlete, or an actor, or a musician, or a businessman, I think people will tell you that staying on top of your profes-

sion for a long period is the most difficult thing. A lot of actors have
won one Academy Award, but how many have won a number of
them, consistently throughout their career? You can start one successful business, but how about being successful in a number of ventures?

That was what motivated me about the record. I've always needed
something to motivate me. Because I worked out so often on my
own, I needed something to drive me. I didn't want coaches telling
me to get in shape, and that never happened. I was always in shape.
But I needed something to push me over the edge to get in the best
possible shape. That had to come from within. The record gave me
something to focus on during some of those years when our team
wasn't very good. It kept me at the top.

I was always fearful that I wasn't in the best shape I could be. I always wondered if I had slipped a little bit. That motivated me. At
Jackson State I used to say that my goal was to be able to play all-out
on every play for a ninety-minute game. I figured if I could play all-
out on every play of a game that long, then I was ready for an NFL
game. I'd probably only play thirty minutes a game in the NFL, so I
figured I would have enough to go that extra mile to make it.

Entering the season I wanted to break Jim's record first. I wanted
to pass Franco Harris even though at the start of the season that
seemed unrealistic. He had a 325-yard lead on me and I thought he
might break the record by the end of September. While I did want
to break the record first, it wasn't because I disliked Franco Harris or
didn't respect the man. That is completely untrue. The man had four
Super Bowl rings and this is a team game first and foremost. I also
liked Franco, I had some business dealings with him, and off the
field he and I were friends, our families really liked each other.

A lot of people tried to make a big deal of the fact that two of us—
Franco Harris and myself—were going after Jim Brown's record at
the same time. People tried to compare the two of us, compare our
styles. It was as if the good news of two men going after a record
wasn't enough.

I was asked at least a hundred times how I felt about Franco's running style, that he was known for running out-of-bounds, while my style was more physical. How was I supposed to answer that question? I said what I thought, which was that whatever style works for each runner is the style they should use, and Franco's style works for him. I got knocked for not being honest. I couldn't have been more honest. I consider Franco a friend. We've worked out together, played basketball together. He is a super person and one of the best running backs of all time. There was no way I was going to get drawn into any controversy about him versus me.

In my opinion, Franco was the best in clutch situations—third-and-two, third-and-three, goal line. He had a great offensive line and used them and they won a lot of games. How can you question his success? Numbers don't show greatness anyway. It's how you feel and the desire you bring to the field.

I said after the game that the motivating drive for me has been for the athletes who have tried but yet still failed to reach that certain achievement. And also the athletes who didn't get an opportunity to, like the Overstreets and the Delaneys and the Brian Piccolos. This simplifies what the game is made of. What I did out there that day was a reflection of those guys because they made the sacrifices as well. It was a tribute to me to bestow this honor on them.

As I got close, I have to admit that it was a lot more pressure than I let on. I tried to pretend it was no big deal and I didn't want to talk about it. But it was. I sure was glad to get it over with. I was glad I didn't have to do that every week. The funny thing is, if people didn't remind me about the specific play, I wouldn't even remember it. I really don't think about that play often. It was all a blur. It was a career thing anyway, so one run didn't do it.

And you know what? In the end, it is just like anything else. When Barry Sanders, Emmitt Smith, Jerry Rice, all those guys, when they come up to break somebody's record or they come up to push my stats, the media is gonna make so much out of it. They're gonna realize, Oh man, what's happening? It's gonna make them nervous, it's gonna make them anticipate, it may even change what they do or how.

I didn't let it bother me. I tried to maintain my own personal level of whatever it was, my own space, my own drum, and keep it away. The thing with records is if you play long enough you're gonna break some records. It is almost a matter of time. I used to joke that I probably gained an extra hundred yards over my career by inching the ball ahead every time I was tackled. When a referee would catch me and move it back to where it belonged I would always say, "Hey, how do you expect me to catch Jim Brown if you do that to me?" Instead of worrying about numbers, what you try to do is you try to do better than what everybody expected. Everybody's pointing at Jim Brown's record and saying, You gotta shoot for that. I wanted to go past that and I did. It really doesn't stand out. I think that is why I talked about the sixteen thousand yards. That immediately became the next unreachable goal. It's one of those things, to chase dreams, to chase goals. Once it happens it tends to lose some of the glimmer.

I don't want, in any way, to minimize the records. Especially this one, because it is special. But football is a team game. The more you win as a team, the better your team gets, and as your team gets better it becomes easier to achieve things individually. But if you're just out there setting records as an individual, it actually gets harder to keep things happening at a high level. Eventually, other guys you play with start to ask why they're not getting the same opportunities you are. Some of them might stop playing as hard. Then you get killed. That's why I'd rather play for a winning team than play for a team where I would set a bunch of records.

So that's why I want to say this. I'm not saying breaking the record or my statistics weren't important to me, but I don't believe I ever broke Jim Brown's record. I don't think anybody has broken it. I think it is still standing. I don't think the record books need to be rewritten, because if you can't do it in nine years and eight games, then you can't break his record. I didn't do it in the amount of time that Jim Brown did. I had more games and I played longer. So I didn't break it.

Jim Brown: I had a lot of respect for Walter when he broke the record. Walter and I were very good friends, and I spoke to him on the telephone. I know I was sitting out on my balcony in California and talked to him on the phone and they broadcast it all over Chicago. I was very happy to acknowledge him because I had so much respect for him. Some people I would not have talked to because I would not have had that level of respect.

But I had great respect for the heart he had and for his abilities and his tenacious attitude on the football field. I'm not like a normal football fan. I don't sit back and enjoy players. I analyze their abilities. He was very strong for his size, very quick, very acrobatic, and most of all he had a great, great heart. He fought for every yard. He was a person I would put with anybody in terms of his work ethic. See, Walter was a very rare individual, in that conditioning was second nature to him. His off-field dedication was that of a true champion, because a champion never waits for a coach to instruct him to get in shape or to learn more. Every athlete who is a true champion knows that he should be in tip-top condition. He and Jerry Rice were very similar in terms of their conditioning regimentation.

But the interesting thing about him was the shoulder strength and the strength he had in his thighs. He had the ability to be a smaller individual with all of that strength. That allowed him to break a lot of tackles, it allowed him to run over people. And then he was extraordinarily quick. Quickness for a running back is the most important thing you can have. So he was extraordinarily quick. He wasn't extraordinarily fast, which didn't matter. The fourth gear wasn't necessarily there, but he was extraordinarily quick. The quickness relates to extreme acceleration. When you can accelerate quick, that's when you can be an extraordinary running back, because you can separate so quickly from would-be tacklers. His balance was also in the same league as his quickness.

So when you take that strength and that striking power and the quickness and the balance and combine it with his intelligence, you have a total package. But the most important part of it was that his tenacity computed to his heart. In other words, he would fight you for every inch, all day long, no thought of running out-of-bounds to get away from a hit. No thought of trying to get away from a hit unless it was expedient to get away from a hit. It was a rare thing that you very seldom ever see today.

Most of these guys today don't even understand that particular level of tenacity. The closest thing you would see to it last year was the second half of the Super Bowl when Eddie George turned on that kind of determination. When I want to use an example of how Walter Payton ran, I say Eddie George in the second half of the 2000 Super Bowl. But that was Walter Payton every day, every minute.

Walter never shied away from contact. And you can't. If you hit the tackler first, if you make him pay a little, then you are always going to get more yards at some point. That's what we know. To give in, to go out-of-bounds and assume somebody is going to stop you, is very weak. But if you take that hit and throw that blow, at some point you are going to get ten extra yards or three extra yards down the road.

People ask me what makes a great back. I tell them to work hard. There's not too much work you can do for your own success. Every back has something different to offer, but all of them can never work hard enough. I think Walter showed that.

You've got to have it as a man. When you see Walter Payton, that's Walter Payton. Men like him don't change. It's right in front of you. A great back is not going to change because God gave them a particular gift. The thing about Walter that's different from most is that Walter had as great a heart as anyone who's ever lived. I always said if I was going to do anything in a competitive field, I would want Walter as my partner. That way I would know that as long as I would keep fighting, he would keep fighting too. So that was where he was very special to me.

I think Walter and I and certain individuals like to achieve things in certain ways. Everyone made a big deal about the record. Well, records are created by other people. Players don't create records. We know performances. As athletes we have a totally different way of looking at each other. We don't even compete when it comes to comparisons such as records. We care only about how a player performs.

The thing about yardage, it is not about how many you got, but the important ones you got, how tough it was to get, did it help your team win. There are so many elements about yardage. That's why most running backs have respect for each other. We know these things. Running backs have to get yardage, we just don't relate to it like newspaper people or fans.

Franco Harris: As far as I'm concerned, I thought Walter was the greatest. With the teams he played on, and what he did, getting all of those yards, only missing one game due to injury his whole career, that's amazing. We had different styles, but I always enjoyed watching him, the way he ran and the way he played the game. He did it all, running, pass receiving, and catching. He was the type of guy who made things happen. And he was just a great guy. We were friends and I appreciated that most.

Roland Harper: I remember Walter trying not to make a big deal out of breaking the record, mostly because he said all the time that records are meant to be broken. He didn't want to be a show-off. He just took it in stride. He said, "We got a job to do. We gotta win this game." That was the most important thing to him, winning the game. Not so much the record, but winning the game.

I know he thought that one was special because he had such respect for Jim Brown. But he didn't want it to be too big a deal, since he knew he'd watch it go away someday, just as Jim Brown did. He joked that Jarrett would break it someday, which was funny because he didn't want Jarrett to have anything to do with football. I'm sure he was counting on being around to see it broken and unfortunately that won't happen.

But he knew his record would be broken one day too. There are so many young guys coming out who are bigger, faster, stronger who will probably break the record. Barry Sanders was still in the game, so he was right behind him. Tony Dorsett was in the game. Eric Dickerson was in the game. These guys were racking up large numbers, so he knew that his record, just like Jim Brown's record, will one day be broken. I think that's the way he approached it, records are made to be broken.

When he broke the record, it gave me goose bumps to know that hey, I know this guy, I played with this guy. For more than half of his yards, I helped block for this guy. This was the greatest feeling. It felt like a great accomplishment for me.

After the game, 'ROOS, the sneaker company KangaROOS, had given him a Lamborghini and he said, "Ro, let's go for a ride." He revved it up and I swear we were at one hundred miles per hour before we were a mile down the road. He loved speed. It was probably one of the greatest, fun rides that I ever had, but I told him, "Hey look, you gotta slow down. It's time to slow down." He loved anything that, like him, went fast.

Mike Singletary: When he broke the record, Walter played it down. I think it was another example of "Okay, yes, I'm breaking a record," but I think he understood that records were meant to be broken. He achieved a great feat, so he was like, "Yes, it's wonderful, but let's go out here and win. Let's not dwell on this record. It's a great achievement and everything else, but let's put a period behind it and not a comma, and let that go. And let's start a new sentence." I think that was his approach, and I understood that approach. And we went out and won the game.

Jim McMahon: When Walter got close to the record everyone was comparing him to Jim Brown. I had never seen Jim in person, but I had watched a number of clips and tapes. The guy was a great player. Man, he had all that speed. I think that's really the only difference between the two. He had a great amount of speed that Walter didn't have. But as far as the power and the drive and the determination, I don't think there was any difference. You see the film clips of Jim Brown knocking people out, same thing with Walter. You never saw either of them running out-of-bounds. They were always hitting somebody. Both of them were so strong, that's why they could do that. I think that is why Jim respected Walter so much. It is why he was happy when Walter broke his record.

I always thought that the fact Walter broke the record on a six-yard carry coming from a basic pitch was fitting. He wasn't a guy who should have broken it on a ninety-yard run or something. Most of his runs, many of the great runs he made, didn't get back to the line of scrimmage. He made some thirty-yard runs that lost a yard. He'd hook and spin and bang into people and bang around just to turn a two-yard loss into no gain. And that's contagious. Guys see that, linemen see that, they want to work harder for the guy 'cause he's busting his ass. All of a sudden everyone is working as hard as Walter and then you don't have two-yard losses. Everything is a gain because everyone is working hard. I think that's why the Bears got so good. They realized how hard he was working and how hard I was working and everybody else, and they wanted to be better. Those guys had a lot of pride.

Mike Ditka: The funny thing about Walter is that the record meant less to him than being the best football player he could be. They used to mention O.J. as the greatest running back. But that's the problem with people who don't understand football making that claim. You have to look at the complete football player. If you ask other coaches around the league who watched Walter Payton block, they'd say he was the best blocker by far that they've ever seen at running back. He got the job done.

As a receiver coming out of the backfield, or throwing the ball, or carrying out a fake, or chasing down the opponent on an interception or fumble, he did everything. Guys in that arena, a superstar like he was, they don't have to do that. But he did it because he was setting the best example he could for his teammates.

But we have a tendency to put people in a popularity contest. There's no question that Jim Brown and Gale Sayers are two of the greatest runners we've ever seen. But when you look at anything

Walter did and how he played the game, I don't think anyone was better. He did everything so well. I don't know if it ever looked easy for Walter on the field. He was always making it happen, working to make it happen. Taking the hard hit on the sideline when he didn't have to, things like that. Some of these guys, it looks easy for them. Sayers made it look easy. Jim Brown made it look easy for him.

But for Walter, it very seldom looked easy for him. He was always knocking people down, running through people, breaking tackles. He was always busting, kicking, scratching, banging. I'm sure that's part of why people overlook him. As I said, for some reason it becomes a popularity contest.

Jim Brown was great in terms of speed, size, strength. I don't know if you could say he was quick, he was just so powerful and his moves were so fluid. He was a big man who could run in the days when the linemen weren't much bigger than him. There was a little bit of difference there, but Jim Brown was a great athlete. He could wrestle, play basketball, lacrosse—he was actually a better lacrosse player than a football player. But Jim was only asked to do one thing, run with the football. And that's what he did. He was a great runner, there's no question about it. Nobody ran like he did. Him and Sayers to me were just a pleasure to watch. But even though I have so much respect for those guys, the best football player I ever saw was Walter Payton, period.

The only guy who could even, I think, approach him is Jerry Rice, because I think he certainly is one of the greatest players in the top three or four I've ever seen. As a receiver, it's a different skill. But he's pretty special. An all-around great player. Still, pound for pound as a football player, Walter is the best I've ever seen.

The way Walter handled breaking Jim Brown's record was tremendous. I think that one of the great traits that anybody can have in their life is humility. I think humility is a wonderful thing. You understand that you are given a God-given talent, do with it what you can. I don't think Walter ever took the credit. I think that even in some hard times, I think that he understood that what happened in those times was God's will. I really believe that. And I think that's why Walter was so gracious with Chicago. He gave back. He didn't just keep taking from the game, he gave back, with his time, with his autographs, with his efforts with kids. To me that's the mark of what it's all about. Do you care enough to give it back? Because we take a lot, we all take a lot from the fans.

When he broke the record he didn't say very much at all. It was really subtle. They stopped the game, gave him the ball, everybody gave him a standing ovation. I know that it was something that he wanted to do, and I don't think after he did it that he thought it was the most important thing. I think he expected to do it. So it wasn't no big deal. If you expect to win, it shouldn't be any big deal, it shouldn't be a surprise. I don't think this was a surprise to him when he did it, because he expected to become the all-time leading rusher.

8

Matt and Me

One of the toughest periods of Walter's professional career came during the early 1980s. His closest friend on the team—and his closest friend in life—the fullback Roland Harper, was physically unable to continue football. Bad knees ended Roland's career before the Bears started to experience real success. Harper's retirement made clear to Walter how fortunate he was never to have suffered like Roland. But it also reminded him that this was a business and he, like Roland, was just a cog in the wheel. No time was wasted mourning Roland's absence. "Move on" was the attitude one had to take. Some who knew Walter at the time suggested he acted more like he was experiencing a death in the family than the retirement of a friend.

Walter Payton: I felt like a part of me was missing when Ro had to retire. We had come in together and immediately bonded because we had so much in common. We were two black guys from the South, who both went to small schools. We loved to hunt and be outdoors. Unlike a lot of people, Ro knew how to listen. He knew how to take me when I was upset and help me keep calm. And there were a lot of those days during those early years when we weren't very good.

Roland Harper: We did everything together. We were so much alike. We're both kind of quiet, but we got to the place where we knew what each other was thinking, whether it was on the football field or in the hunting field. I'm from Louisiana, he's from Mississippi. I guess it was like one of those things where you're brothers in a way, coming from almost the same background.

The Bears replaced Harper with a young stud who had long football bloodlines. Matt Suhey was the antithesis of Roland Harper. Where Harper, a long-shot seventeenth-round pick, had to scrap for a roster spot, Suhey walked in as second-round choice and knew the job was his. A product of three generations of Penn State football, Suhey came to the league polished both professionally and personally. He handled interviews well.

Some wondered how a depressed Payton would take to his new backfield mate. They didn't wonder long.

Roland Harper: Prior to them drafting Matt, I never worried about my position because I knew there was nobody in the league who blocked better than I. But Matt would ask me questions like, "How do you block—how can you do that on the run?" He'd watch me on different things. I think he felt that coming into it he would be a blocking back, he would have to accept that role. I taught him, told him what to look for, how to do it, how to make the adjustments on the run, how to get in the guy's chest and if he was low enough, how to uncoil because that's kind of like the same thing in running. I did it in blocking, Walter did it in running. Right before impact, you've got to be even, even-footed. If you understand that analogy . . . Because a lot of times if you're right-handed you kind of push off with your right foot as you explode into the blocking. In this league, you're not going to be set on your right foot all the time, so you gotta be kind of even-footed. I would tell him basically you got to be able to use both sides and make your adjustment on the run. He picked it up real well and I think he did a great job.

I think what made Matt and Walter such good friends was an extension of what happened between me and Walter. When you've got the right guy in front of you, there's this telepathy that goes on that connects you. He had to know which way I was going to block someone so he could set that block up and cut off of it. He and Matt had that same sort of relationship. And Walter liked people he didn't have to say a lot to. He liked people who just knew, people who just knew what he was thinking or where he was going. That overcame all the differences between Walter and Matt, because Matt grew to the point that he just knew Walter's thoughts.

Off the field, he knew how to fill my shoes too. Walter needed somebody that he could talk with and Matt became that guy. That was always important to Walter, that somebody he could unload on. Matt was perfect there.

Walter Payton: We were Ebony and Ivory before Stevie Wonder and Paul McCartney. I think our relationship really helped break down a lot of lines, a lot of racial lines, on the team and, some said, in the city. Here were two guys who had to have each other, and everything just clicked. Remember, I came from an all-black college in the Deep South. Matt was one of the first white guys I really got to know. He knew I was nervous about all that and he broke the ice by joking around all the time about it. If it weren't for the fact he was an obnoxious Penn Stater, I'd say we could talk about anything.

Matt Suhey: It was tough knowing I came here to Chicago to ultimately replace Roland Harper, who was a first-class A-1 person, and,
more important, who was perhaps Walter's best friend ever. They
were extremely close. Ro hurt his knee, and that type of injury—the
way surgery was medically back then—he just couldn't recover. I
think that at first it was not a great relationship because of all that.

Where Walter and Roland were so much alike, Walter and I were
complete opposites in a lot of ways. He didn't like to sit and talk—
especially to reporters. I enjoyed that. It was funny because he was
the guy that went a hundred miles per hour and I was the calm one,
the one who was more slow-paced. I think it made for a great relationship. Our lives were completely different. I came from a college,
academic atmosphere, born and raised at Penn State with six brothers and sisters, my grandfather, everybody came from Penn State,
raised in that environment. Joe Paterno was my sister's godfather.
My grandfather coached at Penn State, played against George Halas
in the National Football League, coached my father. My father married a coach's daughter. My father played for the Pittsburgh Steelers,
played with Jim Finks, who was the guy who drafted me. Academics and education, those were the goals in life. I married a nice
Jewish girl from Philadelphia, again the emphasis is on academics
and culture. It's a different mind-set. I think Walter eventually
liked that about me.

When I first got there, he used to call me the short white boy—
I'm sure he used to joke around like that a lot—but it intimidated
me a little, since I understood the dynamics here. I dressed right
next to him and eventually that first year, just through joking
around and his sense of humor, a relationship just developed. I was
pretty much a very organized student of the game and was fanatical
about making sure I knew all my assignments, and making sure I
knew the game and all that kind of stuff. Not that he wasn't a student of the game, but he just took a different approach to it. He
knew his assignments, knew his plays, but I knew probably everybody's assignments and that kind of stuff, and his as well.

Walter Payton: It amazed me that this guy was always asking questions. Whether it was one-on-one or in team meetings, he always had questions. Sometimes when he'd start in, we'd groan because the rest of us just wanted to get the hell out of those meetings. Over the course of our career, I can't tell you how many meeting hours Matt added to my life. Sometimes I wondered if he did it because he knew it drove us nuts.

That's what makes sports such an important part of all of us. Sports broke down everything. It made race and where we came from not matter. There's nothing like being on a team, nothing like it. Without sports, how would I have ever met a guy like Matt? I probably wouldn't have. And he turns out to be one of the best friends I've ever had.

Matt Suhey: Walter also knew how to pick me up when I needed it. One time, I fumbled going in for a touchdown in an important situation. I was hurting. We were trotting off the field, and Walter gave me that little half grin. He asked me if I'd ever had a paper route. I said, "What are you talking about?" Then he laughed and said, "Do that again, and you better find yourself a paper route, because you sure won't be playing no more football." It was crazy, but it was exactly what I needed. He got me back from feeling down on myself by teasing.

Jim McMahon: The relationship that Walter had with Matt was a mirror of our whole team during that Super Bowl time. We didn't see black and white. We could joke around with each other and say "nigger" without a big uprising going on. Or they could say "you cracker," or "you hick," whatever it was. It wasn't a derogatory term. It was more like we had respect and love for one another, and we could say things without problems. You say that nowadays, you've got a lawsuit. It's way out of proportion. When you play sports, you can't have too many friends. Guys see a weakness, they just go after it. You gotta be able to take it and give it back. We were able to do that—we never had a big fight in the locker room, a racially motivated kind of thing. I think that's the kind of respect that we all had for one another. That's the same with Matt and Walter. They could say things to each other that they knew weren't meant in a bad way. I think that's just the special relationship we had as a team. Our whole team is like that, and Wally and Matt set the tone.

Connie Payton: I think what Matt understood about Walter was something most people didn't get, was that you don't have to talk a lot to each other to still get along. I think Walter didn't enjoy people who talked a lot, but most people would get around him and feel uneasy when there would be silence, so they would talk. Matt understood that we can still be friends even if we don't talk to each other all the time. When Matt's younger son was born, Scotty, he wanted Walter to be the godfather and I think that meant a lot to Walter that Matt would ask him to be his son's godfather. Walter didn't say much, but he smiled. Matt knew that it meant a great deal to him.

And then too, Matt made it a point to also call Walter and even come by. A lot of people said that if Walter didn't call them that meant he was too busy, so they didn't want to disturb him. Matt knew better. Matt would just drop by. And sometimes with Walter that's how you have to be, you just have to do it. As forceful as he was in football, in his personal life Walter liked people sometimes to just take the lead role. That was Matt and me. We both understood Walter.

Matt Suhey: We had some wild times. We used to go out socially, we played cards and pool. He liked to get the running backs together and have our tight group. As you did back in those days, you spend so much time together, you're in camp for five, six weeks, twice a day. Walter, of course, didn't sleep a whole lot. He was an early riser, went to bed late, loved firecrackers and joking around. And I enjoyed egging him on and giving him ideas for pranks. He was the master.

I remember one time in 1982, we were in training camp in Lake

Forest, and we were driving around, Willie McClendon, myself, and Walter. There was this big estate on the lake, gorgeous big hillside home. The grounds were manicured beautifully, probably fifteen, twenty acres, big iron gates. Typical Lake Forest estate. I said, "Gee, let's go look at this house." So we go driving in there and we're walking around the gardens, which were manicured like an English manor, went by the pool and everything. Now the house was pretty well beat-up, so we wondered if anyone lived there. Only one way to find out, right? We go in the house and look. So we get in this one room there, Willie McClendon, myself, and Walter. The next thing you know we see dog food in the living room and a tray and a pan, and all of a sudden we hear something or someone coming down the stairs. It was either a man or a big dog. Way out the door these guys take off and I'm, of course, the white guy left in the dust. So here I am with two black guys in Lake Forest. Walter's got a gun in his car. He had a permit to carry a gun because he was always worried. I was sure we were either going to get shot or arrested. I was joking the whole time, "They're going to think I'm a dark-haired Hispanic guy"—back in those days I had dark hair and a mustache. I figured they'd call the police for two black guys and a Hispanic guy breaking in. We all made it out. The dog was a Doberman and he came charging around just before we shut the door. That was close, but it was the kind of insane things we got ourselves into. Just us being guys. Look back now and you're amazed we all made it through that period of our lives.

Walter loved to call guys who just got married on the team, pretend that he's a girl, and his voice is very high, and he disguises it very well, and the wives are going nuts. Once the guys were able to convince their wives it was Walter playing a prank, the wives would say, Jeez, who is this guy? He did it to Calvin Thomas and almost got Calvin Thomas divorced or killed.

Even during the darkest of times during the summer of 1999, Walter kept Matt in the deepest inner circle—a circle where almost no

Working out at
Payton's Hill.

BILL SMITH

A poster photographed
at the Hill.

COSTACOS BROTHERS

In action with Matt Suhey. BILL SMITH

CARL SISSAC

With Coach Bob Hill, in the flowered shirt. COLLECTION OF PAYTON FAMILY

At the NFL Hall of Fame induction ceremony in Canton, Ohio, July 1993: Mrs. Alyne Payton, Connie, Walter, Brittney, and Jarrett. PRO FOOTBALL HALL OF FAME

Kim Tucker and Ginny Quirk. STEVE RUBIN

With John Gamauf. BRIDGESTONE/FIRESTONE

With Mark Alberts at Walter Payton's Roundhouse Complex, Aurora, Illinois. ROCKY PINTOZZI

Retirement Sunday in 1987. BILL SMITH

As an Indy car owner.

Walter breaks down at the end of the February 2, 1999, press conference.

An avalanche of support. CARL SISSAC

Fans watch a flight team at the public memorial service at Soldier Field, November 6, 1999. ROB FINCH, COPLEY CHICAGO NEWSPAPERS

one else was allowed. Sensing the sadness that Matt and others felt watching him slowly deteriorate, Walter turned to humor to reduce tension.

Walter Payton: I really believe humor is important, and Matt and I had the same bad sense of humor. In September, I started joking with Matt about how in *Brian's Song,* the movie about Brian Piccolo and Gale Sayers, they had a relationship like ours. But in that one, the white guy gets sick and dies. I said I wondered how come I couldn't have been in that movie. It was funny, but I guess you had to be there. Matt helped me laugh, and after I got sick I needed that more than ever.

Matt Suhey: Walter had an extreme wit, very, very quick. He remembered everything, what you said, what you were wearing. If you said something or you made a promise to him, ten years ago or two minutes, he had a way of remembering. He had a way of putting things. Although he was nonconfrontational, he could twist things pretty good to get you motivated, to get you psyched. When he talked about the *Brian's Song* stuff, at first I didn't know how to react. I couldn't think of him dying.

The reason, I think, that we stayed close all those years is that I felt that he was tremendously loyal to me and he accepted me and my faults. He worked to try to make me better as a player and as a person, and I was tremendously loyal back to him. I got mad at him, I got mad at him more than a few times. He'd get mad at me, but it would take you ten days to get it out of him. There was more of a trust and loyalty that I would be there. I was a good listener and I asked a tremendous amount of questions. I asked a lot about his life, why he did that, why is he doing this? Some of it he would say and be honest with you, or some of it he would just give you a vague answer and he would go on.

He's the type of guy you look at, if you got a problem, if something goes wrong, I know I could turn to him and he would help me out regardless of what it would take from him or the amount of money he would spend. He would certainly be there in times of need, and he's certainly there when things are going very well. I loved him like a brother.

Pam Curry: I don't think Matt knows the depth of gratitude that I have for him because he was there, and he was there from day one. I believe Walter knew back in October of 1998 that he was sicker than what he was—I really think he knew. I think the only other person who knew was Matt. Walter wouldn't let anybody go to the doctor with him except Matt. He wouldn't let Momma go, he wouldn't let Connie go. When he first started going to Mayo, he wouldn't let anybody go with him. He would go with Matt. Matt went with him from day one. When I was in Chicago toward the end, I saw genuine love between two people, because every night before Matt would leave, he would wake Walter. Towards the end, he was getting weaker and weaker, but he would wake him and he would say, "Walter, Walter." He would wake him up until he would talk, he would say, "I'm getting ready to leave." He said, "I'll be back in the morning, okay? Are you gonna be here when I get back?" Walter would say, "Yeah." And then Matt would kiss him on the forehead and he would say, "I love you." And he would leave and he would squeeze Walter's hand when he would leave. I just thank Matt for being there with him to lighten that load for him somewhat, because when I think of it, it was just a tremendous load to bear for Matt. It's something to see two guys, football players, men, strong guys, having a relationship like that.

We were in the hospital—we were at Zion—that Tuesday night before he passed, it was Connie and me and Matt, and Matt was getting ready to leave, and he wanted Walter to bet on the World Series. Matt said he was gonna take New York, and he said, "Walter, you get Atlanta, okay? You take Atlanta, okay?" And Walter said, "Yeah." He said, "How much are we gonna bet, a hundred dollars?" He said, "Yeah." Matt said, "You sure you want Atlanta? You want

New York? You want Atlanta?" Walter said, "Yeah." Then Matt left.
When he left, I said, "Walter, why did you pick Atlanta? Because
New York is up," I think it was three to nothing. And I said, "They
gonna sweep them." I said, "Why did you take them—why did you
do that?" And Connie said, "Yeah, why did you do that?" He said,
"To shut Matt up." So that tickled Connie and me because he wanted
Matt to be quiet. And that night, Connie and I were watching the
game and we were excited and we were yelling because Atlanta was
winning for a long time. And we said, "Walter, you must have
known something, Atlanta's winning." But then they turned around
and lost. It is still one of my great memories.

Matt Suhey: You know, for all the years after football, I considered
us close, but we still only talked every once in a while. I don't know
why, but the sickness seemed to draw the two of us close together
again. I can't tell you how many times in the last few months that I
fell asleep there. We had the same furniture—he had the same couch
downstairs in his basement as I have in my den. I can't tell you how
many times I'd fall asleep there, and at two in the morning— I'm an
early riser, I get up early in the morning and I'm at his house late
that night watching the basketball game. This was like February,
March, April—the NBA play-offs, the whole series. He loved the
Knicks, he loved the Mets. I'd wake him up and then I'd stagger off
and drive home. He didn't sleep that much. I'd wake up and he'd be
looking at me. I told him I knew he loved me, but staring at me was
a little much! I told him that if I ever woke up and he had a hand on
me, the cancer wouldn't get a chance to get him!

Then when we'd go out for a drive, he always complained. He'd
say, "I don't have to worry about dying, you're going to kill me in
this damn car." He didn't like the way that anybody but him would
drive. The doctors told me that he had to get up, and his quality of
life— He had to get up and do stuff, and that would mean a lot to
him. I just felt that he needed somebody and he was too proud to call
anybody, so I never called when I came over. He liked to go every

time to a different spot down on St. Charles, just go by and look at cars, and go look at the track and see who's running the track— finally it got to be he sat in his car and listened to "The Score" sports radio station and talked about it. They'd say something and we'd discuss it. Anything just to get him out.

Every time I'd leave, he'd say, "When are you coming back? What are you doing tomorrow?" I'd tell him my schedule, I'd tell him what's going on. At that point he didn't say a whole lot. We watched I can't tell you how many movies. There was a movie called *Major Payne* that he loved. We watched it over and over. We watched a lot of baseball games. The baseball season, of course all the basketball games, loved dunking. Whatever it was, he liked New York. Of course he liked the Bulls.

Two weeks before he died, he told me he wanted me to take him to Mike Singletary's house. We were driving around and Walter would say, "That's his house." So I'd go to the door and it would be someone who never heard of Mike Singletary. I'd look back and there was Walter sitting in the car laughing at me. He really kept his sense of humor to the end.

When I think about this now, what gets me kind of choked up, he wanted me to get one of those Zagat books, it's a restaurant guide. He said, "You know, I haven't eaten in that many restaurants in Chicago. There are so many great restaurants, let's pick out the top ten restaurants." We're going through books, picking them out. The goal was to pick ten and go to them. We picked out a few but never got to finish the project—all he wanted to do was go eat an appetizer, look at the atmosphere, check it out, look around. The goal was to hit two a night or something like that. You work, you bust your ass, you're running around, and you don't enjoy some of the things life has to offer. Walter wanted to do that before he died and he never got to.

Walter Payton: Once you get out of the game, the truth is you lose a lot of relationships. Matt is my exception. Our lives have been linked, and they will stay that way. Matt led the way when I was running in the NFL, he protected me. And we've stayed close all these years. When I found out about the disease, Matt was right there for me and for my family. I redid my will recently, and Matt will be the executor of the estate. I need him now more than ever, more than when we played together. He didn't fail me on the field and he hasn't failed me since.

9

Super Bears

He was one of the forefathers of professional football in 1920, and in addition to giving America a sport that would forever dominate its landscape, George S. Halas founded one of the nation's most storied sports franchises of all time, the Chicago Bears.

A Chicago native and a three-sport letterman at the University of Illinois, Halas was a former naval commander who had a brief stint in right field for another storied American franchise: the New York Yankees. As a coach for the Bears, Halas won six world championships between 1921 and 1963. "Papa Bear," as he was known, passed away at the age of eighty-eight on October 31, 1983, some twenty years after he was inducted as one of the charter members into the Pro Football Hall of Fame in Canton, Ohio.

As much as the Bears organization missed his spirit, his leadership was an even greater loss. The Bears went through a thirty-two-year drought without a championship after Halas's final title was won over the New York Giants on December 29, 1963, at Wrigley Field. A franchise that had become known for dominance and winning struggled through the late 1960s, most of the 1970s, and the very early part of the 1980s, making just two play-off appearances between 1964 and 1983. After an abysmal 3–6 inaugural season for head coach Mike Ditka (the strike-shortened campaign of 1982), the Bears won five of their last six games in 1983 to finish 8–8. The big, bad Bears were starting to come out of hibernation, and Walter Payton was beginning to growl fiercely with the first of four straight 1,300-plus-yard rushing seasons. In those four years, from 1983 to 1986, Walter unleashed his terrifying combination of rushing and receiving on the NFL and solidified his spot in the annals of the league as its most dominant back.

In 1984, the Bears went 10–6 as Walter rushed for the second-most yards of his career (1,684) and had eleven rushing touchdowns. After stumbling a bit in the final weeks of the season (losing two of their final three regular season games) the Bears traveled to Washington to face the Redskins in the first round of the play-offs on December 30, 1984. Few people gave the upstart Bears much hope against the defending NFC champions.

Walter Payton: We went to Washington and nobody gave us a chance of winning that game, because we were playing on the road. The Bears hadn't won a play-off game since 1963. Why did anyone think that would change against the 'Skins? Our quarterback, Jim McMahon, was out and so Steve Fuller stepped in and led us. Coach Ditka called a bunch of great plays. I can say that because one of his calls was a pass play with me throwing the ball—my favorite thing to do. It went for a touchdown and, to everyone's surprise, we went in there and beat their butts.

Walter led the charge against the Redskins, rushing for over one hundred yards in addition to that touchdown pass. The Bears' 23–19 win enabled Chicago to taste play-off success for the first time in over twenty years. That win put the Bears into the NFC championship game against the dominant San Francisco 49ers at Candlestick Park. The 'Niners and Joe Montana overpowered Walter and the Bears, 23–0, on their way to a 38–16 rout of Miami in Super Bowl XIX. But even with the game already decided, Walter refused to go quietly. On the last play of the game, after the gun had already been sounded, Payton was still fighting for yardage.

Walter Payton: The greatest feeling that I ever had in football and the worst feeling I ever had in football were a week apart. I really believed once we beat Washington that we might go to the Super Bowl, I felt such a tremendous rush. I never felt such a rush in my whole life. Then, after the loss against San Francisco, I was saying to myself, It took almost ten years to get here, it will be another nine years before we get back here and I won't be around. Those are the things that go through your head. I had never felt such a depression in my whole life, and to go from one extreme to the other—I really at that point realized how much I did want it. I remember Wilbur Marshall in particular; he came up to me and said, "Quit holding your head down." He was upset and he was bitter too. He said, "Next year, we're not going to just knock on the door, we're going to kick the damn door down."

The seeds for one of football's most legendary Super Bowl champions were planted there in the loss at Candlestick Park. The 1985 Bears not only kicked the door down, they knocked the whole house to its foundation. With a combination of talent and personality unmatched in recent years, the Bears—with their platinum single, "Super Bowl Shuffle," serving as a backdrop—waltzed through the NFL. The season began with a 38–28 win at home over Tampa Bay, and the combination of a high-powered offense led by Walter, Jim McMahon, and Willie Gault, and a stingy defense led by Mike Singletary, Gary Fencik, and Richard Dent, posted twelve straight wins.

Jim McMahon: That team was magic. There was a special collection of not just talents but personalities. We had the best players in the league pretty much at every position. And we had a bunch of good guys. We had a great time together. We had so much fun in Chicago. Everywhere we went we had a good time. I think that caught on. People got caught up in the excitement of how much fun we had. That's how you saw us—every town we went to, we'd get to the hotel, the damn thing's packed with people, Bears paraphernalia everywhere. I think the fans enjoyed our style of play. We went out and kicked ass and then we had fun after, and they enjoyed that.

Walter was the heart and soul of our team. Hell, that's how we'd win, we'd run the ball. Now, I bitched for years about throwing it more. You got him in the backfield and the offensive line that we had; we were a dominant football team. We could control the ball and Walter was a great part of that. Most important, we knew that he was going to be there every week. They didn't know if I was going to be there, but they knew Walter was. You could always depend on him.

Mike Singletary: During that season especially, I saw Walter having focus, and I think he understood that we had something very special. I think it was that season where he really began to vocalize and verbalize a little bit more of what he felt. For the first time he began to speak, he began to talk in the huddle, he began to talk at practice, and he began to talk before the game—"Hey," he'd say, "let's go out here and do what we have to do." Before the games, and Fridays and Saturdays, he was more vocal. I think that that hunger was there and he communicated that through the way he played, and then, to another step to verbalize what he felt, I think everybody looked at him and said, Wow, this guy is really serious about this. This is it. We can really do it. Walter believes we can do it. We're close, we can get there. Every now and then I realized that we were young and we would lose the focus, and when Walter felt that, he would pull us back into focus—the coaches as well. He was so steady. On that team, you had the flare, you had the obnoxious, you had the style, you had everything. Walter just showed up every day, every game, did what he had to do and more. He didn't complain about it, because he didn't want any extra spotlight on him.

Walter Payton: Finally, after carrying the team for so many years and after being beat-up and bruised—there were days [in prior years] that I couldn't even walk and times that I couldn't even lift my arms. I fought so hard for the city and I felt like I was a one-legged man in an ass-kicking contest. For so many years I was by myself, and then finally, it was like I got one guy here to watch my back, I got another guy there. For the first time I had these guys saying, "Hold on, I'm gonna lift this arm, and I'm gonna lift that arm, and I'm gonna help you up"—and we all pulled together as a team.

We were the perfect unit, and that is the reason. There will never be another 1985 Bears team, because we all worked together. The myriad personalities were a perfect combination to just make it right. Even though we were very cliquish—the running backs hung together, the quarterbacks hung together—we all had mutual respect. We all felt like every guy was giving 110 percent. Every practice, every game.

Connie Payton: That team was really a great group. They were fun to watch and had so much personality and character. You just don't see that anymore. For a team to have that many people with so many different personalities, and everybody stood out. Dan Hampton, they called "Danimal." Steve McMichael, his crazy self. Richard Dent, kind of lovable. Don't leave out Jim McMahon. You fell in love with everyone on the team. They were all so much fun. It was amazing how it all kind of took off. They were America's team. The "Super Bowl Shuffle" was adored by so many people.

Matt Suhey: Walter helped that team feel free to express itself. He was the guy who had such a great sense of humor that everyone felt, if Walter can do it, then I can let myself show a little. He wasn't just the best player on the field, he was the best leader off of it. That team would have exploded had there not been Walter there to keep it together, especially because there was friction from the coaching staff, from Buddy Ryan and Mike Ditka. All the chemicals were there for an explosion, and Walter proved he could instead turn it into the right mix. That was maybe his most important role on that team.

It was amazing how it all just kind of took off. People to this day say they play the "Super Bowl Shuffle." There was just so much character there and so much people could love in life, and you just don't hardly find that anymore on the teams—if you even know anybody.

Walter Payton: Oh, that "Super Bowl Shuffle" video, that was funny. You remember when they were dancing and everything else? You saw McMahon floating across the screen and you saw me floating across everybody else? You know why they did that? Because we weren't there the first day they filmed it, so they did us on the blue background and then they superimposed us on the front. It was wild. That video sold over 100,000 copies, and everybody was happy.

One thing that never made Walter very happy was losing. So when a Monday night game at Miami appeared to be the only thing that stood between the Bears and an undefeated regular season, Walter was especially jacked up for the tussle. Of course, the Bears would be facing the descendants of the last NFL team to go undefeated, the 1972 Dolphins. Not to mention a very talented Miami team led by the rising star Dan Marino. Miami evoked the spirits of past players and wound up defeating the Bears 38–24 to put the only blemish on the Bears' 15–1 campaign. It was a bitter, bitter loss that remained with Walter despite the eventual Super Bowl victory. His memory of and reaction to that game, even years later, is a telling testament to Walter's competitive edge.

Walter Payton: When I think back on that season, the Super Bowl season, the first thing that comes to my mind is the loss to Miami. It was a loss that shouldn't have been. I guess hindsight is twenty-twenty, but I don't think it takes a rocket scientist to figure out that if you have the number one rushing team, which we did, and you're facing the number twenty-seven or twenty-eight team against the rush, which they were, what's your game plan going to be? I think everybody on that team was praying the Dolphins would eventually get to the Super Bowl, because we had a score to settle. It wouldn't have been a contest at all.

That rematch never materialized, as the Dolphins were upset by the wild card New England Patriots, 31–14 in the AFC championship game. The Bears, who had won their two play-off games without surrendering a point (21–0 against the New York Giants and 24–0 against the Los Angeles Rams), were forced to take revenge on the Dolphins' AFC East counterpart. New England captured magic in a bottle, winning all three of its play-off games on the road—against the Jets, the Los Angeles Raiders, and finally Miami. As much as Chicago had captured America's heart with its dominance, its "Super Bowl Shuffle," and its personalities—especially McMahon, Walter, and William "The Refrigerator" Perry—New England rolled into New Orleans for Super Bowl XX relishing the role of the underdog.

Jim McMahon: New England's focus was Walter Payton. They said, "We're going to stop Walter Payton." I mean, everywhere he went during that game, there was two or three guys there with him. The one play I remember—the first play of the second half when we were backed up in the end zone—I faked the ball to Walter and you can see the whole defensive football team go after him. I think that's really what hurt the New England Patriots in that game. Their downfall was worrying so much about Walter; they let everybody else have a pretty good day.

The Patriots managed to keep Walter out of the end zone but could not stop the 46–10 carnage, which at that point was the biggest

Super Bowl victory ever. Walter, as much as anyone, was overjoyed with the title and what it meant for the city of Chicago. But there was a tinge of hurt he carried with him after the game over not scoring a touchdown on the world's biggest stage, the Super Bowl.

Walter Payton: It would have been great to score one, they would have had your name down as scoring a touchdown in the Super Bowl. In the days and weeks after the game, yes, I was bothered by it. But I was blessed to have parents who instilled in me that things happen for a reason. You may not understand it when it first happens, and it might not be something that you're going to be happy about, but down the line there will come a time when it will be shown to you.

Plus, I wouldn't have wanted anybody to have given me anything, and it wouldn't have meant anything if we moved the ball down and then all of a sudden, "It's okay, you're on the 1-yard line, let's give the touchdown to Payton." I don't think it would have meant anything to me. It would have been very shallow and hollow. It was a disappointing feeling at that moment, and then it was like, hey, I realized exactly what it didn't mean, then it was okay.

Jim McMahon: He had played for so long and he had been the Chicago Bears for so many years, and to see him not be able to get in the end zone, it had to hurt. It hurt me not seeing him score a touchdown. But the truth is I don't think anyone recognized it during the game. I know I didn't. On the touchdown that I scored, it was a play designed for Walter.

Mike Ditka: That was probably the most disturbing thing in my career. People say, "Wow, you didn't give the ball to Walter to score in the Super Bowl?" If I had one thing to do over again, I would make sure that he took the ball into the end zone. I loved him; I had great respect for him. The only thing that really ever hurt me was when he didn't score in the Super Bowl, that killed me when I found out about it. I didn't think about it, I really didn't realize it. It just never crossed my mind, to be honest with you, that it was important. And then I realized how important it really was and I felt so bad about that over the years, but I couldn't undo it. In my mind, even when we're ahead 40-something to 10, or 30-something to 10, the only thing I kept looking at, and the only thing I kept thinking about, was winning the football game. I never thought about the individual thing so much. That was stupid on my part.

But our relationship was great because he could talk to me at any time and did. He'd bring things to me, he'd say, "Listen, the guys are having a problem with this or maybe you ought to back off on this," and I did, whether it be the conditioning—because in the beginning we ran like crazy. We conditioned like crazy. All my memories of Walter are good. But not getting him a touchdown, that's the only bad one I had and that was my fault.

I understood why it bothered him too. Here's a guy who set the all-time rushing record—one of the great players in the history of the game, or the greatest in my opinion—and to be on that big a stage in that short a time and not be able to do what he did best, I understood it. In the beginning I didn't, because I had scored a touchdown in the Super Bowl and it meant nothing to me, it was just a touchdown. No different from the one I scored in Green Bay when I played for the Bears. It was just a touchdown. And then I could understand it because I was just a guy, but he was *the* guy, and I should have been more understanding. I understood it after I thought about it for a while.

As much as Ditka regrets not getting Walter into the end zone, the result of the game was what mattered most to Walter. For himself, surely, but for his family, his teammates, his coaches, and his city.

Walter Payton: It was for the fans because they stood by us, they gave us the support. Sure, we had fun doing it, but they were always there for us and because of that we were all able to celebrate together. I can't imagine any city in the league where the fans and the team are as linked as they are in Chicago. It is a great blue-collar town and we were a great blue-collar team. We weren't pretty and we didn't try to be. And our fans understood that. They loved Bears football. Even players from the Bulls will tell you that winning all those championships was great, but Chicago is a Bears town.

Mike Ditka: As significant as all the Chicago Bulls' six world championships were, I don't think they surpassed the feeling the city has for the 1985 Bears Super Bowl champs. Chicago embraced that team and that team embraced that city. I still think it was the greatest sports moment in Chicago history. For one reason, they hadn't had a championship in that city for twenty years—they had won in hockey, that was before that, that was '61 and they had won in '62 with the Bears. It was just so long. And I think the other thing is that the city related to the players on the team. It became the team that Chicago raised—it become a big, strong, loving football team led by a running back who was the greatest of them all. What would you rather be in life, would you rather be revered or loved? I'd rather be loved. Walter and that team, they were loved.

There's a saying that in Chicago Michael Jordan is revered and Walter Payton was loved. Jordan, as great as he is, never made the same connection with the fans. He never made that connection because he's almost like a god. And I think, of all the nicknames I've ever heard, Sweetness really defines Walter as much as any. He had a lot of other good traits. He really was a sweet man.

How integral was Walter to the Bears? After Super Bowl XX, the Chicago front office couldn't decide on a design for the team's Super Bowl ring. They called Walter and he redesigned it. Then, at the dinner to award those rings, he was the first running back whose name was called. Rather than be singled out, he gathered the other running backs and they went up as a group.

Mike Ditka: As a coach, you can't say enough about stuff like that. He was our superstar, but he made sure everyone was included. He was a star that drew people together rather than driving wedges like some stars do. He knew, I guess from those early years with the Bears, that he couldn't do this without them. And he showed his gratitude, which takes maturity and class.

As sports fans have often witnessed, the problem sometimes with celebrations is the lingering hangover that can affect the next season's performance. Favored to reach the Super Bowl again by many prognosticators, the 1986 Bears picked up where they left off by winning seven of their first eight games and their last seven in a row to finish 14–2.

Walter Payton: We were still having some fun that next season, it's just that along with success comes responsibilities in football and outside of football. I think that was taking its toll on the players as well, because we weren't all really as fresh as we could have been when you come to practice. Once you leave practice you have an engagement here, you have something to do there. That, in a way—it's so small—but it still interrupts what we were doing as a team. It kind of separates everybody as individuals instead of being together as a team. The year after the Super Bowl, everyone had new endorsements, everyone had speaking deals. It really did change the team.

When they went back home, they were not just the guys who ran special teams, they're not just the guys who ran the dummy playing for the defense or the dummy playing for the offense. They were not just anybody, they were the Chicago Bears Super Bowl champions. "Hey, let me buy your dinner, let me pay that for you." So you get into that, and you have that success, and you come back the next year. They tasted the forbidden fruit and it was good. When they came back, they wanted a bigger piece of the pie. Guys who were second-team, guys who were third-string who just ran the ball, they wanted to be more in the spotlight, they wanted more, more. And when everybody came back, they weren't just satisfied with just running and helping out where they were needed, 'cause believe me, it takes everybody to win a Super Bowl. That's why I'm in awe of Dallas and San Francisco, because they did it back-to-back. Do you know how hard and difficult it is to keep people hungry, to keep people humble enough to just say, Hey, whatever I can do to ensure and enhance the team success, I'm willing to do it? After you've been to the mountaintop? We had guys coming back, they wanted to score more touchdowns, they wanted to do more commercials, they wanted to be in more interviews, they wanted their names to be in print. Everybody wanted something more. You can only slice a pie up in so many ways, but for everybody to get an equal slice, everybody has to do their part. It didn't happen that way. The Bears had, believe it or not, the same players we had the year before, but just not the same desire, same hunger. We even enhanced our situation by bringing in new players who had the ability to help us in places where we were short at. Then why didn't we repeat? Why didn't the Bears win back-to-back Super Bowls, three or four Super Bowls? Why? Because not everybody deals with success the same way. We had it all. Every piece of the puzzle, we had. But once you shake that puzzle up, it's hard to put it back together, even when you know the pieces. Even when you know there are only twenty-five pieces there and it can only go a certain way, and you've done it before, it still takes you time to do it. We couldn't do it. That's why those other teams that I'm not going to mention anymore, I look at them and think, Wow, it could have been us. We should have done it.

In order for a team to keep on being successful, everyone who's involved, everyone who's working, has to be able to share not only the responsibility, not only the hard work, but also success, evenly and accordingly. Because if you don't do it that way, it's only short-lived. I look back and realize, I beat myself, I said, "Jesus, we had guys like Wilbur Marshall, who took people's head off. We had Willie Gault, who was fast, Speedy Willie." Why wish? It's very easy. Hard work, there's no substitution for hard work. When you work together as a unit, you have to be willing to be giving, to give of yourself.

That's the only thing I regret when I look back. The worst thing in the world is to look back at your accomplishments and look back at what you've done within this organization and the people that you're working with. The worst thing in the world that you can say is that damn, I wish I had. That's a weird feeling. I wish I had. When you say that, "I wish I had," it's too late. We were still good that next year, but we weren't the team we were in 1985, because some of the hunger was gone.

The culmination of those subtle changes showed up in the second round of the NFC play-offs, when the Redskins came to Soldier Field on January 3, 1987, to play the favored Bears. In a shocking upset, the Bears lost 27–13, dashing any hopes of repeating the magic of the prior season. With so many young and talented players standing alongside proven veterans like Walter, many had speculated the Bears could be in the midst of creating a dynasty of dominance.

Walter Payton: Well, we thought that too. But you have to remember, we also thought we were going to beat San Francisco the season before we won the Super Bowl and that we would have then beaten Miami that Super Bowl year. A lot of times people forget how you got there. Everybody who was willing to do everything just to get there, they were a little bit reluctant to go that same path. Consequently, that was why we didn't win. What was so great about that team in '85 was that we all needed and depended on each other.

When you're working with a group and you win, that's the best feeling in the world, bar none. Whatever you do in life, be it tennis, or golf, or running, whatever, you can do all these things based upon your own ability. It doesn't mean anything in a team sports environment. Once you accomplish that, it's nothing compared to being able to accomplish a goal with other people, when you're depending on their effort as well as your own to accomplish your combined goal. When it happens—I'll tell you what, that's something special. You know why? Because there are so many variables that are involved. For instance, there are teams that defy all odds, winning back-to-back championships, like the Chicago Bulls. You know why it's so incredible? Because to do it even once, everything has to go together, everything has to click. Everything has to go just right because everybody is working against you.

One of the days you might come to practice and a teammate has problems—the kids kept him up all night before the game, or someone comes to the game and he's sluggish and he doesn't play his best. There are problems, everybody's gonna have a problem. Everybody's gonna have something that's gonna work against them in terms of them being and fulfilling their best efforts on one particular day. Of course, the good thing about all that is you don't have to worry about just your own performance. When you're on a team, you have other people to pick you up if you're the one having the off day. You had other people to help you when you're small, when you're lacking in your ability to achieve what your goals are.

The Bears in 1985 were a perfect team. We all did the things that it took to win. I am so proud of having been there. I hope no one who ever watched that team will forget how special it was and how special the guys on that team were. I love them.

10

Retirement

Walter Payton: Nothing lasts forever. Nothing.

It is every athlete's toughest decision. How do I leave the game? Do I hang on as long as I can and enjoy this, or do I walk away while I'm near the peak of my career? In truth, only a select few really get to make that choice. Walter was among the select.

Two years after the Bears' Super Bowl run, Walter decided his time had come. He had signed a one-year, $1 million contract that made it evident to everyone that he was on his way to retirement. At the same time, the Bears had used a first-round pick on a powerful running back from the University of Florida, Neal Anderson. The pick surprised Walter, but made his future obvious.

Connie Payton: Neal Anderson was going to be the next Walter Payton, like others who had been mentioned. Honestly, I think he got tired of that. He felt sort of disappointed, because he felt like the Bears wanted him to retire. They would say, "We might as well start paying him more because he's going to be our future running back, and you know you're on your way out." So Walter really started feeling a little slighted because he felt like, Hey, I've had all these great years, and who wants to think that they're getting older and it's time to move on? Nobody does. It was like, I had all these great years and how can they do this? And I think it's hard enough to admit that it is time to get out and to leave it when you love it. Even when you think you're ready, you're really emotionally and mentally not ready for that next phase of your life. Then to feel like they're waiting for you to leave so they can move somebody else into your spot, that was an awful feeling. But I think in his heart Walter knew that it was time to move on. Whether you want to let go or not, you might as well leave while you're on top.

Mike Ditka: Neal Anderson was a great kid, good running back. He had a great burst and he could run with the ball, but it's like apples and oranges. It was so different. That's the hardest thing when it's time to say good-bye—sometimes you know, sometimes you don't know and you want to hang on. In my case when it was time to say good-bye, it didn't matter. I knew it. When I looked at the films I knew it, so I said, Hey, there's no use in going out there and trying to embarrass myself. Walter wouldn't have embarrassed himself, but he had lost the stuff, there's no question about it. So he had to become more of a power runner. He had to really overpower people inside, he wasn't able to dart like he was earlier in his career. But that happens to everybody. There is a lot of inequities in this sport, I don't like it. One constant in life that you've got to realize is that there is always gonna be this thing called change. You may not like it, and you may not understand it, but it's gonna be there. We're all gonna change, physically, mentally, socially, economically. When you're in sports, things are gonna change. Focus changes, time changes individuals, it's just what happens. I knew that, I knew how much it bothered Walter. It bothered me because this is not the way you want people to go out. That's probably one of my biggest faults—I kept a lot of other players who maybe had passed their prime, but I thought that was the way to be loyal, and I think that is. In Walter's case, I didn't keep him past his prime, it wasn't a matter of that. He was still productive, but he had to change his style a little bit. I think he would have been the first one to tell you. After that he became more of a power runner.

Ditka attempted to prolong Payton's career by playing him in the same backfield with Neal Anderson, even though neither was a true fullback. Still, it became evident in that last season that Anderson, the team's leading rusher in eight of twelve games, was the Bears' real go-to guy. Walter had his least productive season in the NFL, gaining only 533 yards on 146 carries. Anderson missed the last two games of the year because of a knee injury, leaving Walter the focal point of the offense once again.

At halftime of his last regular season game, Walter watched as the team retired his jersey. He was asked to speak, and true to form, kept it brief. "I came into this game," he said, "because I loved to play, and because it was fun. It's still that way. Thank you for being here." As he said good-bye, Bears publicist Bill McGrane couldn't help but notice two fans waving a sign. It read: "Santa: Please Send More Walter Paytons. First One Was Perfect."

Walter Payton: I could tell Neal was where management wanted to go. The problem was I still believed I could do it. Was I as fast as I used to be? No, but who is after thirteen years? What I was, was smarter than others in the league. I knew, instinctively, what teams did and how to beat them. But with Neal on the team, I wasn't the focus like I used to be. That wasn't easy to deal with, but I tried not to make any waves. I remember specifically when Neal came to the team. As I had always done with new guys, I always took them under my wing. So Neal actually hung out with me, and I remember going to concerts—one of the Whitney Houston concerts I brought Neal along with some of the other running backs. And I did things to specifically include him even though I was actually fighting the fact of retirement.

Matt Suhey: From the conversations we had then and afterwards, I know he wasn't quite ready to retire. Physically he had probably had— I don't want to say he lost his step, but physically I think he had taken a beating over the years and there's probably some people as good as he was at that point. I don't know if he was quite ready mentally to retire. I think physically he could have played a couple more years. I think that he felt drafting Neal was their way of telling him, It's time. Would they have ever done that to Michael Jordan, or someone else of that stature? I think he certainly would fall in that category. Maybe I'm off base, but that's how he felt. It wasn't that it was the person of Neal, but that they drafted a halfback. Would he be as good? I think Neal Anderson probably was faster. He brought a different style to the Bears, brought a lot of speed. It wasn't the ball-control type of player that we had certainly been used to, he was really faster and had an explosive style. They weren't going to take Walter out of the game, so they put Neal in as fullback. It meant I didn't play much that year. It probably extended my career, but again that was not what I was looking for. Neal took a pretty good beating at fullback. It's different in that position.

The Bears went 14–3 that last year and drew a first round play-off game with the Washington Redskins, the second year in a row that the 'Skins would end Chicago's hope. With Anderson injured, Walter responded by gaining a team-leading eighty-five yards on eighteen carries, his best effort of the year. When the final gun sounded, Washington had won 21–17. But the Bears went down with the ball in Walter's hands. Needing eight yards for a first down and a chance for one last score, Payton gained seven before being dragged out-of-bounds. One yard short.

Walter Payton: My last game that I played in Soldier Field, I sat there on that bench and I sat there after everything was over and everybody had gone in. Everybody said, "Why did you sit there?" And of course the question that everybody asked was "What were you thinking about? Why were you sitting there like that?" The reason is that, think about it, in life—We go through life so fast and so quickly. We miss so much. Think about it. How many of us drive to work every day? How many of us drive to work with somebody else driving? It's amazing. If you're driving to work every day, try trading places. Try being a passenger, drive the same route that you drive every day, but instead of driving, feel the other side. I promise you, you will see things you have never seen before. You may have driven that route for three years, five years, but as soon as you get from behind that wheel and you get into that passenger's seat, you'll see things you've never seen before. You'll see houses, you'll see structures. You'll say, "I never even knew it was there." That's what you have to realize. You have to enjoy life to its fullest. Be able to experience everything.

Believe it or not, I sat there on that bench for one reason. I know that one of these days I'm going to get old and senile or whatever, and I'm gonna look back and try to remember my last game. I know we got beat. But what was it? The game was over, you ran in, you changed, you got your clothes on, and you were on the bus. No, I sat there because I wanted to enjoy every moment, because I knew when I left that field, that was the last time as a player. I wanted to sit there and enjoy that moment, even though we had lost, I still wanted to enjoy that moment. To think back, back in time and think about some of the great games. Just think about every game and every play and everything else. Believe me, I would have still been sitting there, but I was overcome by the fans who were starting to yell my name. Believe me, I would have sat there until they would have turned the lights off. That was my whole purpose, to sit there and just enjoy that moment because I wanted to remember that. I was sitting there and all those things were going through my mind, that was the last time. So I don't look back and say, "You know, instead of running off, I should have sat there and just enjoyed that a little bit more." Don't be that way. If you can do one thing other than being closer to your kids, it's never to have to say, "Oh, I wish I had." They paid me for football, but I would have played for nothing because I had fun. I honestly had fun. It was enjoyable to me. Enjoy what you do, have fun, enjoy the people around you.

Connie Payton: I remember waking up the morning after that last game, my major concern was just wanting him to be okay and knowing that it really— Here you are with all that you've done, it's gonna be so different for you than a lot of other people. He didn't miss games, sit out hurt and know how to deal with not being part of a team. It was like going cold turkey.

But Walter's reasons for retiring after that game in 1988 were more than a lost step or a new teammate. There were forces behind Walter's decision that only his closest friends understood. His longtime agent and business partner, the well-connected Bud Holmes, had begun floating the idea among the NFL elite that Walter would make an ideal candidate to become the first black owner of an NFL franchise. The NFL—particularly Commissioner Pete Rozelle—had made it clear that expansion was on the way, creating opportunities for Walter to align himself with a group that would count him among its partners.

Walter Payton: The way my retirement decision was made, it was my agent at the time, Bud Holmes, who had put the bug in my ear saying, "Walter, you need to be talking about it." Actually Bud had a very close relationship with the Bears general manager, Jim Finks, who at that time was still instrumental in the league, in the organization, all that stuff. Bud wanted to really see me go out on top. He convinced me that if I left the game right then, league owners would think highly of me and might help me become an NFL owner. That was what I wanted as the next phase of my life, so I did as I was told. I can tell you today, if it had been my choice, I wouldn't have retired. I would have definitely played more. I just kept saying, "Two more years." I was not ready to retire, and I think as I got older, I regretted the fact that I listened to the counsel that was around me. I still, even in my last game, had a great game. I was in incredible shape. I worked out all the time and I ate good and really, really felt that I could stay. But under the pressure of the people I chose to surround myself with, I was convinced that this is what I needed to do. So I didn't listen to myself, I didn't listen to my inner thoughts and how I really felt.

It didn't take me long to regret the decision. Sitting there on the bench that last game holding my head, I realized, Wait a second, I'm going through this, and I am a thirty-three-year-old male that could still kick ass and I'm having to walk away from this. Why? Because I was told to? I left very unfulfilled, and it's like I walked into a fog. And in that fog, it took me many years to find the light and to come to grips with what I lost in those two years I didn't play.

Like most athletes, I had no idea how to fill my day when I retired. Prior to that, everything in my life was very regimented. Everything was "Walter, do this, Walter, do that." There was not much in the way of me thinking. I was very much a creature of habit, I was the first to practice, I was the last to leave. I kind of thrived in an environment where I knew what was expected of me. Suddenly, I didn't know what to do. I had gotten into a few business deals, but now all my time was my own. People have no idea what an adjustment that is.

To me, that's kind of the curse of athletics. That's what all athletes are trained to be. And in fact, when most athletes get in trouble, it's when they're free from structure. Many athletes would call the office, especially when they were rookies, viewing me as a tremendous success, because I had my own office. One of the reasons that I had an office was that the people who were around me prior knew that I had to have structure, that I could not just be called at home and go do this. If I went to my office, which was like going to training camp or to the workout facility, I got my orders there and marched out into the business grounds. I went from one playing field to the next. But in that transition, I didn't do very well at first.

Few people knew it, but I was definitely lost those first few years. There were times when I went through withdrawals when it was game time, to get ready, to go to training camp and all of that. That biological clock started kicking in.

Kim Tucker (executive director of the Walter Payton Foundation): The McCaskeys asked Walter to be on the board of directors for the Bears, and being on the board did keep him somewhat involved. He did enjoy knowing what the Bears were doing, because it was such an important part of his life and he looked at it as family. But he was very hesitant to get involved with the different players and different things that would affect the team per se. So it was this conflict, but it was because he hurt. He really loved being a Chicago Bear and an NFL football player. It wasn't out of his system, so he still longed for that and the best way that he could deal with it was to not really be close to it, so he wasn't. He really withdrew a tremendous amount of himself from the league. He was part of it, but he wasn't. That's how he was able to cope with it.

The focus of winning a Super Bowl was all-encompassing to him. Now he's retired and he doesn't have that focus. That goal had already been achieved, but still in his mind I think he felt that there could have been another championship, that there was great potential. Whether that was a reality or not, it didn't matter. It was what he felt in his heart, that he wanted to keep giving to Chicago and to Chicago Bears' football fans.

Ginny Quirk (Walter's executive assistant): When Walter retired, it was definitely a transition from the office standpoint because he was normally only there during the off-season. Even during the off-season he was extremely busy. He'd be shooting commercials, he'd be doing appearances, he would still be working out twice a day. So I interacted with him a great deal, but it wasn't in the normal office fashion. Then when retirement came about, it kind of kept on that same path, where he would come through the office, he would stop by there several times a day. What happened was for about a year and a half, maybe a two-year period after he retired, Walter was doing okay, he really was. Actually interacting with him on a daily basis, seven days a week, I would say that it almost felt like he had taken retirement with a grain of salt. I think a lot of it had to do with the fact that we did have a lot of things going on, many things to divert his attention. And he was still, I think, in the glow of all the hype around the retirement and whatnot.

Kim Tucker: Walter became very hands-on with the office, as far as he was there quite a bit of his time. He would even answer the phone, he would pretend in his woman's voice that he could put on, and answer the phone and ask people how they're doing and things. Kind of like to just check up on, to make sure that everybody was doing good and felt good when they called that office. But also he was very involved in meetings, decisions on all the different business projects that we were involved in. I will say that he would actually just glow when he got to interact with the public. That's why he loved speaking on the motivational circuit. He could be in the worst foul mood, and when he would go to his events, it was just like you were dealing with another person. That's because that's what he enjoyed. It reminded him of his career and that transition from pro-football player to businessman again was something he was able to adapt to, but it wasn't something necessarily that made him the happiest.

There were different periods that we went through just because of his depression at certain points and having to deal with issues in his life that were not always the best issues that a person should have to deal with. There is absolutely no question that Walter went through quite a bit on an emotional level after his years of playing football. We certainly saw that through the various moods that he would go through in any one given day. Internally in the office, we dealt with and saw every aspect of his life. The best that we could do was be a support group for him, and also try to correct him in things, different directions he would take in his life, and try to really say, That's not so much of a good idea, but we were a tremendous support group, the best that we could be for him.

But as far as his popularity, that never ever went away. We certainly saw, when we made the announcement of his sickness at the press conference, that the outpouring was unbelievable. He loved the fans. I can't express the affection that he felt when receiving fan letters; he would take time and come in the office and read a lot of his fan mail and do things that not a lot of other athletes would do. He felt like, Somebody took the time to sit down and write this, I can at least take the time to read it. He didn't get to read all his fan mail, because even in retirement Walter received tens and tens of thousands of letters a year. But he did certainly give that aspect of his life as much as he could.

The only thing that gave Walter direction was his drive to be invited into one of the world's most exclusive clubs—NFL owners. It was not his issue, but the fact that he would become the first African American to own part of an NFL franchise seemed to excite everyone, most notably Commissioner Rozelle. The problem was that before any decisions on an expansion franchise could be made, Rozelle resigned too. And when, in 1989, Paul Tagliabue succeeded Rozelle, Walter became just another pretty face in line hoping for a dance with the NFL.

Walter Payton: All of a sudden I realized that all the promises that I felt had been made to me—"Leave while you're on top and we'll all help you"—suddenly the people who made those promises weren't there. I was told that if I played two more years that I would miss the window of opportunity to become an owner. I was told that everyone would welcome me in the club. Some people questioned how a league that had never even had a black general manager at that time would allow a black owner. But I was assured that because of what I accomplished, if I left then, the gods would smile on me. There was no way I could pursue ownership and still have time to play.

Did Bud give me that advice because Jim Finks couldn't afford to keep me with the Bears anymore? I don't know, but I've certainly asked that question thousands of times in my head. The problem with retirement is that most people—forget Michael Jordan—can't undo it. Did I resent Bud ultimately for talking me into retiring? No question. We haven't talked in a long time, but I definitely have had a hard time forgetting the decisions I was asked to make.

Maybe all of the hurt would have gone away had things turned out better during the hunt for an NFL franchise. Holmes started the process of interviewing the different cities that were looking to expand, seeking a match for Walter. Though he was willing to put cash into this investment, there was no question Walter didn't have enough to buy majority ownership. He would have to settle for a minority stake, but hopefully one that included a serious voice.

Walter Payton: Bud and I spent a lot of time meeting with the potential new teams in the league, and under Bud's direction I kind of narrowed it down, it was between St. Louis and a group from Oakland, both of whom had courted us. At that time St. Louis was led by a guy named Jerry Clinton and a guy named Fran Murray, who was out of New England, who was a part owner of the Patriots. Also, we had met with the people at the Carolina Panthers. And how that Carolina meeting came down is kind of interesting. I had been in auto racing at the time, and did a year of Sports 2000 with a guy by the name of Ove Olsson. We raced under the Olsson Engineering umbrella, but it was Team 34, that was the name. The way we met the Carolina people was that during training for Sports 2000 we had a gentleman approach us from Paul Newman's camp, and he came to our office, Barry Chappel, who did all of Paul Newman's sponsorship. We went and did a test down at Road Atlanta, and that's where the Carolina representative came down to meet with us and talk about what the Carolina group could offer to me as a package.

At the time the league was going to probably place an emphasis on a minority being in the mix. That had been noted, and I was going to use that to my advantage, quite frankly. I certainly didn't have the monetary means to make a difference. All I had was my fame. So basically what I could bring to the table was, obviously, being a minority, and I knew my fame was an asset. I didn't have the financial wherewithal to put this team together and put it together my way, so I was going to have to latch on to someone else.

I knew the position I wanted to play. I wanted to be president of an NFL team. I knew that a kid who once took bales of hay, and learned to flip over them to land on top so that he wasn't hurt and could stay healthy, could figure this game out too. Years ago, I believed I was going to be the best running back there ever was. Now I knew I could be the best president of an NFL franchise.

So in weighing the offers, I had to see who would let me play the role I wanted. The Richardsons in Carolina did not offer anything of substance, it was going to be very much a minority role. Richardson wanted to keep leadership in the family—that was going to be their deal.

People within the league kept saying, Don't ally yourself yet, keep your options open, see what surfaces. Despite that advice, it was shortly thereafter that Bud Holmes made the decision: The best deal on the table here is St. Louis, who is going to give you the most flexibility, the most opportunity. James Orthwine was coming into the picture, the Anheuser-Busch guy who was seventy-seven years old, he was worth $500 million, so he had the pocketbook. Fran and Jerry Clinton, despite the fact they were out front, didn't really have the money. Clinton was worth maybe $20 million and Fran was worth maybe half of that, and they were both—they weren't the deep-pocket guys to make this deal fly. So despite what Fran and Jerry wanted to believe, without Orthwine this deal doesn't come together.

My role was simple but time-consuming. I did an enormous amount of PR. That was what I gave, going and promoting St. Louis. I put three and a half, almost four years into that St. Louis project. I was not paid for any of my time, the promise being that if we won, my small investment would become a 10-percent ownership position and my dream job of being in a senior position with the franchise.

It really looked good for us and I finally had some peace about the early retirement decision. The front-running cities were Charlotte and St. Louis. The dark horse was Jacksonville, but no one believed the NFL would move into a city with that small a TV market. So I felt like I had made a good decision.

Then I started to learn a little more about my new partners and it wasn't pretty. Jerry Clinton was kind of an outcast in St. Louis, in that he had started when he was fourteen sweeping floors at Anheuser-Busch. He worked himself up to having one of the largest distributorships, most successful in the country. So he was not a blue blood. He was not one of these St. Louis blue bloods. So he was never really accepted per se, even though he had done extremely well. Jerry was just kind of an ego guy. A big name-dropper, a big egomaniac.

Even though Jerry was not my type of guy, I always gave Jerry the limelight, always pushed it to him with the interviews. I'd say, "Here's my partner, Jerry Clinton, you talk to him first." I really did, I bent over ass-backwards to do that. Fran was really not in St. Louis all that much and was trying to play a couple of different teams to see where his position was going to end up being. Fran just wanted to make some dough. Jerry wanted the prestige of being the team owner. I just wanted to get a team.

So what ended up happening was the league vote was going to take place in October, end of October. And right around the last week of August, first week of September, there was a board meeting—there were regular board meetings. Jim Orthwine had been in the mix for a while now because he had been the big money guy. Interestingly enough, Jim was not an ego guy. Worth a ton of dough, had always been, made his money in advertising, and wanted a little bit of say-so in the organization, just give some input, but not an enormous amount. For being the one to put down the hundreds of millions of dollars, he was, I think, pretty easygoing about giving other people their space. Because he wasn't pushy enough, Jerry Clinton wanted to give him no say, zero. He wanted all his people, he wanted to hire people, he wanted complete control.

So even though there had been monies invested up to that point—Jerry had probably come out-of-pocket $5 or 6 million, Fran probably about the same, and who can count what Orthwine, who had paid for the whole marketing campaign, had put in—there was a blowup in this meeting six weeks before the vote.

So at this board meeting, the shit hits the fan because Jerry tells Jim Orthwine "I don't want to be your partner," because Orthwine had decided to suggest several people we should be using. It was amazing, here was this guy with a proven track record and Jerry has treated his suggestions as unacceptable. And so Jim says, "You know what, then, I'm going to give you the opportunity to find another partner, to find another money partner, okay? If you don't want me as a partner, and don't like what I have to bring to the table, then I'm going to give you the opportunity." Jerry said, "Great, I want it. I'm gonna take it."

I didn't freak out, but I wanted to. I saw the whole thing crumbling right there. I just kind of sat there and said, "Guys, I think we all have a common goal, which is to get this team." My whole position was "Let's get the team and squabble later. Let's just do what we got to do to go through with it."

Up until that time, St. Louis wasn't just the front-runner, we were head and shoulders ahead of everyone else. Demographics, everything, we blew everyone away. So at that juncture Jerry went out and tried to solicit other partners. You know what? They locked him out because nobody wanted to get in bed with Jerry Clinton. He went to all these other people in St. Louis and found they were all closer to Orthwine than they were to him. The blue bloods of St. Louis wondered why he couldn't live with what they thought was the best deal in town.

So what ended up happening is when we went to the meeting with the NFL and did our presentation—it was at the Hyatt right here at O'Hare—all the groups had big suites. The leaders of each group would go down and do their presentation, and come back. And when the lead guys from the NFL, led by Neil Austrian and Roger Goodell, came in, they said, "You know what, guys? Get this shit together. This is ridiculous. You're there if you can cut the squabbling. We're going to award one to the Carolinas, and we're going to do something unprecedented, we're going to give you a month to get your shit together because we cannot go into this with the possibility of a lawsuit."

What had transpired during this time is that when Jerry could no longer get the financing together, then Orthwine came back in the picture, but under a different group. He didn't want to deal with Jerry Clinton anymore. Orthwine got together with the Emerson Electronics guys and his buddies—they had the money in a snap. So there was a new ownership group that literally in six weeks had been formed.

I tried to stay out of the middle, just saying that I wanted to work with the city of St. Louis.

Now Jerry had to kind of back up. His only way to keep in the middle was to threaten a lawsuit against Orthwine. Jerry said he had the rights to the stadium deal and they couldn't move forward without him. The league, as you know, their track record in court is horrible. That's why they said, "Work it out with Clinton, whatever you guys have to do, we're going to give you a month to get it together, for you to work out your differences."

They gave us a month, but I don't think a year would have been long enough. Clinton wouldn't back down, even though he didn't have the money. As everyone puffed out their chests, the whole thing was blowing up.

What killed that deal—five years of work—came down to three letters: E-G-O.

All the rest of these guys had big careers to go back to. I gave mine up. If we had been able to pull this together, it would have absolutely changed my life. It would have given me a very different direction in life, very different, because it was the first thing to really go off track, that I didn't win at. That was the first loss I had ever suffered in my whole life. And it was a very public loss. It was . . . And as you know, Deron Cherry, who is a great guy, did get some ownership in the Jacksonville group. He played for Kansas City and now owns a huge Coca-Cola distributorship. He's one of those low-key but unbelievably successful guys.

So not only did I lose, but someone else became the first black owner of an NFL team.

I couldn't believe it. There had been so much invested in terms of that's what I banked on being my future, so I ignored a lot of other opportunities, income-producing opportunities. There were business offers that I turned down because I was sure I was going to be in the NFL. I was so sure of it. That was going to be my full-time focus. I couldn't take on anything else, because I really expected that to be a full-time job. It truly was going to be—it would have been my baby. No question. St. Louis was going to be my full-time focus.

Most of those business opportunities, which came to me right after I retired, never really came back. Four years after retiring, I wasn't as hot. Others stepped in and took my place.

I don't hold that against anyone but me. I should have prepared for the possibility of losing. But those six weeks of arguing changed my life.

I had such a legitimate reason to be really upset. I invested a lot. I banked on this happening. I really felt that that was my future, and all of a sudden that's not there. I just decided I wasn't going to ever— It's like writing a chapter in this book and never finishing it and knowing it's on your desk there and you just kind of pull it out and look at it once in a while, but you don't ever accept that you're gonna ever finish that, that you don't put "The End." I never put "The End" to that. Therefore, I didn't have to deal with the emotions with it. I knew that if I put "The End" to it—if I sat down and dwelled on the subject—I don't know if I could have dealt with it. I was very devastated that other people were in control of my destiny again. I was not in control. The egos of these men, it impacted my life in such a way that it altered the course of my life. The outcome of my life—us sitting here talking today, I would be the president of hopefully a very successful NFL franchise. I would be directly affecting all the athletes coming into my team and really getting very involved in the NFL and being able to go in and say, "This is what you need to do to be successful," and I would have had a legitimate forum to do that. I always wanted to be very active with the players, not as the coach, but I would have been very instrumental in their lives and I feel I could have affected many different young athletes. I would see these kids going in and acting like young punks, and I felt I could say, Hey, wait a second, we're gonna change this. You could sit here and say, Well, why didn't you go and talk to people anyway? If they called me, I did. If they called me, I'd spend as much time as they wanted. But if they didn't call me, I wasn't going to go out of my way, because I felt betrayed by some people in the NFL. It was something again that I was pulling away from because now I had to look at what was going to be my future.

The whole St. Louis loss was a blow I think I never recovered from, to be honest with you. In those weeks and months after the decision sunk in, I realized football was over, and there was definitely some depression. More of a more heightened moodiness, more extreme downs. I'd get bummed out. I went into a depression for quite a few years and really the only thing that would snap me out of it was a lot of my speaking engagements, because I could reminisce. The speaking forced me to go out too. I would almost be relieved when I would do some of these events. I know it sounds funny that I needed reinforcement, but I did.

Matt Suhey: Just about the greatest loss in his life was his attempt at winning the St. Louis football franchise. It crushed him. It crushed him so much he didn't say much, a whole lot about it. Which was typical Walter. That's how I knew how much he hurt, because he didn't talk about it. He tried to put it out of his mind, put it behind him and it was gone. That's typical Walter too. Ironically, as much as people might think otherwise because of his running style, in life he was not very confrontational. He avoided it. That just wasn't his style. So when the rug was pulled out from under him on St. Louis, he didn't go public with blame. He didn't complain to everyone he knew. He just kept it inside. Almost no one knew how much it really hurt him not to be an NFL owner.

Connie Payton: I don't think even I knew how much Walter was hurting. He went into a real funk for a while. That was going to be his life, the St. Louis franchise. When things were tough, he refrained from talking about it. He didn't want people feeling sorry for him and he despised people who complained. So he rarely told people what he was feeling. Reporters used to complain about it all the time, that he never let them into what was happening in his life. But he always said that if you want people inside when it is good, they're going to expect the same when things are bad, and he wasn't going to let that happen. He wanted this franchise, but it was not going to happen.

Ginny Quirk: Walter's coaches would set goals and Walter knew what was expected from him. After Walter's retirement, his goals and daily schedule were now solely up to him. The man who used to do two-a-day workouts in the off-season to stay in optimal physical shape stopped working out altogether, cold turkey! Despite being a very successful businessman and motivational speaker, nothing filled the void of not playing professional football. There were many days when Walter was depressed and uncommunicative; however, he would never let the public see his personal struggles.

Walter's deepest struggles came after the St. Louis expansion football team fell through. In his mind, he retired early from the NFL to become the first African-American owner of an NFL team. He was given assurances from certain people that barring something plain stupid, St. Louis would get the expansion franchise. And plain stupid happened . . . and it was all out of Walter's control. This emotionally leveled him. Walter had invested an enormous amount of time and energy and bypassed dozens of lucrative business deals—including an investment opportunity to become one of the first owners of an Illinois riverboat casino—to be an owner of an NFL team. This was the first major goal that Walter set for himself that he did not achieve. He was not prepared for St. Louis not happening.

It was at about that two-year mark that it really started to sink in, and that's when Walter started to in my opinion realize the magnitude of this retirement and what it was going to ultimately mean to him in his lifestyle, and when he began to try and find various outlets to take the place of football. I think that's why he was always looking at multitudes of different projects, because it made it easier for him to divert his attention and to be able to be just absolutely saturated with obligations and projects. It helped keep his mind off of not being in football. It was interesting too because once he left football, he never followed it. Yes, he would go down to the Bears' football games on occasion and hang out on the sideline and play around with the coaches and the players, but he really stopped following football. It was almost like his arm had been severed and he just tried never to use that arm again.

It was kind of interesting, but basically there came a time that was a dark period in terms of Walter trying to find happiness off the football field. This didn't have anything to do necessarily with family, I'm not trying to say that, but just as any of us would have done in that situation, just trying to find something to take the place of it. I would definitely say that there was a good amount of depression going on and that we were certainly working on the St. Louis project, although that was taking longer than expected and wasn't exactly what he had hoped it would be, but was trying to make it work. Walter sank into a really tough depression, which he hid from everyone but his family and a few other people such as Kim and me. That became pretty much a very large part of his life because he would fight it. He tried very hard to fight it, but he often couldn't. It would rule, in many instances, what he would and wouldn't do. He had a lot of cancellations of events, a lot of things that last-minute he just couldn't get himself up emotionally to go to. Now, ironically the one aspect of that that could always get him into a good mood was going to an event, because it would just buoy him by all the public support and the love that was given to him. It was so ironic because I would actually look forward to when he had an event at that time, just trying to do anything to get him to that point, because I knew it would snap him back to his old self.

There were a lot of scary instances, because I had never dealt with someone who had been depressed to that degree and even talked about suicide. I didn't know at the outset if there was any merit to it. I know Connie and I and Kim, we all tried to keep very positive because that's our nature, just to be there and to be supportive. There were cars that were totaled, there were a lot of unpleasant things that went on during the time that was a sad time for Walter, just trying to find himself, and that was a long stint. Walter I don't think was ever really Walter, to the degree that I knew him prior to those couple of years after retirement, in terms of just being the happy-go-lucky guy. He just clicked into another phase of his life; no one would have imagined that he was going through a lot of that pain that he was. He was just trying to feel like a whole person without football in his life. That was an enormous challenge for us because it was very consuming in his business, it affected everything. There were many, many days and weeks and months that were basically pretty foggy for him because of this depression. It struck me as so ironic how everyone viewed Walter as having it all, that if he had gone through this type of depression, then I couldn't imagine all of the other players who had been in football a long, long time and then retired, that they too must have gone through an enormous amount of withdrawal, shall we call it. Somebody who really summed it up well, Vince Evans, a former quarterback—I talked to him this past year and he had retired for the second time at forty-something. I asked him for an analogy of how he was doing with retirement, because I tended to do that. He said something very interesting, he said, "You know, Ginny, it's like being a Vietnam vet. You go in and it's such a different world, and all of a sudden you come home and you're expected just to be normal and you're not normal. You've been treated different all along and now you're just supposed to fit in and you don't know how to fit in." That's I think a little bit what Walter went through too, is trying to find a fit. He had an extremely tough time with that, very, very tough. It was debilitatingly tough and that was sad. That was sad from our end because we really tried to do so much to steer him into positive directions, to get him going, but it didn't work very often. We had a difficult time.

Walter Payton: I learned a lot about the NFL during that time. Remember, I was basically promised this was going to happen by Commissioner Rozelle. It left me with a bad taste in my mouth because I learned some things that I didn't want to know. I learned some things internally with the NFL and with some of the people involved who are in charge of high places. Once Rozelle left, I didn't have the same relationships with the people who followed. You look at this institution and you think it's very stable, which it is in certain areas, and in certain areas it's not. As far as me being an owner, I think my ideas and my views and how I would approach things are totally different from the people who are there now. In a weird sort of way, I guess the fact that it didn't work might have been for the best because I don't think I would have been in a situation where I would have been happy, because the way things are being done now—the way the game has changed and the way I envision the game and the way I played it—it's not the same. So maybe it would have been a bad marriage. I don't want to say it was a blessing, because I'm really torn over it still. But I think things happen for a reason and I look back and I try to figure out, Well, why did this happen? I guess the people that I was associated with in this venture as well as the changing game and the collective bargaining agreement was something that I wouldn't have been able to deal with, so it's probably best that I didn't get into it.

The St. Louis situation ended Walter's close affiliation with the NFL. His disappointment turned to disenchantment as he watched the league and its players change. Though the Bears kept him somewhat involved—they had him interview several potential draft picks—he said he didn't like what he saw. Proud as he was of the years he spent playing pro football, he wasn't, as he said, "proud of the fraternity anymore."

Walter Payton: A lot of people encouraged me to get into coaching when the St. Louis deal didn't work out. I never could even think about it. I could never coach, because I never understood the work-out ethics and the philosophies of any other athlete I ever met. When I practiced I literally would vomit if I had to. I worked my-self and gave all of myself even if it was practice, and when I went to training camp, it was like I was on vacation, because I was ready. I never stopped working out. I understood that I had to be physically fit. I understood that I might not be the best, I understood I might not be the strongest, I understood that I might not be able to have the speed, but I figured if I took all of these qualities that I did have and I put them together, I had something no one else had. So I would be the most prepared for training camp ever, and I was. I trained harder in the off-season than I did during the season, that was my be-lief. And it worked, obviously. It worked real well.

But what I saw in my last couple of years in the league only got worse as time went on. Too many guys showed up out of shape for training camp. Then they missed games or practices because they had pulled muscles. Duh? That wasn't a surprise. How could I coach players who want to sit home and eat ice cream and pies and not even work out once or twice a week, and then only wait until camp? Go out partying all night, and then when camp came, that's when they decided they would buckle down. My philosophy was so opposite, I knew I couldn't—I knew because that's how I was. That was the an-imal inside of me, the untrained animal, and I certainly could not go in there and unleash something that somebody didn't have. I didn't know how I could do that.

I think right now most of the motivation for these players is not coming from within. I think it's based on dollars, and once you use that as a criteria as to how well you play, then it fluctuates because you never have enough. The nature of the beast is to always want more. It comes to a point where if money is your total motivation, then all you feel you have to do is play up to what you think you are earning, not what the team needs. I see that, in my opinion, all the time. It's more "me"-oriented as opposed to team-oriented. Me, all my life I've played as a team player, and it would be kind of hard for me to change from that so suddenly.

Mike Ditka: I think our sports teams have become too Hollywood and everybody is vying for the center stage, and everybody is trying to gain attention for themselves. It's amazing some of the things you see when people go to the end zone, and they actually go through an entire act, they act like they've never been there before. Paul Brown had a great saying: "Act like you've been there before." Walter handed the ball to an offensive lineman because he knew he wouldn't have gotten there without them. Do you ever remember Walter fighting over a contract, really fighting over one, saying, I deserve this? Neither do I. I don't think that he played the game for the money. I think money is a wonderful bonus, and you're entitled to it from the game, but when you play the game for the money, you'll never understand the game. He understood the game, he played the game for the love of the game.

Jim McMahon: Knowing Wally as I did, I know the change in players had to drive him nuts. The game has changed. The money— it's great that everybody's making money now, but I think they lose a lot of desire. That's why Coach Ditka wasn't successful in New Orleans, 'cause Ditka motivates by fear—always has. Back in the eighties, we had to do what he said because we weren't getting paid shit anyway. Nowadays he's probably doing the same thing to New Orleans, I'm gonna fire all of you, if you don't play better I'm gonna bench you. Guys don't care if they get benched anymore. They're making $3 million and $4 million dollars a year. Go ahead and bench me, I'll get a free ticket. They don't give a shit. That's why I got out. Coming in the locker room after a loss, guys are dicking around and don't give a shit, I couldn't take it anymore. 'Cause when we played, our team, we played to win. We had a great time off the field, but when we came to play, we came to play. I think that's what different. We were professional enough that we could have a good time off the field, but when we got to practice or got to the game, we got our jobs done and that doesn't happen anymore. Guys go out and the next day they can't practice, they're sick, they're hungover, whatever. They couldn't do that on our team.

In one of the great ironies, the St. Louis Rams, a team that took advantage of the groundwork laid by Walter and his expansion team, went on to win Super Bowl XXXIV—Walter's jersey number, 34—in the season he passed away.

Walter Payton: So God has a reason for everything happening, and I think he used me to bring the awareness of how great St. Louis was. As I watch their team playing really well this year, I kind of feel a part of it. I think we not only built the interest back up in St. Louis, but we showed the Rams what a good deal the city was. I think now that it was not meant for me to be there, but it was meant for me to be a part of bringing it there, and I accept that. I am rooting for them.

11

The Businessman

While awaiting the fate of his real dream—owning a piece of the St. Louis franchise—Walter continued to establish himself as a businessman. His interests were far-flung, almost all of them spurred by personal interests. During his career he began joining partnerships that owned restaurants and bars, service businesses that allowed him to use his personal magnetism to develop an enterprise.

Walter Payton: Growing up, my father had instilled in me a real respect for those who owned their own business. It said something about you in the world of us versus them, that you've become one of them. That's why as soon as I had money to invest, I wanted to put it in businesses. I became a partner in McFadden Ventures, which at one time owned twenty-six nightclubs—the Confetti's chain, Studebaker's all over the country. There were a bunch in bankruptcy when we bought them. We kept the good ones, sold off the dogs, and refurbished them. In the Chicago market at one time, we had five nightclubs. Remember back then that happy hours were in, in the eighties when it was very lucrative. I had fun with it.

I really hadn't been exposed much to business before that. It was a great learning time for me. I was not a numbers person. I was an idea guy, I was definitely an idea guy. The thing is that if my money had truly been invested the way it should have been, I could have just retired. I didn't make much in the restaurant business. I would have been better in the stock market. But I learned so much being in business with some of the people I was with. I realize that I made the trade-off.

Where I got hurt was that I had an adviser who invested me in lots and lots of limited partnerships, real-estate limited partnerships that were supposed to be very tax advantageous. I never saw a dime out of those, lost lots of money. It was a long time before I figured out how much money I lost. Even though I was screwed over by a few different people who took advantage of my lack of experience in this business world, I never gave up hope in the next person. So where I might have lost money on this deal, or this guy might have been a bad partner and he lied, I never took that out on the next business partner that I had.

Between those limited partnerships and some poor endorsement choices, I really didn't move myself forward financially. On endorsements, for example, I had KangaROOS shoes. I loved those people. But the endorsement wasn't that good because you couldn't find them anywhere. The ironic thing about KangaROOS was that in the height of when I was breaking records, do you know who Kanga-ROOS shoes basically supplied to? The U.S. military. You couldn't find them anywhere. No stores sold them. It was kind of amazing. But I wore my KangaROOS shoes, I had fifty pairs of them. I did, I lived in their stuff. I'll tell you what KangaROOS did, though, they did advertise the heck out of it. I wore the KangaROOS towel. They got a lot of play out of it.

What I learned through all the ups and downs of business is that you have to surround yourself with people that are adept in dealing with pressure, they're very confident and aware of what they do and they do it very well. You need to know those people well, watch what they do on your behalf and talk to them during good times and bad. Then you have to listen to them. You've got to be able to give your people—give the employees—give them a goal. When Mike Ditka came to the Bears, he gave us a goal. He was the first one who said, "We're gonna win the Super Bowl." No one else said it. Everyone else said, Okay, we're gonna get out here, we're gonna play as hard as we can and we're gonna do some things and we're gonna win some games, and we're gonna be better. Nobody said, This is your goal, this is what you shoot for. Give them something to shoot for and then once they reach it, then let them know how you appreciate it.

Mike Lanigan (owner of Mi-Jack Products and a business partner with Walter): We started a business in early '94 called Walter Payton Power Equipment, which was a heavy-equipment company that rented and sold hydraulic cranes and worked with contractors and industry. He was one of the most energetic business partners I've ever had. He was a great reader of individuals. He could tell before almost anyone else whether an individual was a good guy or a bad guy. Walter was actually a very good businessman. If he had any weaknesses, he believed in people too much. He wasn't a typical athlete who showed up, went to this convention, showed up for three hours, and got the hell out of town. He actually got involved with it. He loved getting out there with the guys in the equipment, making them all feel good that they worked for his company. We ended up selling Payton Power in May of '99 and we got real fortunate and made some nice money on it. I'm proud that deal helped make his life more comfortable. Nobody deserved it more than Walter.

Mark Alberts: I became Walter's business partner in 1995 with the Walter Payton's Roundhouse Complex in suburban Aurora, Illinois. Walter was phasing out of the nightclub business and the Roundhouse gave Walter the opportunity to own and put his name on a restaurant/brewpub project. The first time I met with Walter was at a restaurant near his house. It was a pretty big deal just getting a meeting with Walter Payton. Of course, I was a Chicago Bears football fan. Walter was literally Superman on the field. I was such a fan that I was one of those people running around Daley Plaza like a kook in the freezing cold after the Bears won the Super Bowl! So here I am waiting to have a business meeting with my hero, a national legend. Walter walks in to the meeting and I remember my first reaction being, Hmmm, he's not as big as I thought. Then he shakes my hand and crushes it. Walter had the largest hands for a five-feet-ten man I'd ever seen. Walter would love shaking someone's hand and making them beg for mercy.

One of the business attributes that Walter had was that he brought energy with him everywhere he went. I remember Walter attended a city council meeting where, as a formality, the council members and the mayor voted for approval of the Roundhouse development. Well, the council members all had footballs and other memorabilia they wanted signed before the meeting. Walter obliged everyone, which is part of what made things go so smooth for him.

When Walter would visit the Roundhouse, he had this ability of making all of the employees feel special. He had a genuine affection for all our employees. He would come visit through the back door and shake hands or hug each and every employee in our kitchen. At our company Christmas party Walter once put on a busboy apron and served drinks to our employees. To this day, every one of those who worked with him has a story like that to tell.

Ginny Quirk: Walter would often say that all you have in this world is your name. He believed you ought to be able to do business on a handshake basis. Unfortunately, not all of Walter's business partners felt that way. It was a tragedy that during the last year of Walter's life two business issues emotionally devastated him: a lawsuit he originated against his former attorney/business manager for fiduciary malpractice, and his lawsuit filed against Dale Coyne, his CART [Championship Auto Racing Teams] racing partner, for lack of compensation paid. Walter even had to be legally deposed in bed a month prior to his death. The Coyne lawsuit was settled out of court for a seven-figure amount.

Walter was addicted to the telephone. He would call the office a dozen times a day. Walter was one of the first people to test Motorola's new mobile telephones. Only a handful of people had mobile phones at this time and Walter was one of them. He'd call from the sidelines at practice and even from the meeting rooms while reviewing game film. Walter's average cell phone bill was over $2,500 a month!

While Walter was playing, he had endorsement contracts with several large corporations. One of his most enjoyable endorsements was a ten-year relationship of working the Chicago auto show for Buick. Walter kept a grueling schedule every day, signing autographs at the show for hours, making sure that no fan was left out. This was his way to stay in touch with the real Chicago Bears fans. What the true Walter Payton fans don't know is that when Walter went out of his way to sign an autograph or to say a good word to someone, he got as much back from that exchange as the fan did. It was a "feel good" to Walter to make someone's day.

One of my fondest recollections of Walter was his love for laughter and his passion for music. Not a day would go by without Walter pulling a practical joke on someone. He would regularly answer the office telephone in a woman's voice. When traveling, he would tell strangers that he was a male stripper. Walter would spend an enormous amount of time making custom tapes of his favorite rhythm and blues musicians. When Walter found a song he liked, he would play it over and over. He loved to listen to Luther Vandross, Anita Baker, and Freddie Jackson. Wherever Walter was, you would hear music.

While bars, restaurants, endorsements, and public speaking fed Walter's need for public interaction, he had a greater need—the need for speed. A man who loved to turn his car loose on the freeway,

Walter was told by more than one police officer to "save it for the racetrack." Finally, he found a way to do that.

Walter Payton: I had an incredible love for cars, period. I was a car fanatic. You will never meet a person who kept their cars more immaculate. They were detailed weekly. Any car you got into, it was like it was brand-spanking-new. I didn't eat in it—I was a clean person by nature, I liked to keep things tidy, but with my cars, they were meticulous. I took a lot of pride in my cars and I had a lot of them. As you know, I had the Lamborghini, which 'ROOS gave me when I broke Jim Brown's record. I had had a Rolls-Royce, I had my Porsche, and then at any given time we had eight or nine vehicles in my family. I was big on the Lexus cars. I know it sounds crazy, but coming from where I grew up, I just always found cars, fast cars, a kind of "I made it" statement. This past year I had narrowed it down a little bit, so I could go for the Grand Cherokee, two Porsches—the 930 from 1979, and then the one I actually traded the Lamborghini in for. I had a Ferrari for a little bit and then traded the Ferrari for this Porsche. They were my babies.

That love for cars is what got me into a great phase of business life. The gentleman who worked on all my personal cars yanked my chain about getting into racing. He was the engineer for a couple of different people in the Sports 2000 class, a lesser known racing circuit. It's a certain class of car, it's low budget. A whole season was like $75,000. Very inexpensive, with regional races. It's not like I was traveling all over the country, and I was able to practice at Black Hawk Farm, which was just over the Wisconsin border. Ove Olsson, the engineer, said, "Hey, I can get you sponsored, it's not going to cost you anything, do you want to race?" I was for it, said, "Why not?" So it was actually right out of my retiring, like that next summer, I did fiddle around with Sports 2000. We did a couple of seasons of Sports 2000.

At the same time, we were doing lots of appearances. I had all

kinds of things going on, so what the challenge always was with racing was practice time. Honestly, I was extremely good considering
the fact that I put very little seat time in. In the same equation as a
marathon runner, how can you go and expect to run a marathon if
you're not training through the week? I just didn't have the time to
put a lot of seat time in.

Then I went to the next class, and this was when I joined Newman
Racing, with Paul Newman. It was the season after Tom Cruise had
raced with him. Paul Newman and Scott Sharp had been racing for
a while, although Paul would intermittently race through the Trans-
Am series. So they recruited me. A guy by the name of Barry Chappel came to our office at Studebaker's, one of the bars that I owned,
and said, "Hey, we heard you're racing, would you like to move up a
series? We'll foot the bill." And I said, "Great." It didn't make Ove
real happy, because it was a whole different caliber racing, it was the
GT-3 series.

It was great. I actually won a race at Elkhart Lake, they call it
Road America. I did well. That was kind of the perfect car for me because it more or less looked like a street car, and you just hauled ass.
It was like a souped-up street car. It didn't have a roof. So I did the
GT-3 and that was a fun scene that was all over the country. I was
gone a lot. We did a lot of those races. And then we struck a deal
with the NFL. At that time, it was kind of fun because NFL Properties was branching off into all these directions, and they had just
signed up a year prior with Payne Stewart, the golfer, and had a lot
of success with that. They were looking at all these different mer-
chandising venues. They were looking for exposure for the NFL,
here's our leading rusher who can just now get us into racing. We
did a whole line of apparel.

Money was important in all these deals because now that we were
racing Trans-Am, we had a $500,000 to $750,000 annual budget.
That's a lot of dough. So their theory had been, when we originally
pitched them on it, there had been kind of a mutual conversation
'cause I had very good contacts within Properties, and they said,
We've got all these vendors, Hertz and Pepsi and whatnot. What

Properties had initially desired to do was to go in, sponsor us, foot the bill—the half-million bucks—and with that . . . 'cause what I handled was all the hospitalities. At the weekends, they'd have so many guests and we'd have the hospitality booths, just like a normal deal. Well, what they anticipated was turning around and selling off pieces of the car to their vendors. Great idea, which would virtually cost them nothing. And then have this big NFL car and all this stuff. Well, it was at a time when Properties was really going through a lot of changes and they never did pursue it with their other people. There ended up just being a total NFL car where they footed the bill, and we actually did it with them for a couple of seasons, but it was perfect for me because again, this had my stamp on it. I could race to my heart's content because I loved it and was not footing the bill.

I treated racing as a great time, and basically tried not to lose money doing it. I wanted to do it and had I had the opportunity to make money it would have been great. It would have been different, quite frankly, if I had been like, Oh my God, this is going to be my new career. But it wasn't. I was into it during the season, did no testing on the off-season, we were lucky if I got to the race a day before the actual qualifications. And when you think about it, it's a dangerous sport. Those guys are doing 180. In Trans-Am it was 180, in GT-3 it was about 140. That's still fast. That's hauling ass.

I had one pretty horrific accident also, at Road America up in Elkhart Lake, Wisconsin. That was pretty scary because my daughter was up there with me. I walked away, but yeah, it was bad. I don't know if Connie ever went to a race.

Connie Payton: When I talked about retirement with Walter, I would tell him that there were going to be other doors opened to him. His life would be different from other players because of his accomplishments. He was well-loved and respected in the business community. I couldn't understand why this was not enough to keep him occupied. Racing had become his life. I wanted him to tell me why he needed auto racing when he had just retired from a tedious football career. It didn't take me long to understand that he needed

another distraction to keep his competitive juices flowing. Walter
had many accidents during his stint as a race car driver. While Brittney was with him at a race in Wisconsin he had a terrible accident.
His car flipped over two fences, spilled gasoline, caught on fire, then
landed upside down. While the car was burning he was pulled out.
The car completely burned, but miraculously Walter was not badly
hurt. Some of the gasoline had gone into his eyes, he had a burn on
the side of his neck, some abrasions, and a mild concussion. It was
obvious that he had a guardian angel watching over him. There was
no other reason for his car not to explode or for the injuries not to be
more extensive.

Brittney Payton: I was only about six or seven years old when the
accident happened. I was at the track with a bunch of people Dad
had left me with. We were driving a golf cart around the course and
the practice laps had just started. We were getting a drink when
someone came up and said, "Did you see that someone got in an accident?" It didn't hit me until they said it was my dad. I was in
shock. They brought us to the medical area where I saw him laying
there on a table. I started crying and he reached over and held my
hand. He said that everything was going to be okay. He was trying
to make me comfortable. I rode in the ambulance with him and they
took him to a room in the hospital. His eyes were red from the gas
and the flames. They worked with Dad for a while, then sent us
home from the hospital. I was relieved he was okay. I was more relieved when he told me he wasn't going to race again. I didn't see the
accident until later on videotape. I couldn't believe he lived through
that. Having been there that day gave me the feeling he was invincible and that nothing could take him down.

Connie Payton: It was a pretty bad experience for Brittney. She
could hear the sirens, but she didn't know what was happening.
Some child told her that her father had been in an accident. She said,
"Mom, that was the worst feeling. Not knowing if Dad was dead or
alive, or how badly he was injured," and then she started crying. She

soon found out that he was okay, that his injuries were not that severe. Ginny and other friends of the family were there. Ginny was able to drive him home, because his eyes were red and swollen from the gasoline. His vision was impaired.

That was his last time in a race car. I think he realized that he was knocking at death's door. He started to question himself as to what was important in his life. He then decided to go into the race car ownership arena. He hired drivers to do the driving.

Walter Payton: After the accident, I became an owner and that really brought a lot of joy to me through the years. Looking back I realized that the reason I gave that so much focus was because I'm down there in the pit, I'm directing these racers, the cars are flying by, I could relate to them because I had raced for five years professionally myself, and it was again I felt like I was on the field even though it was on a different field, it was a racing field. And it was very prestigious, high-profile. Think of it, I was an owner, an Indy car owner. At the time just about the only minority. I enjoyed being down there with the guys in the pit. I enjoyed communicating with the other racers. It sent me all over the world, they raced all over. I really did get a lot from it.

John Gamauf, vice president of Bridgestone/Firestone: Prior to 1995, Walter's team was racing on Goodyear tires. He was one of the first teams that switched over to Firestone in the '95/'96 racing year. He switched before meeting me, and it was a good place for me to take my customers. Walter and I first met in 1995, out at Indianapolis. I was taking a tour of the Speedway with about fifty customers. As we were going through the pits, Walter was his normal self, signing autographs, doing the normal chitchatting and shaking hands and taking pictures. Towards the end of the session, he spoke to all of the customers and said, "Okay, who's the big cheese? Who's the guy that can get me a deal on some tires for my Porsche?" They pointed to me and I basically just gave Walter my card and said, "When you need a set of tires, give me a call." That was about it.

About a week later he called me and said, "Okay, I'm ready for those tires on my Porsche." I sent him over to Deerfield Firestone, which is up in Deerfield, Illinois, and he went there and made the place go crazy. Walter in a retail store, he took over, he started answering the phones, he started going out and busting tires with the tire men, signing autographs for the customers and waiting on them and just doing crazy stuff that Walter always loved to do. The owner of the store called me up and said that Walter was unbelievable. That's when I first started to see what he did off the football field. I watched him as a kid do all the different things that he'd done on the football field, but you really don't know how these athletes are off the field.

His actions off the field are what really led us to develop our relationship, because as I would go up to the racetrack—I'd go to nine, ten car races a year and I'd always go into the pit and visit with Walter—he would always be so wonderful. He'd say, "Come here, Gam"—he gave me the name of Gam—and he said, "What's going on?" I'd bring customers in and he would never hesitate, he would be a pure gentleman, and he'd be out signing autographs for fans for hours. All the other celebrities in racing, without mentioning names, those guys don't touch anybody. But Walter was out with the fans. He was always out touching everybody. I asked him, "Walter, why do you do this with the public? Everybody else kind of hides in their own trailers and is in their own little world." He told me, "Gamauf, this is where I came from. If I leave these people, if I leave this world, then I'm forgetting my roots. Hey, I was one of these guys a few years ago. These are my roots and these are the people that I never want to leave." No matter where he went on speaking engagements, he would always go for the underdog. He would always seek out the least likely person in that room. If there was a president of a corporation and there was a bellman or something, Walter would go over and talk to the bellman and start asking him questions like, "Are you married, you got any kids? Let me see your pictures." If he was young enough he would say, "Are you going to college, what college are you going to go to, how are your grades?"

He knew there would always be time to socialize with the president and make him feel good. I don't know of any other athlete who can walk into a room and do what he did. Not that Walter was the best motivational speaker—there's tons of motivational speakers out there. It's the way that he was so real about what he said.

We just kept saying, Oh boy, if we could use Walter to talk about more than football, talk about business and how it relates to racing. His message was the type where he'd come around the corner and hit you where you wouldn't expect it. He'd be starting to talk about business or sports, racing, and all of a sudden he'd switch gears and he'd talk about family values. He'd talk about Mom and Dad, and he'd talk right to the audience. He'd pull a kid out of the audience and he'd say, "How are you doing on your homework and stuff?" If the kid said, "Well, okay," then he'd look at his parents and say, "Well, is he?" He'd say, "Hey, Mom and Dad, probably one of the best things you guys could do is start turning off that TV and start talking to your kids. You start doing that, you're not going to have problems with all of the drugs and all of the situations you have with kids nowadays. If more and more parents would spend more time talking with their kids and giving them quality time like back when we grew up, things would be a lot better." Having an athlete say something like that really stuck with people. When we were up in New York, somebody mentioned that he had golfed with Lawrence Taylor. Walter said, "Well that's nice, I like Lawrence, he's a friend of mine." Then the guy said, "Yeah, but about the fourth hole he started to pull over in the rough, in the woods, and he was doing drugs." Walter said, "Well, what did you do about that?" He said, "I just didn't like it, but I kept playing with him." Walter said, "You know what you should have done? You should have walked off the course. Everybody admires these athletes, but if you really want to prove a point to Lawrence, as soon as you saw him doing drugs, you should have picked up your bags and walked right off the golf course. I know that's a tough thing to do because nobody really wants to say, 'I gave up playing golf with Lawrence Taylor.' But what a message you would have sent." He was just using him as an example, it could be any of these guys that are into drugs and all this other stuff. It was definitely a memorable moment.

Walter Payton: Part of the reason I really enjoyed public speaking and CART racing as much as I did is because I felt respected. Not that I didn't feel respected in the NFL, I felt respected in the NFL as a player, but it was different being a leader, an owner. That gave me some form of accomplishment, kind of adding a little footnote to that chapter that never got finished in St. Louis. The fulfillment didn't come from the NFL franchise, so that fulfillment came from somewhere else for me to be able to deal with that type of a blow that life offered me. I really shouldn't say that, because I don't look at it like life offers those things. We are all dealt blows—reacting positively is what we have to do. But again, I was not in control. When I was given the ownership in the CART team, I had a lot of control. My partner there knew that if he had me in the forefront, the cameras would come. So he really exploited that to the utmost. That was the first time I will say I enjoyed being exploited.

I had other business ventures—Payton Power, which was a company that I invested in that had construction equipment—was great. But honestly, there was nothing that really got my juices going quite like my work in racing. In fact, the financing of my start in racing was through Michael Lanigan, my partner in Payton Power.

Kim Tucker: I started developing projects for Walter in 1987, and by 1991 Walter had become my biggest client. In fact, I had opened an office within Walter Payton Incorporated. Tens of thousands of pieces of fan mail would be opened, read, and answered in any given year. A member of our staff would read the mail and pull aside the letters that had significant meaning for Walter to read. He loved sitting for hours and reading letters from his fans. Sometimes when a phone number was included in the letter, he would call them. Upon reaching them you would have thought they won the Lotto. He would only talk ten to fifteen minutes per call, but it was always significant, and usually to a person that needed encouragement.

Anything that had to do with Walter's likeness and image had to be approved through the office. This is where all of Walter's business was done. People could book appearances, Walter reviewed business ventures, and charity decisions were made.

It wasn't always easy working with Walter, but in the end he always made me proud. Walter put a lot of trust in Ginny and me. We would work hard on a daily basis to help make the legend work. However, there were many days between the years 1991 and 1995 during which we spent a tremendous amount of time helping Walter the man deal with a sea of emotions and a future that seemed to be unfulfilling. Ginny and I were on call twenty-four hours a day, seven days a week, and it didn't matter if it was three A.M. If Walter had an idea or a personal situation he wanted to talk about, he always knew we were there to listen and console.

Walter was a perfectionist when it came to his image. It took us two years to complete the video *Pure Payton.* The video highlights his pro career. Walter was adamant with NFL Films that we participated in the production of the video. This video was made for his fans and they were going to get the best. It took a year and a half to prepare for the Hall of Fame—events, licenses of his images, products, and endorsements. Even though emotionally this was a dark period in his life, he wanted the best for his fans.

Walter did very few autograph signings. He didn't agree that fans should pay for a celebrity's autograph, but this is a billion-dollar industry and we constantly found memorabilia being sold that was fraudulent. It was so bad that we met with agents of the FBI who handle fake autographs and they suggested that we develop a hologram that is numbered and says "Celebrity Appearances" and "Walter Payton." One of the only companies Walter signed memorabilia for was Steiner Sports and the Walter Payton Foundation. This was one of the ways the foundation raised money to buy toys.

In any given year, there would be hundreds of requests for his involvement in various business opportunities, but I will say that Walter was very cautious when he did get involved in the business opportunities that he did. Now, not all of them turned out the way that he would have wanted to, or the personalities maybe with him and his different partners would not be what he would have wanted as well, but he felt that he wasn't just going to go out and get involved in just anything and lend his name to just anyone. I will say I did respect that in him, because he saw the value of his name and what he had built and what it had represented. That really is what was the most important to Walter, what his name represented.

So the public didn't really realize Walter's moods or the different emotions or different situations he was dealing with in his life, whether it be business or personal, that he was having conflicts in and he was having to deal with. It was very hard. He didn't want anyone to know that. He was an extremely private person, and I think that that's kind of contradictory in a way because Walter was so famous and was so beloved by everybody, but they loved Walter Payton, that aspect of his life and that part of the person that he was and that he showed them. As with a lot of celebrities, they certainly don't want the public to see them having a bad day or being temperamental or being known as temperamental.

Again, Walter wasn't temperamental to people in general. He was internally with his family, and internally at the office—we saw and dealt with those things and that's it. He wasn't mean and rude to a camera crew that came in to do something, to film something. He was basically good and polite and took time to speak to people. When we would do our events and set up events with companies, not many people—certainly the client didn't know this—but what we would do is we would actually come in a half hour to forty-five minutes earlier and say, if we were dealing at a conference at a hotel and he was going to be the main speaker, we would actually go into the kitchen area, and I would call in advance and they would have their different workers meet there and he would sign autographs and talk to them. He always did that, always. He would say to me that these people would never get the opportunity to meet a celebrity, let alone talk to them that way and get an autograph. He would give them a pep talk and just really be one of them. That was something that I really will always take with me, and even in my career, is how just humble he was and what that really means to people.

It was amazing to me to see all around the world, wherever Walter would go, the popularity that he maintained, because even though I marketed Walter, I was marketing him in the very end, so dealing with his image and all of the aspects of how you package an athlete, he was not the kind of athlete who was really commercial. So we were very choosy on the things that he did, and in my opinion we certainly could have done a lot more, but I also knew what Walter wanted and he wanted to maintain more of a superstar's essence, and that was, they get enough, but not too much. With that, it was just amazing, even in the latter nineties, the popularity was there, it was the same, it never decreased.

He was very observant when he was at an event, and if somebody came up for an autograph, and they tried to come up for another autograph, he'd say, "You know what? I've already given you an autograph and there are so many people here, I appreciate that, but I want to make sure to meet everybody as much as I can." I remember one event where there was an older lady in line and she was very upset because his time had run out being there. There were so many people still left in line and she was far back. She literally went into tears because she didn't get to come up. He said to me, "See where this woman is going." The event happened to be at a huge mall, and so I had my cell phone and I'm following this woman at a distance and when the crowd died down—'cause she had stayed in the mall— I called Walter and told him exactly where she was, and he actually came in and met with her and spent about fifteen minutes speaking to her. She was crying because she wanted to get some autographs for her grandsons. He was just so touched by that that we got her information and sent her a couple of footballs for her grandchildren.

That is what the public— We didn't advertise that. That's why so many individuals have stories about Walter, because when he met you, I don't care if there was a thousand people in the room, he made you feel that you were literally one, the only one there, and he impacted your life. There are so many stories like that.

I remember a woman who volunteers quite a bit at the foundation, and she was telling me that when she was a teenager that the Boys and Girls Club had held an event at a real nice hotel, and it was in a really nice suite at the hotel. It was her and another boy, and they were there representing the Boys and Girls Club and that really no one had come up to them. It was a fund-raiser, so everybody else there, they were all people that had money and were all dressed very nice. These two teenagers were there and they were kind of just alone, nobody came up to greet them or anything. She'll never forget that when the elevator opened and Walter Payton walked out of the elevator, he looked around the room, and spotted them, and everybody's running over to greet him, and he's smiling at everybody and waving and telling them, putting his finger up, saying, "I'll be right back," ran right over to them and grabbed and hugged them, and said, "It's great that you're here, I'm so excited to be able to come and be part of this." She said that when Walter came over, then everybody else wanted to come and meet them too. It was then okay to go up and hug these kids.

That's what he was able to do, he was able to make people feel special and feel good. She said to me she realized that, and she actually went in and is employed with DCFS [Department of Children and Family Services], which is the children that the foundation services, and that's how I was able to come in contact with her.

The things that kept Walter going, he really thrived on helping others. We're going to all miss that because that's what Walter was about. When you lose a good man, it's hard. If Walter had played for two more years, if he had gotten the NFL franchise, certainly his life would have been different. "If" is a very destructive word at times when we look at our lives. That's one of the things I really feel sorry about for Walter is that "if" was part of his life, and it shouldn't have been. It really shouldn't have been. All of those issues couldn't work out or be avoided, but they were out of his control, and that's really what was sad about that.

But I do believe that all in all, Walter did contribute as best as he could and he filled every day of his life with what he could and what he felt was prevalent at that time. Looking at everything, we all worked very hard together, and I think that the main thing, in the public's eye and looking at all the fans who really stood by Walter's side, it shows that we must have all done something right.

12

Giving Back to Charity

In a warehouse in the Chicagoland area, Christmas mornings are made. It is here that the Walter Payton Foundation's most personal charity, Wishes to Santa, is put together. Until 1999, following Walter's death, the Wishes to Santa program was never publicly affiliated with Walter, because he did not want to publicly benefit for his work. He wanted the program to stand on its own. But in many ways, this could become his most lasting and important legacy.

Giant boxes of toys, clothes, games, and gifts are jammed into this huge area as volunteer workers sort, pack, and bag what eventually will become a dream for an unsuspecting child. The Payton gift drive is as impressive to witness as any spin move or power run that Walter made on the field. Its amazing size, its heart-tugging goal, and its glimpse at the generosity of Chicago individuals and corporations alike is everything the storybooks tell us the Christmas spirit should be about.

The goal here is to make sure that every child in the Illinois Department of Children and Family Services, no matter how poor or how seemingly forgotten, has a Christmas. Walter set the goal for the 1999 Christmas, one he was not able to witness firsthand, at providing fifty thousand children with their very own Christmas-morning gift bag filled with toys and clothes worth at least one hundred dollars on the retail market.

Walter Payton: We know that psychologically when things go wrong at home, children blame themselves. We know that when parents divorce, kids wonder if it was their fault, even though it never is. We know that when Dad loses a job, they wonder if it was their fault, even though it never is. But they think that way. For abused children, this is a common feeling. They wonder if the fact that they have been taken from their home, away from their parents, is because of something they did. It is sad.

Then we have Christmas, where America becomes so wrapped up in consuming material goods. Television broadcasts wealth, advertisers tie receiving the latest fad toy or game to self-worth. It's sad because that is not what Christmas is really about. But the children see it, they learn that value, and there isn't anything we can do about it.

So these children who doubt their worth learn that at Christmastime, Santa Claus will bring toys and gifts only to children who have been nice. The naughty ones will be left out. Obviously, that is not how Christmas works. The ones struggling with life wake up on Christmas morning to nothing. But I always wondered, What are we teaching these young kids? They already wonder if they have been bad and that's why they aren't with their family. Now they wake up on Christmas and get no gifts, it is veritable proof to a young child that they have been naughty, that they did not deserve a visit from Santa. It devalues a child at such a young and impressionable age.

Gifts on Christmas for abused and neglected children may not seem like a lot, but it terms of establishing self-worth, confidence, and a feeling of pride, I believe it may mean everything. That's why it pains me to think of a child waking up on Christmas morning with no toys. That's why I worry about the long-term emotional damage such a trauma inflicts. That's why I want no child to go without on Christmas morning. It has a tremendous effect psychologically on these children because they don't have their hero, Santa Claus, coming to their aid. The toy itself is irrelevant. It is the psyche that matters, it is the childhood memories and that's the whole basis of this program, creating happy childhood memories.

That is why I got involved in this. Not that I wanted to do toy drives and go to all the lengths that we go to give the child a toy. My belief is that every child in America, as many children as I can help, I want them to wake up on Christmas morning and feel good about themselves and have self-esteem and self-respect and they deserve just as much as the kid down the street. Because all these kids go to the public schools. So you have a child who's sitting in school, and he's listening to what Katie got and what Billy got and how happy they are, and he's sitting there being taken away from his parents. On top of it, even Santa doesn't visit him, and he feels, What did I do wrong?

Every gift had to be brand-new and still in its original packaging from the store. They had to be first-class products. A Barbie doll had to be the same Barbie doll you'd buy your own child. The games had to be unopened, the clothes not hand-me-downs but off-the-rack stuff you yourself would wear.

As volunteer workers sorted through the stuff from dawn to midnight, individual bags were filled with a collection of gifts, not just a single one. They were divided into groups, based on the dreams and desires of girls and boys at different age groups. Toddlers received *Sesame Street* animals. Preteens got Barbies or unopened boxes of Legos. Teenagers got clothes, computer games, and sporting equipment.

Walter Payton: Can you imagine the impact this has on these kids? Can you imagine?

This was Payton's favorite charity effort and is the perfect example of why Walter Payton was one of America's most generous and caring athletes. His efforts at fund-raising and making a positive impact in the community were more than just raising money at black-tie events or taking part in charity golf outings—though he did his share of those too. He raised money for scores of causes, but his favorite and most important work was hands-on giving. The stuff that touches individual lives, the stuff that makes little kids feel good about themselves, at least for a single day.

Walter Payton: Too many of us only take. We don't give. This is true with all Americans, but especially athletes and entertainers, who are able to take so much but rarely give enough. I myself have never been able to give as much as I wanted. I myself am as guilty as anyone at taking.

It's hard not to. We take because so much is given. Football made me a wealthy man. The community made me famous, made me idolized, gave me a feeling of importance, made me feel loved. I tried to give back on the football field by providing an outlet, a diversion from life for a few hours on Sunday afternoon, but that isn't enough.

Fame is what you have taken, character is what you give. I wanted to have character, because football already gave me fame. I couldn't have been treated better by the people of America, especially in Chicago. So in turn I strived to take care of the Americans and Chicagoans who needed me to help them. It is so easy when you are a star professional athlete to lose touch with real life. Everywhere you go you are treated different than others, treated better than others, all because you can run with an inflated ball better than the next guy. In the grand scheme of things, is that important? Does God care that I could run the ball better than most? Obviously God gave me that ability, but I was always questioning if that was why he gave me that ability.

He didn't do it so I could become rich and famous. He didn't do it so I could make the Hall of Fame or help the Bears win a Super Bowl. He must have done it so I could use my fame and my popularity to rally people and help others. He gave me a gift and I need to use it. I have tried to do that and want to continue to do it after I am gone. It is why I have set such ambitious goals for my charities and challenged people to help me meet them. In 1998 we had 35,000 Christmas bags for children. In 1999 I set the goal at 50,000. In the future I want it to go further. I want to set up a Wishes to Santa program in Jackson, Mississippi. I want to set up similar programs throughout the country. I want this to continue on everywhere.

My understanding of the obligations of fame and wealth comes from my father. He told me when I was young that it was your responsibility, once you've had some success, to reach back and bring someone with you. He'd say that if I was fortunate enough to experience success, then I made it because others helped me along. Teachers, coaches, neighbors, all sorts of people. I don't care how intelligent you are, how driven you are, how great an athlete you are, you cannot achieve great success without being helped along the way. Someone gave to you. That's why it is your job to give back.

And this is not just for the professional athletes or the ultra-wealthy or the recording artist who has truly been blessed. This is for everyone. My father was not a wealthy man by material standards. But he was successful and he gave back. He had a wonderful family, he knew how to live a just life, he knew the basic values of life—hard work, the way to treat people, honesty—that make people successful. And he passed those on. He would help neighbors get ahead. He would show other young people back in Columbia the things he learned. He was a role model to all of us.

I think giving is more than just money. If every American volunteered some time to work with kids in their area, or the sick or the elderly, or with government assistance programs, imagine what our nation could become. You don't need to be Bill Gates to be charitable. You don't even need to give money. You could help a child learn to read, take a veteran to a baseball game and make them feel special, help an older woman manage her bills or do her taxes. Organize a group of friends to clean up a playground or a ball field. Do anything that might make the world a better place for someone.

We have all made it. We have all had some success. Now it is time to give a little back. If you are reading this then someone taught you how to read. Now go teach someone else how to read.

It was easy for me to give back. I became wealthy, I had opportunities to work on big projects after I retired, I made the corporate business connections that could get things done. But anyone can do something. That is why I feel so indebted to the people who help with the Christmas donations. Sure it wouldn't be as great of a success without big companies such as Levi's. But I'd like to thank the people all around Chicago who go and buy a single extra puzzle or extra toy and drop it off. That single act means so much because they are doing what they can.

It is the simplest of tasks that can make such a difference. My entire adult life I have been approached for autographs. So many athletes hate providing autographs, and while I know as well as anyone how demanding it can get, I always approached it with a smile, like it was an honor that someone would ask. Every athlete or famous person remembers the first time someone asked for an autograph. You felt special that someone would care. I tried to keep that feeling years and years later.

I always liked to interact with the person when I signed autographs. It took longer but it meant more, to both of us. I'd ask the person about where he's from, what he's doing. I'd ask about his family, about his life. I have two kids and if they had an opportunity to meet one of their heroes, I would appreciate it if they would give the courtesy to be just a little personable. It is so easy to do so much.

Kim Tucker: Walter was very active as far as donating his time to people. When we would get requests in through the office, no matter what they were, we answered in some way. If he could not attend the event, we would send them a piece of autographed memorabilia or something so that there was an aspect of his presence involved.

The whole evolving of Walter having his own foundation began in 1989 when he was encouraged to form the George Halas/Walter Payton Foundation. Actually he was encouraged to start the Walter Payton Foundation, but Walter throughout his whole life and especially his professional career never wanted to stand alone. He thought that was too arrogant to have the foundation named solely after himself, so he would not do it. He looked for somebody who was his mentor and somebody who he really looked up to, and that was George Halas. So he was given permission to utilize the George Halas name, and the George Halas/Walter Payton Foundation was formed in 1989.

The foundation initially took the role of really helping schools, especially inner-city schools that were home to potential dropouts. Basically, the foundation gave those schools monies. I came into the picture in 1993. I worked with Walter doing his marketing and promotions and was working in my office one night when he came in and just said he'd like to talk to me about his foundation. He really wanted to have a more active role in the foundation and wanted us to develop programming, a variety of programs, that he felt could help people. He wanted to have a more active role in those programs and feel that he was contributing more than just with the financial part of it.

The first program that I put together was on Thanksgiving Day. I went into his office and I said, "Walter, I put the first program together and it's going to be on Thanksgiving Day. Is that a problem?" He never even batted an eye before saying that was fine. And so we checked with his wife, Connie, to make sure that was going to be fine, and she said that was okay.

We put the event together at one of his restaurants at that time, Studebaker's. We had 650 children as our guests from various children's organizations. It was our very first large event with that amount of children. Walter loved it.

Walter stood and took photos with the children. And all these children were pretty small, the majority of them were very young, but I really thought that someday these children would realize that this very famous man took the time out of his holiday to be with them, and they would look at that and have that to cherish as they got older even though they didn't realize it at that moment.

One of the turning points that caused us to create the huge program we have now, the Wishes to Santa program, came at that first event. It came from a little boy who was in line. At the event we had invited Santa and Mrs. Claus, Frosty the Snowman, the Easter Bunny, all of them. Everyone was having Thanksgiving dinner with Walter and the children.

Well, this little boy, when he got up to Walter he was in tears. Walter grabbed him and said, "What's wrong?" He looked at Walter and he said, "I can't believe it, I can't believe Santa Claus is here and that Santa would come all the way from the North Pole just to see me."

Walter started crying and I started crying. Everybody started crying. We realized how important that figure, Santa Claus, was to these children. He didn't even know who Walter was, but he knew who Santa was and seeing him was so important.

Walter looked at me and said, "I really want you to develop a program geared just towards Christmas. I want these children to develop happy childhood memories." He knew that this was going to be very time-consuming and a very huge program, but he was serious. One of the things that I really did appreciate about Walter was the fact that when he was going to commit to doing something, he would do it in a way that was as big as life. That program has helped hundreds of thousands of children through the years.

The program where we would have the children come to the restaurant, we did this on Christmas Day, Easter Day, and Thanksgiving Day for several years. But the Wishes to Santa program developed and evolved to where in the year of his passing, we were able to help fifty thousand children and that was Walter's goal.

He wanted this program to continue to grow and his foundation to grow even though he was not going to be here. The idea of the Wishes to Santa was that we would represent Santa Claus. We wanted to give to all children who are wards of the state, the ones in the Department of Children and Family Services. Walter said he would only do this and commit to this if we were to work with Jeanie Ortega-Piron, who is the guardian of all the children, and currently there's over thirty-thousand-something children in care.

Not only do we collect the toys and put the toys in a clear garbage bag, but we actually distribute the toys to the caretakers of the children. Once we get the toys together, which takes us all year, Jeanie Ortega-Piron sends out letters to all the caretakers. Think about that. There were fifty thousand gift bags at one hundred dollars each. That means we needed $5 million in donated toys. None of us but Walter was sure we could pull it off.

We had nine distribution sites in 1999. We took the toys and we only give them to people who have the proper identification, who can prove that they are the caretaker of those children. Whether it's a group home, whether it's an individual who has only one child, or five children, they have to show five different forms of identification. What the caretakers agree to is that they will hold the gifts and give them to the children on Christmas morning from Santa. Walter realized the significance of taking charge for these children he would never meet and making sure that happy childhood memories were built in them so when they grew up as adults, they would have something to look back in their childhood that they could ponder on, that was happy for them. Most of these children don't have any of this.

I got a phone call on Christmas Day. A fifteen-year-old girl had accidentally been given a gift bag—she was in a group home—for a five-year-old. I was called because the caseworker was very, very upset at this time and said, "Is there any way we can get this young lady some proper gifts to fit her age?" So we got the gifts over to her and the fifteen-year-old's response was "I would rather keep the ones I was given because I've never had a toy." She was in the system since she was about four years old, and it was the first time that she had ever received toys. It brought tears to everyone's eyes. Just the magnitude of this particular program that people don't realize.

We never went public with the foundation and the Wishes to Santa program. No one takes a salary, and so much is done out of complete goodness.

When we started the foundation, we asked for God to ordain the foundation, any programs that we developed, and before any meetings we always said a prayer.

It wasn't until Walter passed that I had to make the decision to publicize all these beautiful programs that we had run since 1993. I did it in order to keep them going so we could continue to help the amount of children that they were helping. I had to make a crucial decision and let the people know what Walter was doing and ask for support so that we could continue. Now we are going to depend on people coming together and making this work.

The wonderful thing is there is such a history that we've been able to build. It is truly part of Walter. This is a living part of him still, knowing that these children are being helped and will continue to be helped. That was his goal. That was something that immortalized him. Even though he didn't look at it that way, I realize that now, because that truly—as well as all the football records and all these things that would potentially be broken someday—what he has done for children is so incredible that it will remain in the hearts of hundreds of thousands of children forever who will never even know that it was the Walter Payton Foundation. Looking now and going public, a lot of them who are older will realize that it was Walter who helped them. We will always keep everything the way that we always had. We tell the kids the gifts are not from Walter Payton or some foundation, but rather from Santa.

Jeanie Ortega-Piron: It was a sunny afternoon in April 1997 when I first became involved with the Payton Foundation. The director of the Illinois Department of Children and Family Services [DCFS] had asked me to attend a meeting on his behalf at the foundation's office. I am the department's guardianship administrator, and as such the juvenile courts appoint me through court order as the legal guardian of all abused and neglected children who become wards of the state. At that time I was the legal guardian for approximately fifty thousand children.

Because of that number and the genuine need to achieve permanency in children's lives, DCFS, its inspector general, and the Cook County juvenile court had decided to partner and hold an "adoption fair" on the grounds of the court. This was no ordinary event, but a real fair in every sense of the word—games, prizes, rides, and lots of food. It was believed that individuals seeking information about adoption could attend workshops at the fair while seeing children free for adoption in their natural state, playing and having fun. But, of course, we needed money to hold this event, hence the meeting at the foundation offices was to ask for some type of sponsorship. And I was dreading this meeting. I've never liked asking for money.

Arriving at the foundation's offices, I stepped off the elevator and looked at a sign to determine which way to turn, when suddenly I felt these very big arms around me. I was startled, a little alarmed, and looked up to find a very famous face gazing into mine. There he was, Walter Payton himself. And he was talking to me. And what he said amazed me. He was asking me if I had gotten lost coming to the office, that he had been waiting and that he hoped I'd choose them to help the children. Choose them?! I was there to ask him for money. What was he talking about? I was soon to find out. He escorted me into their conference room where the foundation's executive director, Kim Tucker, joined me. As we waited for the rest of my group—the DCFS inspector general and representatives from One Church, One Child, and the Cook County juvenile court—I was struck with what Kim Tucker was saying to me. They were going to play a video for us so that we would know the foundation was legitimate and serious about serving the children. The video contained excerpts of past events the foundation had sponsored. All events were for children. Many of the events had been for DCFS wards. The foundation had been providing Christmas gift bags to our wards anonymously for the past five years. They had given close to two thousand bags the previous year. I knew no one in our group knew these things. Kim informed us that she felt that the children needed more help, so she decided to disclose the foundation's anonymous gift giving to us in order for them to do more to help the children.

The group arrived. Kim spoke to us for about thirty minutes as to why the foundation should be chosen to help and then played the video. At one point, the One Church, One Child, representative leaned over and said to me, "Are they trying to sell their foundation to us? Aren't we here to ask for money?" All of us were in awe. But as the children's guardian I was very impressed and very happy. I had found an organization that didn't want to exploit the children and had remained anonymous for many years while assisting children. Often, one can find organizations that will donate things but they want their pictures in the paper giving the donated items to the children. As their guardian, this troubles me because it seems to me that we are sending the message "Here I am, the abused/neglected child who is also poor." I don't want my wards to have to say or think those things. Now, in that conference room, I had found an organization that didn't want publicity but did want to help.

That first meeting was the beginning of a new day. The adoption fair was held. It was a success and the children had a blast, thanks in no small part to the Payton Foundation and the hard work of Kim Tucker. Since that time, the foundation has created a new organization, Walter Payton's Alliance for the Children. Its exclusive focus is the wards of the state. In 1998, their Wishes to Santa program provided over 23,000 gift bags to our wards at Christmastime. They have made a commitment to continue for as long as they can. In addition, they have set up a program with Manpower International to provide employee counseling services to our wards free of charge, have begun a clothing distribution program for our teens, and are exploring ways to develop a scholarship program for our wards.

Throughout these past years I have met, spoken, or prayed with Walter many times. During one of our conversations he revealed to me that he was most comfortable when he was with children, because they didn't really know or understand his fame, they just knew him as Walter, the man who liked to play with them. I know my own children remember him that way. I really believe that when all is said and done, while he may be remembered as one of the world's greatest football legends, his greatest legacy is that he loved the children.

Walter Payton: I have always felt very strong about boosting self-esteem for children. I know from football that when you are very confident in yourself, you can accomplish anything. I was a very confident individual and there was nothing that I felt I couldn't accomplish. Even when I was faced with adversity, I didn't wait and react to it, I took it on. I was very proactive in everything.

That is why through the years several of the programs have evolved, but our main focus with all these programs has been children. I love children very, very much. I think in many ways I always have been a child. I knew that with these children, things were pure and innocent. I know many of the young ones don't even know I ever existed, but that didn't mean I couldn't help.

The reason I started the George Halas/Walter Payton Foundation, which is now just the Walter Payton Foundation, is to be able to take a more hands-on approach to things. Every year while I was playing, I'd have hundreds and hundreds of requests annually for me to do stuff that would benefit a particular charity. I would always try to do as much as I could.

But when I retired, I was pulled in many directions. I worked on so many great charities, from fighting leukemia, the Better Boys Foundation, Make a Wish, and so on and so forth. But I wanted to have more of a clear direction in what I was doing and I wanted to leave an impact on children. The only way to do so was to really develop my own foundation.

Children have always brought a tremendous amount of joy to me and I feel that if you can catch them at a young age you can really change a life. It's like the proverb "If you give a man a fish, he eats for one day, if you teach a man to fish, he eats for life." I wanted to help teach them for life. There are a lot of studies that show that one act of kindness to these children has a 40 percent chance of making that child have a completely different outcome in their life. When I first heard that it astounded me, I was floored.

A lot of the children we deal with come from difficult backgrounds and difficult neighborhoods. The wrong path is clearly marked, but the right one is not always so clear. What you hope is that you can get a kid to believe in something and believe in themselves. You hope they will not be led along by things that are happening around them, like individuals who come talking with smooth tongues and false promises. If they set goals for themselves to look at certain images or certain people and say, That's what I want to be, that's where I want to be when I'm grown up, or, This is where I want to shoot for, and hold on to it, then anything is possible. Anything. Dreaming is important because dreams are all that we have. Dreams are what make this whole country. What made this country was a dream. And if you believe in something and you work at it, then there's going to be hope, there's gonna be a way.

You know what the best thing about helping children was? To know that I was helping them made me feel good and it was very satisfying. I didn't feel that I was helping them. Well, I knew I was helping them, but they were also helping me because it made me feel stronger every day. Even though a lot of children we have helped through the years I've never met, because a lot of this goes on anonymously, I can't explain the inner strength that I've received through knowing all the lives that I've had a hand in changing. Sometimes I get to meet some of the children, and I see on their little faces what a difference I've made. I feel that it's a two-way street. That they've helped me too.

It is the beautiful thing about giving back. You get back also.

After Walter's death, the foundation became a rallying point for many who loved what he had stood for. Calls flooded the foundation with offers of help. Few, though, made the extraordinary effort of Walter's friend John Gamauf, vice president of Bridgestone/Firestone.

John Gamauf: I was in Vegas when I got the phone call from Ginny in the morning that said it was coming very, very close and the time was near. That was about eight in the morning, and then by noon Walter had passed. I was totally upset, I wouldn't come out of my room. I didn't want to see anybody or talk to anybody, just crying my eyes out. I was really, really hurt that I lost a good friend, someone who had taught me a lot about life. Every day since then, when I think I have problems, I think of Walter's fight. I don't have any problems, I really don't. That led me to go down the next day to a meeting with a whole bunch of customers. They all came up to me knowing my relationship and said, Hey, what can we do, what can we do to help? The only thing I knew to mention was that Walter had a charity, the Walter Payton Foundation. I said, Let me check into it and see what we can do. After I got some information about it and saw what a good cause it was, I started spreading the word.

I had one customer, Paul Swentsel in Kentucky, say, "I'll tell you what, I'll help you start out your support of Walter's foundation. I'll give you a check for five grand." I said, "Wow, that's pretty generous, that's very nice of you." He wrote me a personal check and sent it to me, and I called another customer, Larry Morgan, who owns the Don Olson tire stores down in Florida, and he said, "I'll match the five grand." Okay, that was ten grand, this was easy, and it just kept going. All this happened while I was still in Vegas and all these folks were around and I just started picking up these commitments.

Next thing we know, we had dealers that were calling up saying, "I'll tell you what, here's what I'd like to do . . ." and they all had a plan on how to help Walter's foundation. We had a dealer, Target Tire in North Carolina, that was so moved by what Walter did, they sent a letter to all their customers and said, "We would like to contribute to the Walter Payton Foundation and we're going to bill you

$34 on your next statement, and if you have any problems with this, let us know." Nobody did, and they raised $18,000 for the Walter Payton Foundation, just by billing their customers each $34. I got a write up in *Crain's Tire Business* on that one. So that led another customer out in California, Mike Largent, to do another fund-raiser, and he raised about $8,600 doing the same basic thing. He had a business meeting and said, "Whatever donations my customers would like to make to the foundation, we as a company will match it." They raised like $4,300 and he matched it $4,300, and wrote me a check for $8,600. It started going and took off naturally. Went up to Wholesale Tire, where Walter had given that speech a year earlier, and everybody around there at the table started offering up money, and I think we raised about $7,000 or $8,000. By the time I knew it, we had close to $80,000. Then a good friend, Jim Berlin, a former tire dealer, called and asked how close I was to my $100,000 goal. I said about $20,000 away. The next day we hit our goal. We actually ended up with $130,000 last year, and I said to Kim that if we can raise that in basically less than a year, then we should be able to raise the same amount next year.

That's the impact this man had on the people in my industry. We're all proud we can help keep his memory alive by supporting his foundation's efforts.

13

Family

As one of the most private public figures in sports, Walter shielded his family from the media's spotlight nearly as well as he protected the football. Walter always wanted his family to have as normal a life as possible despite his immense popularity, especially in Chicago. Walter would frequently incorporate the importance of his family into speeches he gave to various groups. It was Sweetness's way of showing, however subtly, how very important his family was to him.

For most, the first real glimpse into his family life came when Walter's only son, Jarrett (then twelve years old), stepped to the podium on July 31, 1993, to introduce his father as a newly enshrined member of the NFL Hall of Fame in Canton, Ohio. Out of obligation, Walter had first asked Jim Finks, the general manager who had believed in a little-known running back from Jackson State enough to draft him with the Bears' first pick in the 1975 NFL Draft, to introduce him. Finks was battling cancer at the time and was unable to accept Payton's kind offer. Privately, Walter was saddened by Finks's condition, but it gave him the chance to ask Jarrett if he would like to introduce his dad. He was the first son to ever introduce his father for induction to the Hall of Fame. Not only was the move groundbreaking, it spoke volumes about Walter.

Walter Payton: Well, when it first started out, Jim Finks was supposed to do it because he was the guy who took a chance on a little black kid from Jackson State University. He worked with me and he was very good in terms of getting contracts and everything else and I stayed with the Bears partly because he was there. But cancer prevented him from doing the introduction and he eventually passed away because of that horrible disease. The only other person I would have wanted to share that moment was Jarrett and I didn't know if he was going to do it or not. I just asked him on a whim, I said, "Do you want to do it?" He goes, "Yeah, I don't know." I think he was worried about missing a soccer game or something, and then a little bit later he says, "Okay, I'll do it."

I didn't know anything he was going to say until he said it. When we were together, he would practice in a separate room. It was a surprise to me.

Jarrett Payton: I wasn't that surprised he asked me to introduce him. My dad was different. He was always doing things out of the blue. You could never really predict what he was going to do, so when that came up, it didn't surprise me. I didn't want to do it at first, I was like, No way. It was too scary. I had never done anything like that before, especially when I was only twelve! Man, I sat down and started writing it and then going over it. Then I thought, All right, maybe I'll do it now. And then once I got to Ohio, it was like, I'm still not sure. I was counting the days, I had three days in Canton before I was supposed to do it.

When that day came, I was so scared. I cracked a joke, I forget what I said, and right after that I took a deep breath and I just said it and that was it. It was fun nevertheless. Once I got done, I was still shaky and bouncy. There were just so many people who were out there watching. Plus I was thinking about how many people were at home watching, I said to myself, Man, if I screw up, everyone's going to know it.

Jarrett Payton (at the induction ceremony): I'm gonna try to get this thing over with. I'm very privileged and honored to be chosen to induct my dad into the Pro Football Hall of Fame. This is a historic event which my dad, Walter, and members of the Payton family will treasure for the rest of our lives. His friends and fans will recall this memorable occasion. My dad had played football thirteen years, only missing one game and breaking all running-back records. These and other records have placed him in sport annals and that's why we are here to honor this superstar. Not only is my dad an exceptional athlete, he's a role model. He's my biggest role model and best friend. We do a lot of things together, play basketball, golf, go to the movies, to name a few. I'm sure my sister will endorse this statement: We have a Super Dad. My father has always been involved with charitable organizations. As a matter of fact I can safely say he is a philanthropist. On behalf of my mom, my sister, Brittney, and all of our relatives, I congratulate you, Dad. On behalf of your friends, and your fans, I say congratulations too. Thank you.

Walter Payton: I've had so many people come up to me and tell me when he got up there and started his speech, big lumps came into their throats, and I've had people saying they were crying like babies on their couches. I think it was one of those moments where football became human, it became more of a family as opposed to coaches, players, and owners. I think it transcended that. Heck, I had tears in my eyes when I got up to hug him.

Jarrett Payton: I didn't actually see him cry, because I turned around and gave him a hug, and after I gave him a hug, I sat down. And I could only hear it in his voice when he was talking.

Walter Payton (at the induction ceremony, following Jarrett, fighting back tears): When I first got here, we made a wager of who would be the first one to break down in tears, and I was the first one to say that I wouldn't, and I was the first one to say how strong I was and everything else, but as it goes to show that a lot of times, when you are amongst your peers such as these great athletes over here, you try to be something that you're not.

After hearing my son get up here and talk, I don't care if I lose the bet. There was a guy that was supposed to be here today to co-introduce me with my son—Mr. Jim Finks, who is having a bout with lung cancer. And I wanted to let him know that our prayers are with him because he was the guy who gave me my start. He was the one who called me when I was at Jackson State University the day before the draft, and he asked me a question. He said, "Walter, this is Jim Finks. How would you like to play for the Chicago Bears?"

My answer to him was "Jim, I'll play for anybody." And that was the way I felt at that particular time, and I think if I had answered that question any different than the way I did, I would have probably been playing for somebody else, maybe even Pittsburgh. Every day, every offensive lineman that played for the Chicago Bears helped me get that sixteen thousand yards, and I thank them. But the thing that I'm most proud of and the thing I'm most ashamed of coincide with each other. You saw my son up here a few minutes ago, and believe me, I had a lump in my throat that was so big it was unbelievable. I also have a little daughter, Brittney Jene Payton, and I think about her also because their mom was with me for those thirteen years that I played, and believe me they were not all good. I was not the easiest person to get along with. And because of my wanting to give to so many other people, sometimes you tend to neglect the people that you truly love the most. And I want to stand up here and say at this point in my life that Jarrett, Brittney, and your mom—you guys will never have to worry about anything in your life, no matter what the situation or how it ends. Because just as running up that hill and trying to catch the runners such as Jim Brown and Gale

Sayers motivated me to do more than I thought I possibly could do, you three will motivate me to make sure that your lives are happy and fulfilled.

Everybody that you meet, you can learn something from them. Everybody that comes in your life can influence your life as well. Just as these people here have, just as you have, because the fans are what make this game. Without you being out here and coming to this Hall of Fame, it wouldn't be professional football. So I stand here and I applaud you for supporting and staying with the National Football League and these players here. Thank you.

As special as that July day was for Walter, his family, his friends, and his legions of fans, there was one very important person who wasn't there. Even in one of his proudest moments, Walter could not stop thinking about his deceased father, Edward Payton. The elder Payton's absence made the family photo taken that day—a rare shot of nine smiling Paytons—incomplete.

The circumstances surrounding the elder Payton's death in 1979 are still, to this day, a sensitive subject in Columbia. Edward was arrested by a white police officer in Columbia for what the officer reported was "driving under the influence." Family members agree that was highly unlikely because Edward rarely drank and was never drunk. Put in a jail cell to "dry out," the fifty-four-year-old suffered a brain aneurysm while in the cell and died there. In retrospect, it is believed that Edward was most likely having some type of seizure when he was arrested, but wasn't coherent enough to explain the situation.

Regardless of the specifics, the bottom line is that Edward never got to share in the greatest successes of his younger son, Walter.

Walter Payton: Well, when you look up there in the audience and you see my mom out there and my brother and my sister, and my father would have been a very young man at that point and for him not to be sitting in the audience, it was a moving moment.

But I was at peace with things, I think that things were cleared up surrounding his death. What happened was that he died from a brain hemorrhage and I think the doctors and a lot of people understand that when that happens, it's something that happens slow, it's very painless and what happens is, once it's reached a point, you start to lose your equilibrium and your motor skills, simply because the blood that's pressing up against the brain just went away.

A lot of people wanted to see it in racial terms. I don't believe it was. I grew up with most of the people involved. They knew it was my father when they arrested him. I think some people were looking to light a match and burn down the city. I wouldn't participate in that.

I'm at peace with what happened and how it happened, because things happen. The only thing that really upset me, and I cannot deal with it to this point, was one of the comments that Paul Harvey made on the radio about the incident.

I'm still not comfortable talking about it and it is still is a very bitter pill to swallow. It was a derogatory remark that Paul Harvey made and he didn't even know the facts and he made a comment. To this point now, he has not apologized for it. He has not retracted his statement. I never brought it to Mr. Harvey's attention because I didn't feel I should make the first move. He was wrong, he should have apologized. As a matter of fact, I was in Chicago several years back and I was one of the Lincoln Award recipients and he was one as well. We were on the same dais together and I couldn't even shake his hand.

But as far as the situation itself, who is to say in a situation where if my father had been a white guy and the same thing had happened, and I had been the police officer, I think I would have assumed the same thing, that he was impaired. You want to get angry and blame people, but that wasn't the way my parents had raised me.

Eddie Payton: I still think about the circumstances of my father's death, and whether I'm convinced or not at this point, it doesn't matter—you don't harp and you don't harbor, that's the way we were brought up. He could have been walking down the street and if it was his time to go, it was his time to go. There wouldn't have been a thing that anybody would have been able to do. The good Lord sets you here for X amount of years and only he knows the day that you're gonna leave. He knows the way. Whether he would have been in a jail cell, been driving home, the outcome would have been the same. It would do no good for that community to do a lot of things that wouldn't have brought him back and probably wouldn't have yielded any different results than what we figured happened. Now, whether there was negligence or something that happened, when you look at it, you say, Well, there probably was. They could have done this and they could have done that, they could have done this, but they didn't. They did not.

I think as a family, the decision we made and the way we decided to handle it was something we all would be able to live with the rest of our lives because we feel that we handled it the right way. The way our dad would have wanted us to handle it.

Connie Payton: It was a pretty sad situation surrounding his dad's death. It was the way the whole thing happened. If there was any reason for Walter to really look down on his hometown, it would have been for this reason. Mr. Payton was arrested for being drunk, which he wasn't, and no one tried to find out what was really happening to him. It was a disturbing experience for the entire family.

He was really hurt that his father was treated that way. During the summer of 1999, we were watching the ESPN special honoring Walter as one of the "Top 50 Athletes of the Century," and they did a little bit on his dad and the circumstances of his death. Walter left the room and cried. When he saw his father he realized how much he missed having him around all those years and his father not being able to experience his having success. His dad loved pickup trucks and Walter said that it would have been nice to buy his dad a new pickup truck, just to see him drive around in it would have done Walter's heart all the good in the world. I think it was the first time he dealt with the whole incident emotionally. He had handled it intellectually, but it wasn't until that moment that he dealt with it emotionally.

As emotional as Walter was about losing his father, he was equally passionate about his own family. In all discussions about Walter's legacy, one is often forgotten. His family, whom he infused with his personality, lives on. And Walter lives on through them most assuredly.

Walter Payton: Probably the greatest thing I regret in my life is that I had to get sick in order to understand how lucky I am to have such a great family. The things that stand out the most to me in my life are the small things like seeing my first child smile at me. Seeing him take his first step, or the friendship that I've developed between myself and my children. These things stand out more, they mean more to me, than the actual activity on the football field.

I certainly will say that all things in that area of my life were not as I wished they were and had been. For instance, in 1994 I filed for divorce. I felt myself being pulled into many directions. I was in a very confused state of mind. I was very unhappy and wasn't sure of myself or anyone else. I felt that I needed some space. Connie allowed me to have the time I needed to clear my mind and my heart. With some time I decided that my wife and family were the most important people in my life.

My getting ill also made me review and refocus my relationship with my wife. I will tell you that I have enjoyed the closeness that we shared during these trying times and I enjoyed her driving me around town looking at the cows—and you know, I've got to tell you that she's not a good driver! She is not a race car driver, but I've enjoyed that time with her and I wish that for all those years I was off traveling and taking almost every speaking opportunity I could get, my priorities would have been different.

Connie Payton: I think Walter knew from the beginning that I was just real and I was who I was. It didn't matter to me who he was, and I never got into the fame, even from early on when Bob Hill was trying to get us together. That wasn't important, but I really liked him for him. And I'm sure that for most people that's what they want. They really just want to be loved for who they are and not for what they have.

Walter surprised me on our tenth-year wedding anniversary by arranging a surprise wedding ceremony, the one we never had. He flew up the minister from my home church, my mom, and everybody else, and had them all in hotels. Oh, he planned it. He worked it out with the neighbors across the street to park the cars there. He fooled me by taking me out to a real nice dinner. All of a sudden we get this call that we had an emergency at home, Jarrett had fallen. And I thought that wasn't a fun way to get me home—he was supposed to have hurt himself and they weren't sure if he needed to go see a doctor. So we had to leave dinner and we had ordered champagne—we had already even started ordering food, but they were all in on it. I thought, Of all the times for him to fall—leave dinner, have company with us, go home. We walked through the front door, at least they had me walk in the front door first. I said, "Where's Jarrett?" And all of a sudden, people just started coming out of closets, everywhere, and saying, "Surprise, surprise, surprise." I was in total shock because I had no idea. It was wonderful. It was perfect.

Walter Payton: My children have brought me tremendous joy. Each child represented different levels of joy and different things that they brought to my life. Of course, my baby girl brought me just a tremendous ease in my heart, and just a tremendous feeling. My son brought me tremendous joy and inspiration and I looked at him like he was going to be my hero someday.

Jarrett Payton: We were close, but like I try to tell people, we were so much like each other that it was scary. It wasn't just that he was an exceptional athlete, he was a role model. He's my biggest role model and my best friend. I'm one of those people who it won't matter— Sometimes my dad would do a lot of stuff and would not ask people how they felt about what he was doing. He did things for himself sometimes, and that's just kind of how I am sometimes. You don't understand—me and my dad used to fight all the time. About stupid things. Like, I'll give you an example. We came home one night and I went downstairs and me and my mom were watching TV and we were talking. The next thing you know, I was about to go upstairs and he came down and told me to hug my mom. And my mom was like, "For what?" She's like, "I don't want a hug, for what?" He used to joke and I could tell he was not joking. I said that no, she didn't want a hug, and he took my car away from me.

Our heads would always butt for certain reasons and he'd ask me questions and he knew it would get me upset and he would just always want to see how I would react. I was like, "He wanted me to give her a hug just because he wanted me to?" And the easiest thing would have been for me to just give her a hug, but no, not me. I want to fight about it, so I said, "No, I don't want to." So then I don't and I go to walk away and he grounds me from my car the whole month. Just silly things like that.

Walter Payton: I allowed Jarrett to be in the limelight, but I shielded Brittney from the limelight. I was very protective of Brittney, I really was. But she's now coming into her own. I started, as she got older, to tell her how proud I was of her running. She was the fastest. She was much faster than I ever was.

I respected my daughter all the time, I really did. The accomplishments, even though I publicly didn't talk about her as much because she was a vulnerable point to me, and I didn't want people to criticize her the way that they did Jarrett. All of a sudden, because he started playing football, Jarrett had critics, and I was not going to allow Brittney to have critics. I relished everything that girl did. I really had a special place for my daughter. Not that I didn't for my son, but my daughter was very different. I'll tell you one thing I always did for Miss B, that's what I called her, was I would always shop for her. I loved buying her clothes. Wherever I traveled, and I traveled an enormous amount, there were hours spent picking out clothes for Miss B.

Connie Payton: He would find the most stylish clothes for Jarrett and Brittney. Back then, when Jarrett was a baby, they didn't make cute boys' clothes. He took so much pride in finding all these different outfits for Jarrett. He was always saying, "Put them on, let's take a picture. Put this outfit on him now, let's take another picture." He was the most well-dressed child I knew.

He would call our friends and say, "Come over and see what I bought for Jarrett." It was the same way for Brittney. He would come back from his trips and he would have all these gorgeous clothes for Brittney. He loved to take pictures. He really was a good father. He adored his kids so much.

Brittney Payton: There were so many wonderful moments that we had together. He was so funny, he was such a joker. He loved movies. Even now when I see an Eddie Murphy movie, it reminds me of my dad.

Walter Payton: The kids are basically what this country and what this society are going to be. They are the most important resources that we have. They are the most precious thing that we have. Just like anybody else, like for instance, if you are a farmer, if you had a crop out there this year, you wouldn't just let it go to waste. You wouldn't just let weeds grow in it. You would fertilize it, you would nurture it. You would make sure that it would give the best yield possible. Same thing with our kids. Why would you treat them any differently than you would deal with a field of corn, or a field of potatoes, or a field of anything else? Please, spend time with your kids.

Make sure they are very important to you. Make sure that they are your focus, because if your children and your family are in focus, then when you come to the workplace, you'll be a much happier person and you're going to be a much easier person to get things accomplished with. It's amazing.

It's sort of like a booster shot when you spend time with your kids. They can turn you on to some things that you never knew. All I ask of people I talk to and meet is that they spend at least thirty minutes—just start out with thirty minutes a day—and sit down one-on-one talking to your children. Find out what they're doing, what their life is all about, what their problems are and what they feel is important to them. It's the best medicine you can have, better than chicken soup.

Make sure your children know how important they are to you, because you never know when you won't get a chance to say it. Always do that, so they know.

I didn't get to say some things to my father before he died. I always regretted it. And I made sure the same thing would never happen to my children. It was, in my life, another lesson learned the hard way.

14

Walter Gets Sick

Walter often joked that the one professional game he missed in his thirteen years of football was a game that the coaches should have let him play in anyway. "I was hardly ever sick and when I was, I would fight through it. Remember this, that one of the most important aspects of playing professional football, for me, was about blocking out the pain and continuing to perform," Walter said. "I didn't take time off for an ingrown toenail."

That made picking up signs of Walter's serious illness all the more difficult for those around him. In retrospect, the earliest indications of Walter's illness probably came in the early 1990s when he underwent a routine physical in conjunction with his CART auto racing team. After some further testing with Jay Munsell, a former Bears team physician, it was determined that Walter's liver enzymes were abnormal. But because Walter was such a physical specimen in every other aspect, the doctors, and in turn Walter, never gave the test results much thought. This was a guy who was so healthy, in fact, that he didn't even have a personal physician!

So, even during the summer of 1998, when Walter began getting stomachaches every day, he tried to fight through the discomfort and figured it was just a temporary thing. Walter was convinced his discomfort was the result of what he believed was some bad crab he had eaten during a trip to Panama.

Walter Payton: When I started getting those daily stomachaches in the middle of the summer of '98, I didn't initially take it too seriously. I had been traveling between Chicago and Panama for a potential business venture and I figured I must have caught an intestinal bug, maybe from eating some undercooked crab—I had been eating a ton of crab in Panama, I loved it. But the pain and discomfort didn't go away. Each day that summer I felt a gradual progression of fatigue and just an overall sense of feeling lousy. Then strange things started to happen. I started losing my sense of taste. You see, I would love to suck on Brach's Star Brites mints— I would go through dozens in a single day. Now, all of a sudden, the taste just wasn't the same. Then the scent of colognes and lotions began to annoy me. I always enjoyed wearing some kind of scent and now I couldn't stand any strong odors whatsoever. My face was breaking out in pimples. Obviously, I knew something was wrong.

Next the whites of my eyes began to yellow. I began to wear sunglasses all the time to hide my eyes. In August, I began my weekly radio show on Chicago's sports talk station, WSCR. It took everything I had to make it through that first show. I went to see a doctor that day.

The first doctors I saw diagnosed vitamin toxicity. After a period of time, as I saw I was not getting any better, I decided on my own accord to check into Rochester's Mayo Clinic. I felt that Mayo was the best medical facility around. If they didn't know what was wrong with me, no one would. Unfortunately, the lead time to get into the Mayo Clinic was several months. I scheduled an appointment for the earliest possible time, which was early December, and just "bulled through" not feeling well. I was frustrated that I just didn't feel well. I wasn't used to being sick. It doesn't enter your mind that you may have a life-threatening disease.

I felt that Mayo was the best that was available to me, so I wanted to wait for the best. And one of my former business partners, Jim Sheerin, who was a man of a lot of means and could go anywhere, had always gone to that place for his stuff. I just knew that it was very well respected in the Midwest and they deal with people from all over the world, that's why the wait is so long sometimes to get an appointment. And I felt there would also be privacy there, not that there aren't many fine institutions here in Chicago, it was just that Mayo was the place I felt I could go, check in, have a battery of tests run, and they could come up with what the deal is and get me on track for what I could do to resolve the situation.

Again, I was not panic-stricken at this point. That was not the case at all. I realized, I've got to find a resolution. I've got to find something that's going to make me better.

Ginny Quirk: Walter had a weekly radio show, was the color commentator for the Chicago Bears' preseason games, wrote a weekly newspaper column, gave motivational speeches, and was pursuing a new business venture in Panama. He had a very demanding schedule and traveled four out of every seven days a week. During September and October, Walter didn't have one day off. So when he started to complain of being tired, which he never did before, I didn't think it was very unusual. The pace Walter was keeping made his illness that much more difficult to diagnose. Imagine someone who had never been seriously ill in his life and having a business schedule like a madman. . . . No one thought he had a serious health problem. Walter was invincible. But now his health was affecting his business schedule. I had to carve out some time for Walter to get some rest so he could try to shake off what was bothering him. Little did we know he would begin to spiral downward.

John Gamauf: During the summer of '98 we were together out at a CART race in California. Walter and I would always try to get together at Laguna Seca and we were scheduled to do a bike ride, but he had called through Ginny and said he wasn't feeling good. I got up to the race the next day, Sunday, and it was the first time I'd seen Walter since my dad had died. He pulled me aside and said, "I just heard about your dad and I'm real sorry." This was between the warm-ups and the actual race. He was really classy about it and there were a lot of people standing by and he just focused on my dad's death. That's when he asked for my mom's phone number also, because Walter then started calling my mom. He knew how she felt since his own dad had died and how much of a void there was and he started calling her for six months. He'd call once a week or once every two weeks to just say hello for five or ten minutes. He didn't have to do that. Anyway, he came up to me, and he was leaning up against something, and I said, "What's the matter?" He said, "I don't know, my back is killing me. I don't know if I picked up something or whatever, but I'm really hurting. I don't even want to stay for the race." For Walter to say, I don't want to stay for the race at Laguna Seca, it's like giving a kid a bowl of ice cream with whipped cream and cherries and then he says, I don't feel like eating it. He was just really hurting. He said, "Do you have some connections to get me a helicopter? I want to get out of here." Laguna Seca is not near anything and for him to catch an airplane to get out of there, he would have to use a helicopter, otherwise he would be jammed in there. So I went looking for one and got him out of there.

That summer is when I started to notice Walter getting a lot of acne and his skin color not being quite right. In June of '98 I flew with my two daughters, Michelle and Melissa, to meet Walter in Lexington, Kentucky, to visit a tire dealer there. It was a big event, in fact the coach of the Kentucky Wildcats, Tubby Smith, was there. Everything was good and we're flying back and just talking in a private jet when I began to notice that his skin color wasn't good and he also had a lot of acne. At the time he was eating a lot of nuts and he was saying there was good cholesterol and bad cholesterol, and how certain nuts are good for you. That's the first time I noticed that there was something wrong by just looking at him. Then everything just kind of went out of control, and that's when I was shocked with a phone call from Ginny in early January a week or so before he announced the situation. That's when I got a phone call saying he had a liver ailment.

In early December 1998, Walter finally was able to find a time to go to the Mayo Clinic that worked with his busy schedule. It was then that his drastic reduction in body weight began, with Walter losing close to fifty pounds during December and January. An extensive battery of tests was run over the course of about two days in December at the Mayo Clinic.

Walter Payton: They came back with an initial diagnosis, saying it's definitely something with my liver and my bile duct, and they told me they needed me back as soon as possible for a more extended stay. That way, they explained, they can really focus in on that portion of the body and do more definitive tests. So I went up there on New Year's Eve and I stayed for about three and a half or four days. I actually stayed at St. Mary's—at the hospital and everything. It was after that round of tests that they came back with a diagnosis of primary sclerosing cholangitis (PSC). That was when we knew it was serious, that was when they told me I was going to need a transplant.

They explained the different levels of how serious things get, and it was like Level 1A is when you've got hours to live; 1B is you've got weeks to live; 2A is like a month; 2B is a few months. I was at a Level 3, where they figured I probably had a year or two at that point, that's what they said.

Walter was placed on a liver transplant list, a list that disregards human accomplishments such as winning a Super Bowl or being in the Hall of Fame. He was simply and sadly another name on a long and growing list of sickly patients who needed healthy livers.

Walter Payton (to Larry King): Well, you have to accept what they tell you, because if you ever go into denial, you waste time. I realized that at this particular point the doctors that were working with me were the best in the business, so it was sort of like when I had Coach Ditka. I just said I'm going to believe in his philosophy and I'm going to do as he tells me because he's going to take us to the Super Bowl. It was the same way with this doctor, I just used the same philosophy.

Mike Lanigan: Walter was supposed to get five treatments of chemo, and I think he only took three because there was some test that indicated his cancer count was going down, so he thought he had it beat. He had a difficult time handling the chemo, and so when his count went down and his liver was continually starting to fail, they actually considered giving him a transplant anyway. They brought him in to make sure that the cancer did not spread, because they knew there were two small tumors in the bile duct. If it did not spread, they were going to give him a beeper. They wanted to go in and do an exploratory. They cut him from rib to rib—in fact, Crazy Guy showed it to me two days later; I almost puked. When they opened him up he got the bad news that it had spread to the lymph nodes. I called up Ginny that next morning, because I was in Panama at the time, we have a branch in Panama—she said he had three months to live if he doesn't do anything, six months if he goes through chemo but it won't save his life. She told me, "You better give him a call, he's really down in the dumps." I called him on his mobile and acted like I was not aware of what he was going to tell me. I said, "Walter, how are you doing?" He said, "Well, Mikey, I got some good news and I got bad news. Which one do you want to hear first?" I said, "What do you mean, Walter?" He says, "What do you want to hear first?" "Tell me the bad news." He says, "Mikey, I'm not going to be around very much longer." I say, "Oh, don't tell me that, Walter. . . . What's the good news?" "I'm alive today." Think about that. That was his attitude from then on. He knew he wasn't going to live long, so he wanted each day to be special.

I was crushed. Obviously, number one, there's not that many Walter Paytons in this world. The example he left to the young people . . . they just don't make them like him anymore. Walter never turned down an autograph for a kid, ever. I went to a lot of car races with him, I hung around with him for a long time in public. He always had a smile on his face and he never turned down an autograph. I was with him at a race in Miami. Have you ever seen these transporters where they carry the race cars? Well, it's a big fancy trailer that they put the race cars in, and they work on the cars and all the tools are in there. He's sitting on the end of this thing, and there is a line of people that just went on and on and on. He's just autographing and getting pictures taken with the young people. The line never stopped. I think he was there for at least forty-five minutes, minimum. He went in the back of the truck to get a glass of water, and I closed the trailer. I said, "Well, that's it," I started closing the door because I figured he was done. He chewed my ass off. He told me, "Don't you ever, ever close me off when there's children out there, don't ever turn them down." He was an amazing man.

15

Press Conference

It has become a rite of passage for the elite-level high school athletes in America—a sort of preinduction induction into the hoopla that surrounds big-time college football and basketball. The setting is usually the athlete's high school, usually in the dingy gym, and usually with wide-eyed classmates waiting alongside the unblinking eyes of local television cameras and slovenly newspaper reporters. In the front of the room, at a podium or a table, will be the young man, flanked by those who have been the most influential in helping him reach this moment—his parents, his coach, maybe his teammates.

So it was, at Chicago's St. Viator High School on Friday afternoon, January 29, 1999, that senior Jarrett Payton—the nation's fifty-eighth best football player overall according to *The Sporting News*—sat with his mother, Connie, and his father, Walter. The only son of Connie and Walter, Jarrett was born the day after Christmas in 1980, less then a week after Walter finished his sixth season with the Bears. During that 7–9 campaign, Walter rushed for 1,460 yards and six touchdowns on his way to his fourth of nine Pro Bowl appearances.

Jarrett's neon-bright smile was so very reminiscent of his dad's grin, and his fledgling athletic career another reminder of the apple falling so close to the tree. At St. Viator, Jarrett had been a standout soccer player before turning to football, where he played quarterback, tailback, and receiver, accumulating 2,842 all-purpose yards in his All-American senior year. Used sparingly on defense, he had also managed to pick off two passes in his final season.

Admittedly the Payton name attracted attention, but it was Jarrett's athletic skills—at six-feet-two and 210 pounds, he ran a 4.3 in the 40 and bench-pressed three hundred pounds—that intrigued the major college scouts the most. When he had finally narrowed his list of suitors down to three Big Ten schools—Wisconsin, Indiana, and Penn State—and one Big East program, Miami, Jarrett and his parents sat down on that Thursday night and hashed out the particulars of each institution. Just before midnight, Jarrett made his decision.

At the press conference the next day, Jarrett said: "I almost didn't take my last two visits to Penn State and Miami. My mom, who came with me on all the visits, was getting tired of all the travel. But like a trouper, she went.

"When I went on my visit to south Florida, I fell in love with it. I enjoyed being in a place where it is warm," he said. "I also liked that it is a smaller, private school where I can get a great education."

Jarrett Payton, the son who had introduced his father at Walter's Hall of Fame induction ceremony in Canton, Ohio, had chosen the University of Miami.

Unfortunately, as the Payton family discovered when they turned on the local news that evening, Jarrett's announcement wasn't the only news of the day. Instead of reveling in Jarrett's big decision, the Paytons heard the local sports reporter Mark Giangreco utter, as footage from the press conference ran, something to the effect of "The man there who looks like Gandhi is the former Walter Payton."

It was a cruel, cheap shot from an irresponsible member of the media. Beyond the element of shock the words delivered, there were also slivers of a truth Walter had been avoiding for several months: Walter's appearance was so bad that now everyone was wondering what was up. Despite the fact it went against his very private nature, the decision was made to announce Walter's disease publicly. One of the toughest, most durable, and most competitive men to ever put on a uniform was being weakened by a rare and horrible disease, primary sclerosing cholangitis. The man known as Sweetness was at once sad and sickly. Not to mention, as he would boldly admit, scared.

Deep brown eyes that once darted from linebacker to safety were now yellow and lifeless, often hidden by sunglasses. He was everything we always wanted in our athletic heroes—he touched many with his fierce approach to the game, his dedication to excellence, his sense of humor, and his humility. Walter Payton's life went beyond what he accomplished on the football field, and now his life—and his disease—were going to impact a nation.

Walter Payton: At the time of Jarrett's announcement, I had lost so much weight and was visibly sickly-looking. My face was broken out. I had lost a tremendous amount of weight. I looked and felt very tired. The doctors had explained to me how serious things were, but I had not digested what had been said. They hadn't really sat down and mapped it out for me, so I did not have the full end result at the time of Jarrett's announcement to tell anybody what I was going through.

At Jarrett's press conference, I wanted to deflect attention from me and I wanted the focus to be on my son, so I made a comment that I was doing a lot of running, training for a marathon, which was me being my typical jokester self and I think I did that out of self-defense.

But that night, as we watched TV, Mark's Gandhi comment was certainly an impetus for me going public about my health. Nobody likes to hear that stuff about themselves. You see, in today's world of journalism, every reporter has their "thing" to get them noticed. It seems that smart-aleck comments, which may be comical at someone else's expense, are acceptable. Sure, I took it to heart. That upset me beyond what you can imagine. I had felt betrayed. They, the town of Chicago, wanted to—if they could have had a modern-day lynching—they would have with Mark because it was very apparent that I was very emotional about him and what he had said.

That comment from him stirred the pot to the masses. Eventually, I made up with Mark over the incident; life is too short to hold grudges. I can't waste my time being angry at anybody. But at the time, it got to me. It hurt me.

Connie Payton: Walter was going to have to do something because it was obvious to people that something was wrong.

We told him, "We can't hide it." And Walter would say, "But it's nobody's business," because he was such a private man, but I'd say, "Maybe it isn't, but you're not any ol' body, and you're out in public, and people know you and they know what size you were. And they know something was up when they saw you go from 210 pounds, or whatever, down to the 180-something." I told him, "Sure, I wish we could just live this and do it ourselves, but we can't, we can't."

He really just didn't want to have to deal with the public with it, he really did not. But then when Mark said that, I think it really took that to get him to understand. It was hard for us to put up that façade, honestly. And then you get to the point where you don't know what to say anymore, and you don't want to take the phone calls, and people are still seeing you and wondering what's wrong.

But you know what? The way I look at it—it was almost a dream come true to have what happened with Mark happen. Because now you have to address it, and you might as well get it off your back because you can't hide it. Why not just go on and make it public? Let people know and then you're free to not have to tell people that you're training for a marathon, when you know you're not. But when

Walter saw that and then the phone started ringing from everybody else who had seen and heard it, then he knew.

We were shocked when we watched it, we couldn't believe that. It was like, "No, he didn't just say that, did he?" Brittney was like, "That's mean," and I said, "I know dear, I know it is."

Right after that I said to Walter, "People may as well hear the truth from you," and then he realized he had no choice and it was time to have a press conference. I just think it was something he was dreading to have to do.

Walter Payton: I felt that this was nobody's business. Why couldn't this be a personal fight? Everyone was telling me the same thing about needing to make things public. They said I had to do it because it wasn't fair, it wasn't fair to myself and it wasn't fair to my family. People were starting to think it was AIDS or whatever, so my staff really sat down with me and said, "Walter, listen, this has to be addressed."

Ginny Quirk: On Monday, February 1, when Walter came in to the office, we had one of the most difficult conversations in my decade and a half working for him. Too many people had been inquiring that something was very wrong with Walter. . . . They were speculating that he had contracted the AIDS virus. Since this was definitely not the case, it was not fair to Walter or his family for this type of rumor to exist. Due to the fact that we had just learned a week prior as to the actual diagnosis of PSC, we needed to hit this speculation head-on. We needed to call a press conference and set the record straight. By coincidence, Walter was scheduled for his last weekly radio show at a suburban restaurant the next day. Walter's response was that if we have to do it, then let's do it tomorrow.

The day of the press conference felt surreal. Behind the scenes it was an extremely emotional experience. Walter didn't want to burden his family with the public intrusiveness of a press conference even though Connie and Jarrett were there for moral support. Walter tried to make the press conference very matter-of-fact, but that just couldn't be done. Walter was emotionally taxed and broke down at the end of the press conference. This was to be the beginning of a journey of which we had no idea where it was going to take us. We hadn't put in the due diligence to even begin to understand what a liver transplant would truly mean. That would be forthcoming in the following weeks and months, when we would come to realize how grave the situation actually was.

Kim Tucker: A man who didn't acknowledge weakness was about to face his in front of the world. Walter was a here-and-now personality, so when he made his decision, he said, Tomorrow seems good. So within twenty-four hours the world was to share in his pain. No one in our office could ever have imagined how our lives were about to change.

Before Walter went to face the world he asked Jeanie Ortega-Piron, a friend, to say a prayer. With his family and friends by his side, we gathered into a circle and were led into one of the most beautiful prayers I had ever heard.

After the press conference, Walter had to fly back to Mayo for some tests. Ginny and I were still at the press conference talking over strategy when Walter called and said, "Meet me at the airport." I'll never forget pulling up and seeing Walter dancing out by his car with the music real loud, and he looked so peaceful and so happy. He said he was spending some time with God and felt like dancing, which was so fitting because it was one of his favorite things to do. At that time we discussed some of the issues. We wanted Walter to know that we were going to take on the full burden of dealing with this issue concerning the media and the public, and we assured him that we would handle everything to the best that we could. We wanted him just to focus on getting better and not worrying about all the things that he would worry about. Walter was always concerned about his fans and making sure that all the phone calls were answered. Well, all of a sudden floodgates were about to open and we were to receive hundreds of thousands of letters, so many phone calls that we could have stayed on the phone twenty-four hours a day. We just assured him that we would handle everything in a very professional and very polite way, but all we wanted him to do is just get better. We ended the meeting with a group hug because we always had our group hugs. At that point Ginny and I tried to stay strong. We drove him to the front of the airport. When he left and was walking off, that was the first time that we just couldn't control ourselves and we had to sit there for a while and just cry because it was a major turning point and we knew it at that moment. The reality of the situation had just hit us in the face and there was no turning back.

Upon my arrival home, my nephew Bradley Pardo Tucker, whose legal guardian I am, was waiting up for me. He was very upset that I hadn't told him Walter was sick. He had seen the conference on TV. Bradley looked at Walter as a father figure. Bradley told me he had a solution to the problem; he would give Walter his liver. I proceeded to tell him that he couldn't live without his liver. He said, "It doesn't matter, Walter means so much to so many people. I am only ten years old and the world would not miss me, but it will miss Walter." I said that he couldn't give Walter his liver and he started crying hysterically.

Later on that night Walter did *Larry King Live* and he called to say how things were going and to tell me that afterwards, when he had walked through the airport, for the first time ever, he walked through that airport and no one recognized him. No one approached him for an autograph, no one came up and said he was their favorite person. I think he knew when he wasn't recognized that everything's about to change, and it did. But through all of this, we all stayed together as a unit and as a team. I think all in all with God's help, we did the best we could to provide the information and comfort to the public and the media. We all knew then, all the years of working together and all the hard work, that we all could be very proud of our accomplishments with Walter, and proud that we were here at this time in his life to help him through one of the most difficult challenges that he could ever face, and for us to be able to say to him that he will not have to face this alone was the biggest gift we could give back to him.

Walter Payton: I knew deep down that I had to be proactive. If I did it on my terms, I'd be in the driver's seat. If I was reactive, I wouldn't have been. Like I said, it's not that I wanted to do the press conference, but at the same time I understood the merit. Things had happened so quickly, my appearance had changed so quickly, literally in an eight-week period from December to January. I realized that I had to take control. I knew that I couldn't hide my physical appearance.

And at that point also, because I knew that I had no choice but to have a liver transplant, it then became an issue that I couldn't handle it without people knowing about it. I knew at that point that I wouldn't be able to get through it all without all the information being out there. So I realized I might as well just lay it out on the table, and just get it out there so people would have the accurate information.

I was scared. Again, I am a very private person. I really did have a lot of hesitation and I really went into deep thought about it because my private life was all I had. That little part of my life was all I had, because I gave everything else away, publicly. To now know I was going to be completely public, I wasn't going to have a private life anymore—I had to really think about it. In doing so, at that point I really understood what it was to be a parent in the respect that I came out because of my children, not even so much for myself. I didn't want Brittney going to school and hearing things. I didn't want Jarrett going off to college and having me be the brunt of jokes with my visible weight loss and all these things. So at that point especially, after I really thought deeply about it, it didn't take me long to realize I had no choice. Really, once my people met with me and really had a heart-to-heart talk with me, I had to go with it. I knew if I thought about it too long, I would hedge or maybe I wouldn't do it. I wasn't willing to give up the only part of my privacy I had left, but I knew after those talks, I had to.

I couldn't talk about it to anybody, I just had to do it. Just run that hill. You get up that hill to a point that you can't turn around, that the hill's controlling you, and that's how I thought about this situation. The situation at this point was controlling me. Remember that I knew about the seriousness of the illness only ten days before the press conference. It's not easy to just orchestrate a press conference and tell the world about a very personal and intimate problem. To add to matters, my personality is that of a loner. I always have kept my problems to myself. If it were entirely up to me I would never have had a press conference.

The press conference was held at Carlucci's restaurant, in Rosemont, Illinois, on February 2, 1999. Walter, in black-frame sunglasses with a rose tint, wearing a black leather Fox Sports jacket and a gray button-down shirt, sat at a table with Jarrett to his right. He kept his emotions in check until he neared the end of the press conference, when he was asked if he had a message for his fans. Fighting back tears, his shaking right hand holding a local radio station's microphone, his left hand rubbing his forehead, Walter said, "To the people that really care about me, just continue to pray. And for those who are gonna say what they want to say, may God be with you also." At that moment, Jarrett reached out to hug his father.

The man who Chicago fans never saw run out-of-bounds, who never gave up in his pursuit of the goal line, was being overcome by emotion in the realization that his most fearsome opponent was something unseen and not to be explained in a scouting report.

Walter Payton: It was awkward at the press conference. I have spoken in front of large gatherings hundreds of times, of course. But talking to the press after you rushed for two hundred yards is a very different thing than talking about a private health issue. Most of the media that were at the press conference covered me during my play-ing career. I know these guys. So answering personal questions to this group was very uncomfortable.

I almost made it through without breaking up. It just kept build-ing inside of me until I couldn't hold it in any longer. I just broke up. I remember Jarrett reaching out for me. Funny how it comes full circle—he was there to pick up his old man. Jarrett and I just hugged each other. We didn't say any words. We didn't have to.

You know, during the press conference I said I wanted everyone to pray for me and that's also when I said, "And for you that are going to say what you're going to say, may God be with you too." I was di-recting that statement at Mark and the people who I heard had been whispering that I had AIDS or was doing drugs.

At the press conference, it was just a strange feeling for me, a very strange feeling. For years I felt I had carried my team. I was the one they could look to. But there, at the press conference, at that time, for the first time, I felt I needed to be carried, and I needed to be car-ried by those who loved me. I came out and explained what was going on for those people, not my critics.

Connie Payton: The day of the press conference was the first time I had seen him cry about his illness. At that time, all we knew was that he needed a liver transplant and there was no doubt in our minds that it would happen, then he was going to be fine. We didn't have the other condition to think about yet. It hurt me to see him vulnerable.

Walter is used to being strong and in control, therefore it was hard for him to sit there in front of all those people admitting his ill-ness. He wanted to deal with this chapter of his life with family and close friends, now he was telling the world. We were dealing with the situation, but how would the rest of the world handle it?

It was just going through all the preliminaries to get to this point. But I sort of felt that once we got through the press confer-ence, it would be fine, because it would be a monkey off his back and he could relax. Even though he didn't owe anyone any explanations, he still had to feel a little bit freer.

The reaction to Walter's announcement was one of shock and sadness, but also one that very much represented what Walter was all about. Almost everyone who had known Walter, or had been touched by him in some way, knew that of all people, Walter Payton would be strong enough to battle through his disease.

Mike Ditka: The one thing I told people after the press conference was that Walter would show us how to fight. He'll show everybody in the world how to fight. I thought, Maybe that's the lesson that's gonna come out of this, that people have to learn that you never throw the towel in, you'll never quit fighting—because that's what I was sure Walter was gonna show, I'm telling you that.

The news, and the press conference especially, hit even the most hardened of Chicago's legendary press corps, not to mention the national media that flocked to the story. In the days following the press conference, Walter appeared on *Oprah, Larry King Live,* and *CBS This Morning,* to name a few. His announcement was front-page news throughout the country and columnists from coast to coast shared the emotion of the moment.

Walter's tough decision—telling the world he might be dying—proved a lesson for many. His plea for prayer led thousands to light a candle for him.

The day after the press conference, the *Chicago Tribune*'s John Kass wrote:

It was his pride, and that can't be translated by highlight films of brilliant runs. It was in that perfect technique on meaningless plays late in the game when he wasn't even carrying the ball. It was in his determination to deny what hurt him, to distract focus away from the vulnerability, such as the broken rib. Walter Payton tried to use the same techniques of distraction on Tuesday, first on his radio show and later at the news conference where he formally announced that his liver was diseased and that he needed a transplant to live. Instead of a bad shoulder or a ripped toe, what threatened him on Tuesday was emotion. He tried to keep it away from him, to deny it. But this time it didn't work.

He was gaunt, his flesh receding—but if his liver was ruined, his heart was the same. . . . Payton didn't want to break down. He said he wanted to keep his emotions private. He didn't want to cover his head with his arm and cry. It's not his way. It never has been. But we in the media aren't linebackers. We understand the emotional harmonics of vulnerable people in public situations. It's a technique of the ear, an unfortunate skill, to listen to the empty spaces while prodding. So the tuning forks were properly pitched, and the rhythms were noted and reinforced. The photographers got ready. And the result was inevitable.

Earlier, on his radio show, Payton avoided the questions about his health, slapping them aside. He reluctantly agreed that his son, Jarrett, who will play college ball in Miami, is faster than he was, and wisecracked his bad time in the 40-yard dash was "my white man's speed." . . . Then it came time for Payton and his doctor and family to sit down at that table and tell their story of his illness. He said he held the news conference to knock down wild speculation about what was wrong. . . . After he said he wanted a transplant and was praying for the best, there was a push for more from him. He knew what they wanted, and it wasn't about the liver.

He saw it coming, and several times he said he'd only answer a few more questions. You could see it in the tightness of his mouth, how he waved his hand nervously, as if to stop it all before he broke. Payton knocked down a few of those questions with some jokes. But the rhythm had already been set. Someone asked if he was scared. "Am I scared? Hell, yeah, I'm scared. Wouldn't you be scared? But what can you do? Like I said, it's not in my hands anymore. It's in God's hands. . . . If it's meant for me to go on and to be around, I'll be around. If it's not meant for me, it won't be meant for me."

Then another question about his future, and another about family. And finally, the one about whether he had a message for his fans, as if we hadn't been listening. That was the one that did it. And we cried with him.

The media cried. Like Walter and so many others.

16

Organ Donorship

It's a simple thing, really. One of those things that certainly requires some thought, but once the decision is made, the act itself—agreeing to become an organ donor—is quite rudimentary. But there are over 12,000 people on the national waiting list for a new liver, and over 55,000 on the waiting list for an organ transplant of some kind. Both of those lists could be drastically reduced if more people agreed to become organ donors, an action as simple as signing your name.

Still, the need for organ donors and general organ donor awareness is something many individuals and organizations alike have been trying to educate people about for many years. What makes the campaign so important—especially for liver donations—is that the success rate for liver transplants in adult patients is better than 80 percent.

Obviously, when a high-profile celebrity like Walter is put into the spotlight, it draws attention to the cause. Granted, the number of cadaver-donated liver transplants steadily increased from

1988 through 1998 (according to data supplied by the Richmond, Virginia–based United Network for Organ Sharing), the numbers are still not where they should be.

As uncomfortable as Walter might have been sharing his disease with the nation, he knew that his situation might be able to make a difference in the lives of others, and therein lies one of the most significant and enduring legacies of Walter Payton.

Almost immediately, Walter became a very desirable spokesman for organ donation. He himself was an organ donor and he was also on a waiting list for a liver. Within days of his February 2, 1999, press conference and the announcement that rocked the nation, Walter was contacted by producers of the CBS television show *Touched by an Angel*. They wanted Walter to tape a commercial encouraging viewers to agree to donate their organs. Suddenly, the man who wanted to keep his health concerns private was being asked to do very public things in hope of helping others.

Walter Payton (in commercial): For the past few weeks, *Touched by an Angel* has been exploring the true meaning of honor and courage. Along with me, over sixty thousand Americans are awaiting organ transplants. Only half of us will receive them unless a real hero steps forward like you. Please consider signing your donor card, and make sure you discuss this with your family. Thank you.

Maybe the most amazing thing that can be said about Walter Payton is this: By the time he was able to tape the commercial, Walter had learned that he had cancer and likely would not be getting a transplant. Still, he stood before the camera, never mentioned his plight, and begged America to give. He didn't pout. He didn't cry.

The man who never ran out-of-bounds and never avoided contact was, once again, moving ahead with full force. Several large national and regional organ donation groups reported a significant increase in inquiries in the days following Walter's announcement and his various appearances on national television shows. Walter's word was making a difference.

On February 4, an editorial on page 22 of the *Chicago Tribune* read in part: "Only now, the one they called 'Sweetness,' the running back who carried the Chicago Bears in the years building to Super Bowl XX, that same Walter Payton is utterly dependent on another human being. And that human being could be you. Or someone in your family. Payton may hold the National Football League's career rushing record with 16,726 yards, but his name will now become just one of 12,190 on waiting lists for a liver transplant. Then again, if his being there helps shorten those lists, score another victory for No. 34. It's likely that the greatest running back in NFL history, now just 44, will be dead in two years unless he obtains a healthy liver from an organ donor. . . . Sweetness needs help this time. Next time it could be someone you love."

Walter Payton: I guess what surprised me most as I read and learned more about organ donation was how few people participate, but how those who do have the greatest peace in death because they might provide life for someone else. I learned that families of organ donors deal better with death because they know—in a strange way—that part of that person lives on. Their death had some sort of a happy result. All that is real. So why do people not sign up? Did you know that in Illinois alone, less than half of those eligible have signed on to the donor registry kept by the secretary of state's office? Here in Illinois alone, I read there are 3,700 people on the waiting list kept by ROBI [the Regional Organ Bank of Illinois], more than a thousand of them waiting on a liver. When they first told me that I would die only if they couldn't get me a liver in two years, I thought, No problem. What are the odds that won't happen? Then I found out the odds might not be so good. Think about this: Ten Americans die every day while waiting for an organ. It doesn't make any sense. Think about this too: There is no way, if everybody agreed to organ donation, that there would be any list at all.

If I can say anything in this book, it is *please* sign the donor's statement on the back of your driver's license; make sure you're listed as a donor with the right group in your state; and tell your family about your wishes. That last thing is really important, because some states still require that your family agree to your decision. So make sure they know this is what you want to do.

At first, because I had such a hard time going public with my disease, I wasn't really concentrating on what the reaction would be and what the obligations would be. But I knew, after being the teammate of all those great Chicago Bears players throughout the years, it was time for me to join some new teammates. Those teammates—that's what I started calling the twelve thousand people waiting for liver transplants and the 55,000 other people waiting for a kidney, heart, lung, or other transplant—those were the most important teammates of my life. It was an incredible eye-opening experience for me. To be honest, it made me realize how vulnerable I was, how vulnerable we all are. I had always been the picture of health, I always took care of myself. And then this happens and I'm just kind of in awe for a little while.

People ask if I have yelled at God for this or if I ever questioned, Why me? Truthfully, I haven't. I don't feel sorry for myself, because that's the first step toward giving up and I'm not giving up. I know something good is going to come of this. I just haven't figured out what it is yet. Maybe it is organ donation and that's what I started to focus on. I think my good friend and former coach Mike Ditka put it best when he said that the greatest gift anyone can give is, through death, to give life to another person by being an organ donor. I knew I had that chance to help others and I knew I had to do it.

Matt Suhey: I believe that he always felt strongly about organ donation, but he didn't want to appear that he only became involved in it due to his own circumstances. That was hard for him, because he didn't want it to seem he was jumping on a bandwagon. That kind of reaction always bothered him. I know he was really touched when he heard people were signing their cards and calling donor groups after his press conference. He asked me to help him with one appearance for organ donation awareness, and I couldn't have been prouder.

Walter Payton: It's kind of strange when you think about it—being a pro football player for thirteen years, I probably wore out just about everything in my body, but if there's something in there that somebody can use, well, I think they should be able to use that. Again, I go back to what Mike Ditka said, how in death you can give life, and there is no better gift than that. I think a lot of people should look at that now. I know there are religious reasons and everybody thinks of other reasons, but I'm just letting people know that it's something we can all, at the very least, look at.

Perhaps what made Walter's announcement even more shocking to those around him and those who had watched his Hall of Fame career was that Walter was always the very specimen of physical strength. Many of those who had played with Walter or closely followed his career were amazed that a man who had always played through pain, and had always been so physically dominant, was stricken with this debilitating disease.

Jim McMahon: Well, that's what was tough because he was the strongest guy I'd ever seen. If anybody could have kicked this, it would have been Walter. I think had it just been the liver problem and not the cancer, then maybe, but I've seen it eat away people like that. He must have weighed 120 pounds when he died. It's like ninety pounds that he lost in less than a year. It was devastating. It sucks, man. Life's unfair sometimes, you know. Here's a guy that did everything to his body, he couldn't break it in thirteen years on the field. This one little thing, though. . . . There were all kinds of weeks that, at midweek, he couldn't practice. He could hardly walk. He didn't want medication, he didn't want to get shots. He refused to get shots. Then, come Sunday, he'd play. He was Mr. Consistency.

And that was because he had such great conditioning, such great health.

Walter Payton: Yeah, there's some truth to that. I'd play games where I couldn't raise my right hand above my head. I didn't have enough strength in it to raise it up. But I wasn't going to miss a game because of that. There were times when you get hit, when you bounce back up, then it instills in the person's mind who tackles you or who's hitting you that maybe he hit you with his best shot, maybe you felt it but then you didn't show it. Maybe he thinks, he says, "Wait a minute—I hit this guy with all I had and he gets up like that?" And I've never let anybody intimidate me, because if they intimidate you, then you may as well not even play the game. That is how I think you should approach everything. If you admit defeat, why play?

Mike Ditka: I used to watch him even when I was an assistant coach at Dallas when he was playing with the Bears and we'd marvel at some of the things he did. He was a good player, but I don't think you ever understood how good he was until you saw him every day in practice. His conditioning he did on his own. His regimen was much harder than any NFL strength coach's regimen. He had a regimen that defied what the U.S. Marines were doing. He came to camp in the best shape, he never asked to be taken out of anything. At the end of his career, his knee blew up a little bit and we'd cut down a little bit in practice. He was a warrior, he was an old-style football player. You could not describe his running style if you wanted to. There's no way. You could say, Who does he run like? He doesn't run like anybody who's ever played. Nobody runs like him. Nobody has the ability to change direction and run with the power he had. He only played at 195, basically, that was his weight. Maybe he got up to two hundred, but it was always around 195. He was a power back who had great change of direction, great anticipation, great instincts, great vision. He didn't have overall great speed. Speed wasn't the greatest asset he had. He had the ability to stay

ahead of people chasing most of the time, but that wasn't his
strength. His strength was his heart because that's the way he played
the game, with his heart. He willed himself to be what he became.
He became the best football player, like I said, I've ever seen, and I
think he willed himself to that. If you were gonna say that the talent
would have taken him there— There were guys who had more talent, but they didn't have the will to do what he did.

Walter Payton: I think basically it's total concentration and a little
mind control. If you think hard enough and you will things to happen, they're gonna happen. If you think negative about things,
they're gonna be there. So what I try to do is I try to get in a positive
frame of mind, think of something that happened in my life that's
good, or something that might happen in my life that's good, and
then concentrate on that and that blocks out a lot of the pain.

With all his amazing skills and his health throughout his youth, the
question does persist: Why Walter? Why would this happen to such
a good and decent person?

Pam Curry: I never questioned God. I guess that was instilled in us
at a young age, because if you believe anything—there are some
things you have to take a stand on, some things you have to believe
in, and I believe the Word of God. He said all things work together
for the good of those who love the Lord and are called for His purpose. His purpose may not have been for Walter to play football, or
it might have been for him to play football and to accomplish what
he did at that time, but also to carry this cross to allow people to
know there is a need for organ donors. I hope that's his legacy. I hope
that's his legacy, more so than even football, because when you look
at it, that's so much more important. How amazing when you touch
a life and that person can live and become anything they want to become.

Kim Tucker: Out of all the business and charity work Walter and I were involved in together, the most important bond we shared was our love for Father God. Even though there were times in Walter's life he may have backslid, he always knew God had blessed him. I will never forget the countless hours we spent talking about heaven and angels, especially the archangel Michael. We both share a very special connection to the chief warrior angel. We also discussed how magnificent spending eternity with Jesus would be.

Eddie Payton: I had seen people close to me endure through cancer, so I understood the stages that they go through and how quickly it happens. The body is just a machine, anyway. When the machine breaks down, it rots, and it no longer functions. It just can't. The body can't heal itself regardless of what you were, how great an athlete you were, or how your body had taken care of you for all those years. When it stops, there's nothing you can do about it and you are gonna go back from whence you came. We put all the time into building our body, weight training and watching our diet so it can work at maximum efficiency. It's just a machine, and when the machine breaks down, it can no longer be fixed, it's gonna rot. When you've seen it and you have to deal with it, you can understand it. I know that Walter understood that and wasn't upset. He wasn't upset with himself, he wasn't upset with God or anybody. It's kind of a matter of fact in our family. We got it from our mother and father both. I mean dying is a part of living. From the day you get here— Dad always said from the day you're born, your clock doesn't run forward, it runs backwards. So you got to get the most you can out of every day that you're here. Walter did that. We all should. The one thing Dad didn't think of was that by giving organs, you can keep the clock running in someone else. That's what I got out of all this.

Mike Singletary: I will always remember Walter the great football player and Walter the champion for life. But there's something that I realized, and something that I always knew but I had never really seen it that way—that's a man who is created by God and was given a message to deliver. All of us are vulnerable at any moment, and as I looked at him in those final days I just— The glory of God was never more apparent to me than at that moment. When I say, "Walter was courageous," I mean courageous in coming to a realization that life is more than touchdowns. Life is more than all the great runs and everything else. Life is to be lived at every moment and you gotta be courageous in life and in death, and he was. He made a difference. We should all be so lucky.

Roland Harper: You do wonder and you say, Yeah, he was so young. But you know, we have a life on this earth that we take for granted each and every day. So many people do. Within a blink of an eye, if it's your time, it's your time. It's a sad thing because you're used to seeing a person walk on this earth, and you're used to talking to that person. My whole thing is that eventually I'm going to see that person again in heaven. I know that Walter is looking down and saying, Hey, I'll meet you up here when I can. Walter, like all of us, probably took his health and his good life for granted early on. But through his death, we've all learned something.

Walter's 55,000 teammates hope Roland Harper is right.

17

Like a Train Going Downhill

In the months between Walter's February 2, 1999, press conference and his death on November 1, 1999, many stories of Walter's rapid deterioration surfaced and many half-truths or outright lies were generated. It was during the fallout from his press conference that Walter asked his friends and confidants to grant him one wish: Don't tell anyone anything, keep the true state of my health here in our little circle. Tough as it was sometimes, Walter's friends did just as he asked. In answer to every question, they told the world Walter was just waiting for a suitable match for a liver transplant, the same statement Walter gave at the press conference.

Within weeks after the press conference, Walter's physician, Dr. Greg Gores of the Mayo Clinic, dropped another bomb: Walter was diagnosed with cancer of the bile duct, a vessel that carries digestive fluids from the liver to the small intestine. The exploratory surgery on May 10 revealed the cancer was in his lymph nodes, which was devastating news and certainly not the news Walter had wanted to hear.

"The malignancy was very advanced and progressed very rapidly," Dr. Gores said. Because the cancer had spread so rapidly outside his liver, a transplant "was no longer tenable." Walter found himself in a devastating catch-22—now that he had cancer, he was ineligible for a transplant, yet without the new liver, he really didn't have the strength to go through treatment to fight the cancer. When the cancer was discovered, things became even tougher for Team Walter— especially for the two women, Ginny Quirk and Kim Tucker, who were running Walter's office.

Kim Tucker: What people need to understand is that Walter could deal with getting a new organ. He understood that he needed it and with it, he could live, he could have a life. Walter himself was unwilling to accept the fact that he was gonna die. So, as the people in his life who were running his businesses, taking in the fan mail and doing those things that made WPI function, we were not going to take away his hope. If we had gone public and allowed everyone to know what the real situation was, it would have been in all the headlines. They would have ripped that hope out of his heart. When he was sick, he was watching television all the time. He was reading papers and magazines, something he never had time for before. Now he's laying in bed, he's tired. Now he was very aware of things he wasn't aware of before. He was watching the news all the time, and we were not going to allow the news reporters to just pound it into him that "you're gonna be dead soon." We owed him that hope. And we had to take the brunt of it as we had to take the brunt of everything throughout his career, as far as if somebody was unhappy. He could not be all things to all people. So to all those that he couldn't be, we got the beating, his office did. We were willing to take the beating for this because that was something he deserved, every person deserves.

Ginny Quirk: I believe we bought him time by keeping the truth from the public. Argue the point if you want, but that is what we wanted most . . . more time for Walter. From knowing where he was in early August, and the doctors said that it could be weeks, his strength and sheer belief that he could overcome anything is what kept him hanging on as long as he did. Imagine if Walter hadn't been able to sit outside on the porch and soak up the August and September sun and if he hadn't been able to go on drives with his friends. If there were cameras and reporters around the house, I believe he would have been taken much earlier. Those simple things were all he had to look forward to. He kept saying to me, "If I could just put on a little more weight, if I could just get my strength up, then I could go back to the Mayo Clinic and do some more chemo." I believe in my heart of hearts, that until the very end Walter believed that he was going to beat his disease. He felt he had the ability to lick anything that would come in this path.

Matt Suhey: When he got sick, the one issue that he felt very strongly about is that he wanted to be private, he wanted to beat this thing by himself, and he wanted to handle it like he wanted to handle it. He didn't want anybody else knowing about it.

Kim Tucker: He would sit there and eat and drink, just force it down, and that's when we were making the decision on the title of this book. That truly is why we decided on *Never Die Easy,* because Walter did not die easy. He fought to the very, very end. I think that one of the things that anybody reading this book can relate to is that you have to feed on the positive things. You have to have those around you being positive. If you've got everybody around you trying to throw reality in your face, that can't happen. No matter what the odds were against him, we were gonna give him that fight. He deserved that. He was in the boxing ring now one-on-one, and he didn't wind up winning, but he gave it a fight. A great, valiant fight.

Connie Payton: No matter what the doctors said, Walter made me promise that I wouldn't keep anything from him, that I would let him know everything. He wanted to know what he was up against. But I promised him that whatever they said I would let him know because he needed to know. He just wanted to be prepared. In other words, he didn't want anything to catch him by surprise.

Some of the doctors weren't sure about how much they should be telling Walter, but I told them I knew Walter better than most people, and I thought he should know because he deserved it. I would want to know what I'm facing if I was in his position. There's a sense of freedom in knowing the truth.

When Walter heard about the cancer—they actually always called it a tumor, so it never sounded so bad—it was almost like, Well, Doc, it's not what I wanted to hear but that's okay. That's okay because we're going to beat this thing. That was his thing.

Ginny Quirk: Right before the press conference and in the weeks thereafter, life was literally a blur. The media was relentless with requests for Walter interviews. Our response, for the most part, was that if Walter did one, he had to do them all, and that just wasn't feasible. Of course he did do *Oprah, Larry King,* and *CBS This Morning,* because of those shows' vast reach, but we had to be cautious, or the media, I believe, would have taken full advantage of the situation. In fact, members of the media who thought they were close to Walter couldn't understand why they weren't included in the loop.

Friends and family saw the weight loss and loss of strength and it shocked them. A man whom they had known for so long as a rock and a pillar and a physical specimen was shrinking before their eyes. But through it all, they remained positive so Walter would remain positive.

Mark Alberts: For the next eight months everyone close to Walter put on their game faces and did whatever we could to make things go as smooth as possible for Walter. We made sure he had chartered flights to Mayo and comfortable living arrangements. Matt would go to Rochester and keep Walter company. Matt organized a dinner for about ten ex-Bears, where they just shot the bull for hours. We always talked positively, thinking positive thoughts, not even entertaining the possibility that Walter wouldn't make it. If anyone could beat the odds, Walter could.

One of my fondest memories is Walter calling up and wanting to get out of the house and go for car rides. Connie, Matt, and I would alternate taking Walter for a drive. We would go to KFC, go for ice cream cones, go into the city and look at the cows on Michigan Avenue. We didn't have to say a lot to each other either. Sometimes we didn't say anything for fifteen minutes at a time. . . . I just drove with the sunroof open and Walter was freed from the confines of his bed for a couple of hours. Walter loved giving directions. He'd shout, "Turn here, hurry!" or "Make a turn over there. . . . What are you waiting for!" He loved to criticize my driving. . . . This coming from a man with *his* driving record!

One time, we got stuck in traffic and he started getting pains in his stomach. His cancer was very painful, and if he didn't self-medicate in a timely manner the pain would be severe in his stomach. Walter would try to rock himself until the pain went away. That time, I had to turn off the expressway and take side streets back to his home in South Barrington.

Every so often the media would call the office and want a statement of Walter's condition. "Everything's status quo," I would say. Once Walter went to a local hospital to get a simple treatment in lieu of going to Mayo. Well, some fan saw him at the hospital, called a sports station that Walter was admitted to a hospital, and the news stations ran the story, of course with the tone of impending doom. We physically had to go to the hospital and take him home. He flew to the Mayo Clinic the next morning for that "simple procedure" because of the press.

Walter would still have good days and bad days. On his good days he would actually get in his BMW and drive to the office, honk the horn outside of Ginny's window and motion for her to come down.

Once she went down to the car and saw a big dent in one of the head-lights. She said, "You shouldn't be driving, what happened to the car?" He said that he just "slipped" off the side of the road and knocked down a little tree . . . that's all.

Connie Payton: Being in his presence twenty-four hours made his weight loss somewhat unnoticeable. It was after returning from Miami in August 1999 that I truly noticed how frail he was. I made the comment to myself that he was fading away right before our eyes.

I then became thankful for the trip, which just days before was the saddest for me because I was taking our son, Jarrett, off to college. I hadn't been looking forward to acknowledging the fact that we now were the parents of a college student. Where had the years gone?

Walter and I had some serious decisions to make. His condition was getting progressively worse. His pain had become unbearable and the weight loss even more evident. I was frightened, but fear had no place because we were at war, we needed our minds to be clear.

We had not told Jarrett and Brittney about the cancer. Walter didn't want to burden them. I'm not sure if we made the correct de-cision, not telling them, but it worked out for all of our good.

Pam Curry: When my father died, then Walter took his place as being my pal and I would call him, or call his office, or call his cell phone. If something was bothering me, I would tell him. In certain instances he was more like a big brother than a little brother. Some of the things I remember when he was sick, and I told him—I sat on the bed and he was sitting down—and I told him on that bed, I said, "Daddy is gone. If you leave me I won't have nobody. You're all I got." And he hugged me and I cried. I didn't want to give him up and I didn't believe that I would have to.

He just held me and we just cried. He never wanted me to worry—I think he never wanted anybody in the family to worry. It grieves me and it hurts me to know that he carried this burden by himself.

Matt Suhey: Towards the end it was hard to see him fade the way he did. He was irritable when you would talk to him. He was pretty irritable towards the end. He was in excruciating pain. Yet he never complained. That was most amazing to me. He internalized everything. He didn't lean on anyone else.

All the times we went out for drives—to Dairy Queen or wherever—he never wanted to talk to anyone, and that wasn't like him. You looked and you'd see him for a couple of seconds, but the way he would look was . . . Boy, he was so thin at that time. He just didn't want to be put in that position, and he didn't really vocalize how he really felt about it. He didn't trust that many people. Why? I don't know. I have wondered that, especially in the last six to eight years. He just didn't believe in— He kept a lot to himself.

When people did recognize him, he was as gracious and as giving—especially to kids, especially to older grandmothers, those types—he was gracious and as polite and nice as anybody you'd ever want to meet, and very sincere about people. To be hounded and to talk to people day in and day out—to do it constantly, wherever you go out, you'd be mobbed, he was amazing. Wherever you are in Chicago, wherever you are, just the patience he showed was incredible. Walter was nice to everybody and just so gracious.

I went to the hospital three or four times, or I'd take him—he did not want the press to know that he had cancer—and we checked him in under other names so no one would know he was there. He wanted to fight it by himself, and I think he had every right to do that. That's the way he wanted it. So I was going to uphold that.

It wasn't easy getting him in and out of the hospital. As a patient, he hated needles. I mean, hated needles. Here we are, it was the best thing for him, and he's looking at a needle. It was difficult to get him to take that needle. The doctors were patient with him, but I think a few couldn't figure out how this tough guy could be frightened by needles.

When we went to Mayo for his radiation treatments—the radiation treatment itself, it would take about forty-five minutes to set it up—I'd look in the window and be nervous while he'd be joking around. He was so nice to those nurses and they were nice back to him. It is a remarkable place, Mayo. They were first-class. They were just incredible. The treatment didn't bother him that much, I was surprised about that.

Some people would recognize him. We went to a Timberwolves game one night, against the Lakers, and we saw Dick Stockton, and Hubie Brown was another guy. Of course, everybody recognized him. After the game we were outside the locker room waiting for the players to come out. Shaquille O'Neal came up and gave him a hug and told Walter that he had been Shaq's hero. It was such a classy thing to do, encourage him, that kind of thing. All the players did.

Mike Singletary: I first found out that he had cancer when he had come back from the doctor, several months before he died. He had this huge cut on his stomach and he said, "Man, this is painful." He told me he went to the doctor and they cut his stomach open, looked in there and found some things that they gotta work on. That's kind of how he talked about it, he never said the word "cancer." I think for him, to say "cancer" was like being in a game and saying that it's over. I think Walter understood the power of the tongue, the power of language. You don't speak death, you speak life. I think for him, cancer meant that. So it was just one of those words that I don't think he really wanted to say, and he didn't feel comfortable saying.

Roland Harper: It's amazing that he went from where he was in February to where he was in May, when he actually knew that he had cancer, and yet in that entire time no one knew anything. There were some rumors, but Walter managed somehow, as high-profile as he was, to maintain some privacy. That's the way he lived his life. He drew back from everybody and nobody knew, and he wanted to keep it that way. Toward the end, even at the time of his death, no one knew. I knew. I was there, I didn't go inside the house, I was outside. But I knew. It was the mental telepathy and I could just feel it.

John Gamauf: After he made the announcement of his illness on TV, I talked to him that same day. He was driving home, I called him on his cell phone, I said, "I saw you on TV, buddy, I love you. I'll do anything I can for you." About three days later, he calls me and he said, "Gam, I just do not want to sit around the house. I do not want to look at the four walls. I've got treatments, I've got this, I've got that. But I would love to continue speaking to your customers as I do with you because it's so enjoyable for me." I said, "Walter, we would love to do it," because I had like half a dozen speaking engagements lined up in January, February, March, April, right into May. He said, "As long as my health holds up, let's do it." I said, "Fine, and obviously I'm not going to let you fly commercial or anything like that, I'll get you a jet and we'll just start trucking."

We went to New York and that's when he did probably his most motivational talk, at a dealership called Wholesale Tire up in Long Island. It was his first real appearance since he made the announcement on TV, so obviously his weight loss was tremendous. A lot of these customers saw Walter at my meeting in '97 when he was built like a brick house. He had flown in the night before, I had picked him up at the airport, we got him a room in the presidential suite, and we just talked for about two and a half hours about life, and a lot of personal stuff. Walter either let you in or he didn't let you in. He let me in and it was really neat. He gave such a moving speech that day that it just made everybody really happy about what you have in life. He brought a kid up onstage, talked about family values, and was very unselfish about his health situation.

He reiterated what he said on TV—"Hell yes, I'm scared, but I'm not going to sit here and worry about it. The Lord's got it in His hands, and I'm going to say all the prayers I can and I appreciate all the prayers everybody else can say." He got it over with in about a minute or less. So it was like, Okay, that's that and now I'm here to talk, and that's what I'm going to do.

At that stage he knew he had cancer, but he didn't tell me. I think he kept that very tight between Ginny and his wife and Kim, and maybe a few select other people. He really kept that under lock and key. But I could tell he was getting sicker and sicker. After New York in March, we went to Cincinnati in April to do an engagement at Michel Tire. Also in early April we did Avellinos Tires in Philadelphia. His last one was in early May at the Tire Rack in South Bend, Indiana. Let me tell you, he was sick. When he got off the plane, he was doubled over, and I felt so bad. I said, "Walter, why did you bother coming?" He said, "Because I made a commitment and I really want to do this." I'd take him up to the hotel room and let him lie down on the bed for about a half hour to forty minutes just to kind of gather his energy. But then when he went downstairs and he came out in front of three hundred people, it was like nothing, he just hit it off. This was a real family business, the Tire Rack is, and they brought all the kids and relatives. He gave one of the most moving presentations ever.

Did I know that was going to be one of the last times I saw Walter? No. Did I know he was really, really sick? Yeah. Did he let it affect him? No. He just gave such encouraging words, and I can't remember everything he said, but he pretty much told everybody the same scenario—it's all in God's hands and God will take it from there. Whatever is meant to be is meant to be.

If you watched him in his playing days, you know how Walter was hurt so many times, but nobody ever knew it. He said so many times he was hurt so bad he couldn't even raise his arm above his shoulder, but he would never let anybody know about that. He would never let the defending team know, because then they would know there would be a weakness. So he would pretend he was invincible. That's the same way I saw him that day in South Bend. That's the same way he performed during his illness. He would never show the public that he was hurting. I thought that was so courageous that he would do something like that.

During the months after cancer was diagnosed, Walter continued to do public service announcements advocating organ transplants and tried to live as normally as he could. When Jarrett was called home from college, missing a game, all hell kind of broke loose, according to Mark Alberts. The press picked up on Jarrett coming home and one radio station in Philadelphia had actually reported that Walter had died. It became an ugly feeding frenzy and exposed the worst side of "real-time journalism." Walter had needed a liver transplant to survive, but due to the cancer, he would not be eligible for a transplant and therefore there was no solution—only the inevitable conclusion.

18

Remember Me

The letter arrived for Walter a few days after his press conference. It was one of thousands he would receive and be touched by. The outpouring of support and sympathy was something Walter was too humble to even conceive of. One letter in particular, which was later published in the *Chicago Tribune,* affected Walter deeply. It came from a little boy who wasn't even born when Walter was working his magic on the field, but the boy's magic letter had nothing to do with football. It had to do with life, which is exactly what Walter was focusing on:

Dear Mr. Payton,
My name is Christopher and I am nine years old. . . . I have [a liver ailment] too. My doctors don't know how I got it and they don't know what caused it. They don't even know a name for my sick liver. . . . I've got an enlarged spleen too. I can't play any sports so my spleen won't bust. I need it to help my

liver. I'm real popular at the hospital. They keep taking my blood to run tests, but they can't figure out why I have it. . . . I'm sorry that you have to go through all of this. I'll pray for you. Mommy said that God will take care of you, just like he's going to take care of me. Don't be scared, please. Maybe you can do tests with me at my hospital. Will you please write back?

> Yours truly,
> Christopher Cash
> Jonesboro, Georgia

Walter Payton: That letter . . . I read it over and over, even cried. How could I ever feel sorry for myself when there were tens of thousands of letters like this flooding into my office? All those letters and all those stories gave me perspective. I knew I wasn't going through any of it alone. I always knew I had my friends and family and loved ones for support, but letters like this showed me how big my support network really was. How far it reached. I think it also helped me to see that I had a unique position. I could help others by sharing my story and becoming active.

I had always been involved with children and organizations during my playing days. I always tried to help in any way I could. That letter brought back some memories of those days and it gave me some energy and drive to do whatever I could to help others and spread the word about transplants and their benefits.

All those letters I received keep me going. It is not often that you get to find out how many people you've touched. Through all of this, God has given me the chance to find that out. I want to say thank you to those who lifted me up.

Fan mail was always very important to me. I wanted to feel how my fans were feeling, and what impact I was making on their life because by reading them and understanding that, it kept me grounded and more in touch. It made me realize the effect I was having on an individual, and I did realize that I could spend five minutes with somebody and alter the course of their life in some small way. That is an enormous responsibility and I don't think enough of us take it seriously.

Connie Payton: I think it kind of blew him away, all the letters and the outpouring of love. If he ever doubted that people really loved and cared for him, he knew now, but I don't think he realized to what extent. It was a true sign that he really made an impact on many people's lives. It surprised us all. It really made him feel good. He knew too that all these people would be praying, because he had asked them to pray for him during his press conference. He really did believe in the power of prayer, and I did too. Just to know that people cared and were praying was a huge source of encouragement and strength. Walter was receiving from family, friends, and fans alike the greatest gift of all, *love.*

Walter Payton: I never had a problem in talking to somebody, and I realized that people listened to every word I said, so therefore I chose my words when I was around people. Even though I was a jokester with people, I did like to keep that side of myself within my circle of friends and family because that was truly me, but I looked at myself as a counselor in many instances when I was out in public. I took that to heart and I wanted to have a message. I always wanted there to be a substance so that when people look back, they would know I wasn't full of BS, that I had meaning in what I was saying.

Bill McGrane (former Bears publicist): Some years ago, he agreed to meet a boy before practice. The boy was ten, but he wouldn't see eleven—he had a brain tumor.

When Walter came out on the field to meet the youngster, a crowd began swarming, wanting autographs. He was polite but very firm. "After practice," he told the crowd. "I want to talk to Kevin now." He took the boy who was dying and the two of them walked to a far corner of the practice field, where they sat down on a blocking dummy. The boy had on a baseball cap because he didn't have much hair left. Walter grabbed the cap off his head and replaced it with his helmet. He wore the boy's cap. They talked for a long time. That fall, I heard the boy had died. I told Walter. He was upset about it, but he said something interesting, something poignant. He said it was all right, because the boy hadn't been fearful.

Likewise, of course, Walter was fearless in his battle the same way he was fearless on the field. It was a trait he was proud of, and a characteristic that had been ingrained in young Walter from an early age and reinforced in later years.

Walter Payton: My college coach taught me that—never die easy. I wasn't the biggest. I wasn't the strongest or the fastest. I do think I was the smartest. I was probably the runner who wouldn't go down easy. Like one of those cowboy movies where a guy is coming at him and he gets shot once and he gets shot again, and again and again, and he's still walking and then all of a sudden a big explosion goes boom, an arm over here, arm over there, leg over there and they're still trying to get him down. That's the type of runner I was.

Eddie Payton: I think Walter would most like to be remembered for the type of effort he gave, every play, he played like it maybe was his last play. He wanted that for people who watched, who may never get a chance to watch him again. He wanted to be remembered for giving his best on every play. It's amazing, when you go out and people see you do your best effort all the time and you do it in a professional manner, with respect for the game, it seems to help you rise above the average guy who does something average, jumps up, pounds himself on the chest, and says, "Look what I just did!" And fifty thousand people say, "You just did what you were paid to do." Walter never did that. People appreciate him for the blue-collar effort that he had and the manner in which he did it.

He never really talked to me specifically about how he would like to be remembered. All he said was that he wanted to perform for the guy sitting in row double P of the stadium, who works nine to five for minimum wage and brings his family and that's the only place he can afford to sit. I want him, when he leaves, to say, "I saw Walter Payton at his best." And whenever he went out to play, he went out with that in his mind. It's not for the people in the box seats who can afford to come to every game, it's for the guy who can only come once and you never know when that guy is there, so Walter was performing for those people.

He wanted the fans of Walter Payton, the football player, to remember him the way they saw him the last time he was at Soldier Field, when he was saying good-bye. A healthy, virile young man, he didn't want to be pitied, he didn't want any of that.

What he did want was to be remembered for what he did off the field, more so than what he did on the field. Maybe that was where Walter differed so much from some of today's prima donna athletes. There is always a perception by older generations that the younger generation doesn't do things the way they did. But for Walter, it went beyond that. It wasn't all about the game on the field for Walter. It went well beyond that.

Walter Payton: Athletes today don't understand what it is to be a hero. They are so caught up in the money and they are so caught up in the fame. Because when I started playing, there wasn't as much fame. The NFL wasn't a billion-dollar business. I started when it was pure football, it was the game. I played for the love of the game, and sheerly for the love of the game. I loved the game. The by-product was money and eventually for me, fame. But I was not in it just for that. Athletes today don't have team loyalty. It would have never occurred to me to leave the Bears. Never, ever. It was just home to me and I wasn't about to make another home elsewhere. I started there and I was going to end there, because otherwise it would have been selling out.

What happened when I looked at the international fan mail that came in after the announcement, there were, for the first time, letters that didn't want anything like an autograph or a picture. They were just people saying, I'm praying for you, I want to give you something, because I just respect you. That meant more to me than anything—knowing that people respected me.

I knew then that I accomplished what I had set out to accomplish when I entered the league, and that was to be a hero. I realized I did that through the respect of people, because you respect your heroes. I realized that for the first time and it gave me complete peace. I felt more at peace than I ever had with all those letters I had received when I was playing. I could never express to people how much I really felt their letters and cried at night and wished they were with me, not just their card, but that they were with me and holding my hand.

When I was able to look at the hundreds of thousands of lives that I've affected, I'm blown away. Because you know, you think, Well, I went out of my way to go and speak to this person, oh, I did this. You'd think after all these years, they would have forgotten. I've gotten fan mail from people that I met fifteen years ago and it still meant the same to them as the day I talked to them. I didn't realize—I really, for the first time, got it.

Mike Singletary: Walter taught me to smile and he taught me to be courageous. And the other thing he taught me was to be a professional and how to handle myself. There were some games that we played, there were times that he played against some great athletes. I don't care who they were, sometimes he would get the crap knocked out of him, bounce right back up. Bounce right back up. Wouldn't say a word, he would turn and give the ball to the referee, straighten up his helmet, and go back to the huddle. You knew at that moment he was saying, I'm coming back. Get ready, I'm coming back, and I'm coming with all I got. To me, that's what he exemplified. When I looked at him, no matter what I felt like before a game—when I saw him run with such courage and authority—I don't care who you were, he was going to dish it. He was gonna hand it out, he was gonna do the punishing, he was going to set the tempo.

What's amazing to me is I look at his life and I look at those last days and I know there was so much that he wanted to accomplish. I know there was so much he wanted to do. I think he was looking forward to getting back to "I cannot wait to get back, to get this over with so I can get back to telling people what life is really all about." He didn't get to tell anybody what life was really all about, but he got to show them. Life is about a fight, life is about a struggle. Life is about every day of your life being thankful for getting up. Life is about making a difference every day. Making a difference. I never heard him say, "Why me?" I want to tell you, I know I would have been saying, "Why me? Why me? There are other guys out there killing people and doing this—why me?" I never heard Walter say that.

Walter Payton: If you ask me how I want to be remembered, it is as a winner. Is a winner somebody who has success and basically accomplished something or wins a game or whatever? That's not a winner. You know what a winner is? A winner is somebody who has given his best effort, who has tried the hardest they possibly can, who has utilized every ounce of energy and strength within them to accomplish something. It doesn't mean they accomplished it or failed, it means that they've given it their best. That's a winner. That is what a winner is all about. It doesn't mean that, Oh, God, I've got a lot of money, I've got a lot of success. Everybody knows me and pats me on the back. Everywhere I go they open the door for me and they're giving me this, and they're giving me that. That's not a winner. That's fantasy. Everybody wants to live in that world, but it's not reality. What is reality? Hard work.

I want to be remembered as a person who, whenever he played the game of football, he left everything he had out there on the football field, did everything he possibly could for the team to win, not for himself. For the team to win.

That's the way everyone should really want to be remembered, that whatever they did, they did it as best they possibly could. That's all anyone should want in our life. It's not being the best, it's not winning this or not holding this record . . . but for people to say, While he was on the football field he gave all he had, and then when he was off the football field he was just that much of a person that you could relate to, that you could talk to, that he had feelings. That's what you want to be remembered as. Because football is a business. Walter Payton is a human being. If all I'm remembered for is a bunch of yards and a lot of touchdowns, I've failed. That was just my work. I want to be remembered as a guy who raised two pretty special kids and who taught them to be great people. Please have them write that about me.

All the honors are great, but personally I would ask that anyone who wants to pay tribute to me, for any reason, I would say there is one thing you can do above everything else and that is: Never let a day go by where you neglect to tell your loved ones that you love them.

Every day you live is a special day, even though sometimes it might not be easy to see that or understand that, but every day is a wonderful day, because you make it wonderful.

Make every day count. Appreciate every moment and take from those moments everything that you possibly can, for you may never be able to experience it again. Talk to people you have never talked to before, and actually listen. Let yourself fall in love and set your sights high. Hold your head up because you have every right to. Tell yourself you are a great individual and believe in yourself, for if you don't believe in yourself, it will be hard for others to believe in you. You can make of your life anything you wish. I hope my story is at least an example of that. Create your own life and then go out and live it with absolutely no regrets.

Most important though, if you *love* someone, tell him or her, for you never know what tomorrow may have in store. Remember, to-morrow is promised to no one.

19

The Memorial

Walter Payton died shortly after noon on Monday, November 1, 1999. Within hours, plans were in place for two memorial services, one private service for family and friends and one celebration of his life on Saturday at "Payton's Place," Soldier Field.

The private service drew many of those Walter knew as a child and those he grew to know as his celebrity multiplied. It was powerful and poignant. The media was not present, though a few reporter friends were invited as guests. It was, as the invitation said, closed.

It had the potential to be a difficult time, since determining who would be invited became an almost political exercise. Marcus Allen, for example, said he wouldn't come if O. J. Simpson was there, leaving those managing the event to inform O.J. he wasn't invited. The personal feud between Allen and Simpson surrounding Simpson's late wife meant the two couldn't even be at the same funeral together.

Though a few members of the media were invited as friends, no working reporters were allowed into the private service. Five speakers were chosen: Jarrett, Eddie, John Madden, Mike Singletary, and Mike Ditka. The stories that were told and the message that was passed embodied Walter. There was laughter and a few tears. But mostly, there was a feeling of relief. Walter was not in pain anymore. He was in a better place.

In this book, the Payton family wanted to share with readers the words of those who spoke at the private ceremony. It is the most memorable gift that the family felt it could give to Walter's fans.

Jarrett Payton: Thank you. Ladies and gentlemen, on behalf of my mom and my sister, I thank you for sharing with us in this time of sorrow and paying tribute to my dad. At the age of twelve, my dad asked me to deliver his induction speech to the Pro Football Hall of Fame. Little did I know at that time that six years later, I would be standing here before you with our family and our friends underneath these circumstances. I am honored to share with you some of the fine memories of my dad, Walter Payton. He has taught me many valuable lessons that will be with me forever. The values of setting goals: The best way to achieve my goals is through hard work and determination and the importance of maintaining a competitive spirit. Dad also taught me the value of compassion, and the importance of respect, and the value of humor. He also taught me that we have a responsibility as children of God to share our good fortune with others, which is one of the ways we can ensure the making of a meaningful difference, one that can carry over to the next generation. Although this is a time of loss and sorrow, my mom, sister, and I also want everybody to see this is a time of celebration of my father's life. For those of you that saw my father as a great football player and businessman, I would like you to know that he was also my hero, my dad, and I loved him. I will stop getting on a serious note, I have a story I would just like to tell.

When I was a kid, my dad always had a whistle that whenever he needed me, he'd whistle. No matter where I was, in the yard, on the football field, I heard his whistle and when it came to me, I knew it was important when I heard it. I knew that if I heard him whistle to turn around and find him somewhere and he would tell me, if I was on the football field, to calm down and let things come to me. Or if I was outside causing trouble in the front lawn, he'd tell me to get inside, since I was in trouble. It commanded my attention and it was something that I became trained to, kind of like a dog with a whistle. I knew when he said something—when he did that whistle—it was time for me to turn around. I think the hardest— It's hard because being in public and when he would try to talk to me, we talked very little in public because it seemed like everybody would want to listen to see what he had to say to me, so it was kind of hard for us to actually sit, if we were in public, and talk. I remember a time when I was playing football at St. Pat's and I got off the bus, and it was the first day—I was actually gonna play tailback for my first time, because the starter got hurt, we won't talk why, but he got hurt and he left me putting on his pads and playing the tailback position for my first time ever. I got off the bus and he didn't say anything to me, but the way that we communicated was through that whistle, where he whistled at me and I turned and I looked at him and he gave me a head nod, and I looked at him and I gave him a head nod back. And that was just like him saying, Go out there and do a good job and represent me and do everything that I've taught you. I remember, it was after the game, we won the game. I gained over two hundred yards, I scored four touchdowns, so he was really happy with my performance. It was like when I was leaving the stadium, I heard the whistle again and I turned around and he kind of nodded to me in approval that you did a good job and I'm proud of you. From there, every time I always would hear the whistle, something came over me. I remember we were playing Boston College and we were in BC and we were playing the game, and for some odd reason I was just standing on the sidelines, and I swear I heard the whistle and I turned around. Knowing that my dad was at home watching the game, I still was looking around and trying to find him and see where he was. I know I'll never forget that moment ever.

In closing, Dad, we love you and we miss you. But we take comfort in the knowledge that you and the Heavenly Father are watching over us. You are resting in peace and there is no pain and there is no sickness and there is no sorrow. One day we will all join you. I recognize that millions of people will miss you because of what you've done on the football field and the lives that you have touched. I will miss you because you were my dad.

Eddie Payton: A great man once said it's not a celebration unless you have a group of friends. This truly is a celebration because all of Walter's friends are here. As late as last night I wondered, one, if I'd be able to do this, and two, how long I'd be able to do it before breaking up. I asked Connie, "What do you think Walter would want me to say?" She said, "Just wing it." And five minutes later she came back and said, "Look, let me explain what 'Just wing it' means. Keep it clean and keep it short," so I'll try that.

I went to bed not knowing what I'd say this morning when I got up here, but when I woke up the only thing I could think of is, What would Walter do if he was in this same position? What is it he'd want this group to know? I jotted down about six things because my memory is like my stature, just a little short, but not bad. Kind of bear with me as I go through this.

I think the first thing he would want to do is thank the media. The way the media in Chicago handled his situation and what his family was going through speaks of the professionalism that we need more of. It would have been easy for them to jump and start rumors, but they didn't. They allowed Walter to have dignity, the privilege to have dignity and pride during his last times here. The entire Payton family is sincerely grateful. . . . This is a lot tougher than I thought it would be.

Secondly, we'd like to thank his mother and sister for doing the things that only a family's true love allows them to do during his last week. Shaved, massaged, anointed his head, and prayed, you know. Especially for the good-night kiss and the good-morning kiss that he got every day during those last couple of weeks. I should be so lucky.

Third, his wife, Jarrett, and Brittney, for being by his bedside always smiling, always encouraging him to hang on, it's going to get better, always being positive. Continue to fight. Not ever letting on that they were worried in the least. They made it possible for him to fight on and try to live every moment, every precious moment so he could spend with them. I know he'd say thank you.

For Matt Suhey and all of his teammates that he played with: Matt, for being an honest man and a true friend. Teammates, for making all this possible. Without you and without your help, Walter Payton would have been ordinary. You made him special, and he would thank you if he was here today.

I'm getting close. The state of Mississippi and Jackson State University: for nurturing him, educating him, and supporting him all his life. He'd say thank you and thank you very much.

For the Chicago Bears and the Halas family: for having the faith and giving him the opportunity to prove he was as good as anyone who has ever played the game and the privilege of doing it with class. He would say thank you. He would say thank you very much.

I would say the same to the late Jim Finks, but I'm sure by now Walter has already told him and the first person he looked up.

For the city of Chicago: for having the greatest fans in the world. Fans who were there through good times and the bad times, and who were there now at the very end. He'd say thank you.

And then he'd probably look at me and say, "Slick, tell me one to make me feel good." And I am probably a jokester, not a prankster. So the one I like best, and I didn't know which it would be until everybody that passed by kept saying, Man, I looked at you and you looked just like Walter. Or said, Man, I thought you were Walter. Y'all are the spitting image. Obviously those were people who couldn't tell true beauty when they were looking at it. But that's always had its advantages and disadvantages. I was driving to south Mississippi, to the rural community to speak at an athletic banquet, and I stopped to get some gas in my car and the attendant came out. As he was pumping gas he was kind of staring at me. I kind of looked at him and smiled, he says, "You're that Payton boy, ain't you?" I said, "Yes, sir, I am." He said—rural Mississippi, now, I say,

"Yes, sir, I am"—he says, "I followed your career for a long time. I watched you when you ran up and down the field at Columbia, Mississippi, and I was a big fan." I said, "I appreciate that." He said, "You don't understand." He says, "I watched you at Jackson State College and I thought you were the best." I said, "I appreciate it." And he was about to finish and fill up, and I started walking to him, he said, "You don't understand. I watched you play in that professional league and you was about the best I've ever seen." I said, "Thank you, I appreciate it." He says, "No, you really don't understand, I am your biggest fan." He says, "To show you what a big fan of yours I am, Walter, I'm gonna give you this tank of gas free." So I did the only thing I could do. As I got in my car, I looked him straight in the eye, and I thanked him [puts on sunglasses], and I told him if he was ever in Chicago, look me up and I'll get him two tickets.

A lot of people ask me—I'm on a roll now, I feel better, thanks, guys—a lot of people ask me what motivated Walter to excel in everything he ever attempted. When I look back I think of a great saying that became my motto and something that he lived by and something that I hope Jarrett will take with him down to Miami, as he leads them to a national championship, and then to the NFL, the greatest professional organization in the world.

If I can get through this here: Each new day the good Lord gives me an opportunity to be good, better, or best. Each day I pledge to the Lord I will not rest until my good is better, and my better is the best. Thank you.

John Madden: I had the opportunity to watch Walter Payton throughout his whole career. I know that he was much more than a football player, that whatever he did he was great. He was great before he came into the NFL, he was great when he was in the NFL, and he was great after he was in the NFL. I was a coach when he first came in, and I'll say if you look at all those games where Walter Payton gained over a hundred yards, you'll see the Oakland Raiders were after them. I was subject to that so I know it, I know it firsthand. I

know it from watching him while broadcasting more games of
Chicago Bears at that time when all these great players were playing
there with Walter Payton, who I think was the greatest. And I say
that, and I believe that.

You know, we always have an argument in sports, who's the best,
who's the greatest? Walter Payton was the greatest and I'll argue
that. I'll argue that with anyone. Because you'll say, Well, how did
he run? Well, if you needed a yard, who would you want to give it
to? You'd want to give it to him. How about if you needed a block,
who would you want to block? Walter Payton. How about if you
needed someone to catch the ball, who would you want? You'd want
Walter. How about—and the Bears did, they had some bad teams,
he played in some bad teams—how about if you had to tackle after
an interception? He had eighteen of them one year. That's no fun,
but he did the things that weren't fun.

You know, there are three kinds of people in the world: There's
those people that make things happen, those people that watch
things happen, and those people that don't know what's happening.
Walter made something happen. When he made something happen,
it was good, it was always good. It wasn't only in football, it was
everywhere. He made people happy. I remember once talking to him
about what's the favorite thing, what's your favorite play? Now, you
ask most running backs, and all due respect to great running backs,
they'll say some run. I ran through here, I broke through the hole, I
straight-armed, I hit this guy, boom, I dove in the end zone, gave a
move, and all that. Walter said, "The greatest play I could make is
having a blitzing linebacker coming, boom, hit him, knock him
down, and my quarterback, Jim McMahon, throws a touchdown
pass." That's Walter Payton, doing the tough thing and enjoying it
and being special.

Remember, I had just a few years ago, I had an all-time Super
Bowl team, and Walter Payton obviously was on the team. Walter
Payton would have been captain of that team. And we had a locker
room scene, and after the locker room scene—and this wasn't

scripted or anything—Walter just had everyone come up and he said, "Okay, make a circle and everyone put their hands in there," he said, "We're the best, we can whip anyone, let's just go out and enjoy it and have fun." That's what he did. He did it, he did it better than anyone else, and he had fun doing it. I had the opportunity to do his last game, the last game Walter Payton ever played. It was here in Chicago. I travel by bus, I don't fly, so I had my bus out here and we were out at Lake Forest and the drivers were out there. So after practice—there were people from all over the world—there were newspaper people, the league, the whole thing, looking for Walter. No one could find Walter. It was in essence the last day he ever practiced. So maybe he had to go here, he had to do this, he had to do that. So I talked to— When I got out to my driver, he said, "You know who was here all afternoon?" And I said, "No." He said, "Walter Payton." I said, "Walter Payton was out in my bus?" I said, "What were you guys doing?" He said, "We were watching *Soul Train*." I was just talking—I have the same driver, my driver Willie—I was talking to him about it this morning, I said, "What were you guys talking about?" "Well, Walter was telling me about when he was on *Soul Train*." He said, "Walter was on *Soul Train* and he took second place, and he was upset because he said he would have taken first place if he had a better partner. And then he said— he waited and he thought a while—and then Walter later said, 'You know, she might be saying the same thing, that she would have won if she had a better partner.' "

But that was Walter, the day before his last game, he's sitting on a bus talking with one of my guys, watching *Soul Train.* That makes him special, and this is a tough one, Connie. I had an opportunity— Kevin Kelly is here, he remembers this because he was there this day. One time, when I was at CBS I did a television show and I said the best football player in the world was Walter Payton. So I did a feature on him. So we did the thing, the running, the hills, the whole thing. My son and his friend were like sixteen, and they idolized Walter Payton. So they wanted to come to meet him, to see him, to be there at the interview. So my son Mike and his friend Carl were there. So we go, it was when the house was new—brand-new house. So we go in this room and they have these beautiful floors, wooden floors. I think the floors were like from Spain or Italy, or some special wood. Walter said, "Just don't scuff the floors, my wife will kill me." So you know, in sports we have this thing: You don't tell a pitcher don't walk a guy, because then he's gonna walk him. Don't throw an interception, you're gonna throw an interception. Don't miss something, you're gonna miss something. Well, this kid Carl, as he pulls— They start to take the camera out and there is a steel plate that holds the camera, and he goes to pull it out and he drops it on the floor, takes a divot out of the brand-new floor. This is the tough part, but Carl didn't know whether to cry, to run, to hide, to duck. Walter just laughed, put his arms around him, and said, "Don't worry." He said, "It'll give it some character. She won't know anyway." Connie, to this day I don't know if you know, but on that brand-new floor, we're the ones that put the divot in it. We're sorry, but that was Walter. You think what you would do. I know what I'd do if that happened to me, but I'm not Walter. I wasn't.

I was honored, someone sent me a clipping a couple of years ago, Walter was going to do a fishing show. He was going to take people out there and go fishing with him and then talk and do all this stuff. And they said, Well, who are you going to do it with? He said one of the people in the story was John Madden. So I'm looking, you get all puffed up, you're feeling good about yourself, John Madden. Then later in the article it went down and they asked Walter, Why John Madden. He said, Well, I'd like to get him out in the middle of the lake and dump the boat over and see if he can swim. That was Walter. It was whimsical. He did things and he had fun. A treasure—we talk about greatest—we're going to hear, Walter Payton, a great man. We talk about a treasure is something rare, something special, something unique, it's something that we dig in deep and look for all our lives. And if we ever find it, we keep it forever, it never leaves us, we never forget it. It's always part of us. Walter Payton is a treasure.

Mike Singletary: One of the things that I decided to do all along was first, make it through. I've been asking the Lord, What would you have me say? I've been thinking about Walter and thinking, What would he have me say? My mind began to go back to my first year in Chicago and I remember working out in Houston, Texas, on a hill. The gentleman that was training me at that time, he began to get on my back, he began to get on my case. I guess I was complaining a bit. And then he began to talk about Walter Payton. He said, "Mike, you're getting ready to go to Chicago and there's a guy there, they call him Sweetness. You know what, Mike? This guy will take your heart. He's unlike any other running back you've ever met. The guy runs up hills taller than this, and he runs like a stallion, his legs kick all over the place. And he runs with a lot of grace. Mike, I've seen some guys hit him with their best hit, and he just popped right back up. Mike, he's never been hit. Mike, that's who you're going to be practicing against every day. If you don't want to do it out here, when you get there, he's just going to take your heart. So what's this going to be?"

Well, I remember a few months later being in Chicago, and everything that my trainer told me was right. I couldn't wait to go in the game and play and hopefully get three-and-out and be on the sideline to watch Walter Payton run. That was a tremendous incentive. I remember the first time I saw him run in the preseason, and Todd Bell and I were standing on the sidelines looking at each other, and we just kind of looked and went, *Wooooooo*. But he really had something special. And then I began to meet the person of Walter. This guy was so funny, and to be honest with you, I really didn't like being around him because I never knew what to expect. The first night of rookie camp, Walter Payton put a firecracker outside of our room. Another player and I were scared to death, we didn't know what happened. And the veterans were walking around laughing, saying, "You'd better watch Walter, you'd better watch Walter."

I remember the jokes. I remember Walter giving everybody names: Binky, Big Back, Ozzie, Reedy, Chocolate City, Doug Blank, the Assassin, hit you in the back anytime. I also remember the hug that Walter Payton, coming up to you, there's no way in the world you can ever get out. You'd hear a few bones crack in your back and he'd let you go and he'd say, "You okay?" And you'd just kind of walk away a little stiff.

Coach Madden talked about Walter Payton and all of his greatness, and you know all of that. You know about the day that he broke Jim Brown's record, and you know about all of the hundred-yard games that he had, and you know about all of the great stuff that he did, the running and the blocking, all of this stuff.

But then I have to take a step back and I have to give you the message that I think he would want you to hear. The first one would be this: This is a celebration. And I think as he looks down, I think he's saying, Whoever it is in the audience that is crying, he's saying, Hold everything. Don't you understand what just took place? I am here on holy ground, and I'm running hills, man, I never thought I could run. I'm running clouds and stars and I'm on the moon! Wow! Walter to me reminds me of the prodigal son who struck out on his own and who's going to conquer the world. And as he strived to do everything that he could do, conquer everything that he could conquer, one day he woke up and he came to his senses. As he looked around in all of his greatness, as he looked at the fame, and he looked at the power and he looked at the status, and he looked at the money, I think Walter did a reevaluation. I think he asked a question, Is this it? And as I listen closer, the thing that I am hearing is this: Don't cry for me, I am here. I am home.

But for those of you in this audience that do not understand the message, and do not get it, one day we must all leave. One day we must all exit this earth and all of our greatness and all of our records and all of the things that we have accomplished in life, it will stay somewhere on a chart. And then the true story is revealed when we stand before a holy God. As I look at Walter and I understood what he was saying, I can even hear the questions of: Mike, listen to me. Matt, listen to me. Connie, listen to me. Jarrett, Brittney, listen to me. Mom, Eddie, listen to me. Pam, listen to what I am saying. And it sounded something like this: As I lay here, I see it. I see what life is really all about, and I'm going for it. I'm going for it. And I want you to know, in the fourth quarter, Walter was a fourth-quarter player. When everybody was down and out, you could always look for Walter to make the block, make the run, make the catch. He was a fourth-quarter player. All great players are fourth-quarter players. And in the fourth quarter, it was his finest. It was his finest. To all of his teammates, you would be proud. You would be proud because I'm telling you, I saw it. A peace. So as you go forward today and you leave this place, all of you who are tired and weary, all of you who are suffering from whatever it might be, all of you who are lonely and afraid and angry, you ought to be saying, Let it go. I saw it. I didn't know it was going to be this easy.

As I come to a closure, I want to tell you this: Walter made one last great run. Fourth down, no time-outs, and he looked across the line of scrimmage and they were all there. He didn't have any blocking whatsoever. And as he looked, he saw them and they were there to take him out. Hate, fear, unforgiveness, selfishness, everything else that you can imagine, they were there. And Walter was asking the question, How do I get past this? And as he looked forward, he just looked up and Christ was there saying, Walter, touch my hand. Grace is yours today. And Walter took His hand. He didn't have to run, he didn't have to jump, he didn't have to earn it. It was free.

To Walter's teammates as I close, let me say this, to the coaches: Walter would say, Let's not wait until an occasion like today. Call somebody, be there for somebody. Pray for somebody. Uplift somebody. I want you to know that I am so blessed, so blessed to be a part of this tradition, the Chicago Bears. I don't even understand it. All of the players here today, I am blessed, and I know that he is saying thanks. God bless you. Thanks, Walter.

Mike Ditka: The first thing he would say is whoever put these speakers in order screwed up. I'll tell you that. I should not be last. And I'm not good at this, but I think it's important and I don't know if I can be as strong as Mike or Eddie or anybody else. Let me tell you a couple of things that I think: I know I loved him as you all loved him. But I loved him before I met him. 'Cause I saw something in the way he played football that was special. He was a warrior, he was a gladiator. He was up to the challenge, he wasn't backing down for nobody. I saw that in his college days and I tried to encourage, along with some other offensive coaches in Dallas, we tried to encourage Coach Landry to pick Walter in the draft if we had that chance. And I'm not sure why we didn't. But you know God had a better plan for Walter Payton. He wasn't supposed to play for America's team. He was supposed to play for the greatest franchise in the history of the National Football League, the Chicago Bears. They are, because the man that founded them was Mr. Halas, and he's the one that founded this league, that we all, or some of us, still work for.

In 1982 I was privileged and honored to have the opportunity to be the coach of the Chicago Bears. At that time I thought I knew how great a player he was. I had watched him on film all the years he had played with the Bears. I actually saw him in person almost destroy the Cowboys in a game they lost 10 to 9. It was a one-man show and a darn good one. But I really didn't know anything about him until I got to see him every day, until I got to see him practice, until I got to see him coming around the locker room. He simply was the best runner, blocker, leader, teammate, and friend I've ever seen. He truly was the best football player I've ever seen. And as Coach Madden said, I'm not going to talk about— You try to describe his running style, you couldn't. Who does he run like, or whoever runs like him, you couldn't. Everybody has a distinct style, and it's great. He had no style, he just got it done. I think Coach Halas has finally got the greatest Bear of them all on his heavenly team. You know, when you think about all the guys who have gone before us, Nagurski, Luckman, Piccolo, Stydahar, Galimore, Farrington, Osmanski, George, Lee, Marconi, Dave Whitsell a couple of weeks ago, all those great Bears that have joined George Halas. He's saying, Hey, I've finally got the final piece of the puzzle, I've finally got the final piece of the puzzle. I've got the greatest Bear of all.

Never have I met anybody that had the success, the prestige, was idolized like that man who wore the mantle of success with such great humility. It is a great lesson for all young athletes to know and to see and to emulate. The game is greater than the athletes in the game and it always will be, it always was. Walter knew that above all. But when they make a mark against his name, it's not going to be whether he won or lost, but how he did play that game, and man, he did play that game. He really played that game.

Now what will his legacy be? Some 16,700 rushing yards, leading receiver in Bears' history, best blocking back, best—well, I would say—best blocking tailback I've ever seen. Two of the best blocking fullbacks are here today, Roland Harper and Matt Suhey, that I've ever seen. But he was the best blocking tailback that I've ever seen, that's ever played the game. There's no question about it. Well, what's his legacy going to be, really, is that what it's going to be? Or is it going to be what Mike just told you about? And I'm sure a lot of people will remember Walter for that over-the-top, that high step down the sideline. I saw a film the other day, it was the greatest run I've ever seen down in Tampa Bay. I don't remember what year it was, '83 or '84. Hugh Green was a great football player. I've never seen a guy make a guy look so bad on one play. It hurt me to watch him cut that way.

His real legacy is going to be the mark he left on all of us. It's going to be Connie, it's going to be Jarrett, it's going to be Brittney, his mom, Eddie, sister Pam. The lessons, values, the principles, the ideals that he lived for and he taught. That's going to be the legacy. They're going to pass them on to their children, and their children to their children. That's what you leave behind. That's a heck of a lot better than scoring touchdowns, gang, because he was something special. He was sweet.

Now, the Bible tells us very simply that all men are like grass and their deeds are like the wildflowers. Now, the grass will wither and the flowers will fall, but the word of the Lord will live forever. And I believe this in the bottom of my heart, I really do, and I've believed it for a long time. I know the two great commandments that we are given, I know that Walter loved God. He honored God with his whole heart, and his whole heart and soul. I believe that, that he always kept God in front of him. I believe that with my whole heart and soul because I watched him deal throughout his career with people. To love God is to love your fellow man, and I think he did that exceptionally well. I think he did that outstandingly well. I think he shared, he gave. If he didn't care—he didn't have to have a foundation to help people. He could have said no a lot of times, but he always said yes. So I know that he put God in front of him. He loved Him with his whole heart, his whole mind, and his whole soul. And Paul in Romans tells us simply, which is very fitting for this day or any other day, whether you lose a football game or whether you lose a friend. He says, "Consider that our present sufferings are not worth comparing to the glory that will be revealed to us in Christ Jesus." That's simple. I loved Walter Payton. Thank you.

Afterword

Our nation has suffered a great loss, but the legacy of Walter Payton will live on through his foundation, which has helped hundreds of thousands of needy children, and he will live on through the countless lives that will be saved through the awareness he has brought to organ donation. We as a people have always embraced this humble sports hero with respect and love. Every time a young boy runs with a football, or the Bears score a touchdown, we can look into the heavens and say, "That was for you, Sweetness."

Walter had a great love for our Father God and he was blessed among men with fame, fortune, beauty, and talent, just to name a few. However, who God really blessed was all of us, because Walter brought joy and happiness to so many people and to his city, which he made Super Bowl champions.

We thank everyone for their love and prayers. God bless.

THE WALTER AND CONNIE
PAYTON FOUNDATION
104 North Barrington Road
P.O. Box 154
Streamwood, Illinois 60107
(847) 605-0034
www.payton34.com

THE ALLIANCE FOR THE
CHILDREN
P.O. Box 5128
Elgin, Illinois 60121
(847) 645-2112

Acknowledgments

Any project that is as emotionally draining as this could never be done alone. I have many people to thank for their cooperation, their time, and their love for Walter. Certainly, credit has to start with those closest to Walter. Connie, Jarrett, and Brittney all opened themselves up to discuss Walter in ways that made all of us cry. And Ginny Quirk and Kim Tucker, who spent most of the last decade working with and for Walter on a daily basis. Ginny and Kim, who were like family to Walter, saw and lived a side of Walter that really contributed to the full flavor of this project.

I am also indebted to two fellow journalists, Dan Wetzel and Dave Scott, who were of great aid when the writing grew tough. Along those lines, the work of some top-flight journalists who followed Walter's life proved invaluable. The *Chicago Tribune*'s Don Pierson, whose reputation as one of the best NFL writers in America is well deserved, penned stories that led me down the many trails of Walter's life. *Sun-Times* columnist Rick Telender shared insight, both in writing and phone conversations, about fifteen years of conversations with Walter. It was a quote from Rick's 1984 *Sports Illustrated* story on Walter that provided the inspiration for this book's title. Veteran television journalist Armen Keteyian was also a great help, especially with his work on a Super Bowl XXXIV pregame tribute to Walter. I also tapped dozens of important stories from *Sun-Times* writers Jay Mariotti, Taylor Bell, Ron Rapoport, and Lacy Banks and *Tribune* writers Skip Bayless, Bernie Lincicome, and Ed Sherman.

Mitch Albom's bestseller *Tuesdays with Morrie* was a book I turned to regularly in an effort to keep in touch with the emotion of what was happening around me. Like millions of others, I was grateful for the lessons Morrie taught. I was a little more fortunate in that I had Walter to teach me graduate-level classes in the same course.

At *Sports Illustrated,* where I work with the best editors in the business, Craig Neff, Rob Fleder, Bill Colson, and Peter Carry all provided me the support to work on this book. Linda Wachtel in the *SI* library has been not only a friend but a true resource.

Never forget the agents: David Vigliano and Ed Breslin. They offered strong guiding hands early. And at Villard, thanks to Mannie Barron, who started this project, and Bruce Tracy, who finished it. Their faith in our ability to deliver was unshakable.

Closer to home, my assistant, Jill May, helped with going through interviews and editing the manuscript. And Sen. Jim King, my close friend and confidant, was always there to keep me on focus and challenged.

Finally, something this challenging could never be done without the love and support of my family. To Denise, Billy, and Katie, I say thank you and I love you.

—DON YAEGER

DON YAEGER is the coauthor of the *New York Times* bestselling *Under the Tarnished Dome* and the critically acclaimed *Pros and Cons: The Criminals Who Play in the NFL*. He lives in Tallahassee, Florida, with his wife, son, and daughter.